Sexism in School
and Society

"Critical Issues in Education"
Under the Advisory Editorship of Louis Fischer

Sexism in School and Society

Nancy Frazier

Amherst, Massachusetts

Myra Sadker

Assistant Professor
University of Wisconsin-Parkside

Harper & Row, Publishers
New York, Evanston, San Francisco, London

Contents

14455

Editor's introduction

In a diverse, pluralistic culture the institutions, policies, and practices of education will be influenced by the major disagreements of the times. Education in America, a diverse nation searching to define its brand of pluralism, most certainly reflects the major conflicts of the culture.

The dominant tradition of our past attempted to keep the public schools above or away from the controversies of the times and attempted to transmit a common core of learnings. Those tranquil days are gone, perhaps forever. Today, consistent with John Gardner's phrase that "education is the servant of all our purposes," various interest groups try to influence and even control public education. Such groups represent political and economic diversities; racial, ethnic, and religious preferences; business interests, conservationists, internationalists, isolationists; proponents of women's liberation, sex education, and sensitivity training, to name but the best-known voices. In addition to these influences from the culture at large, developments more indigenous to schooling must also be considered. Among these are the various forces urging innovation, accountability, professionalism for teachers, and community control. They are concerned with combating institutional racism and sexism, violence in the schools, the civil rights of teachers and students.

Teachers must become informed about these issues and

conflicts if they are to function as professionals. Toward this end, a beginning must be made in teacher education programs and continued into a teacher's maturing years. The titles in this series were conceived with such a goal in mind. Each volume can stand on its own, yet the several volumes are easily relatable. This arrangement maximizes flexibility for professors who may select one or more volumes, while the student's budget is also respected.

The authors were selected on the basis of their competence as well as their ability to write for an audience of nonspecialists, be they teachers, prospective teachers, or others interested in the dominant issues in our culture that influence the schools.

Louis Fischer
Amherst, Massachusetts

Preface

Myra Sadker is an assistant professor of education who has experienced and observed the effects of sexism both as a student and as a teacher. Nancy Frazier is a journalist who writes books for children and is active in the women's movement. Chapters 1, 2, 3, and 8 were written by Nancy Frazier, and Chapters 4 through 7 by Myra Sadker.

Our personal involvement in education and in the women's movement has encouraged us to add our own experiences to the research that we present in this book. Although our backgrounds and experiences differ, we are working toward a similar goal and share a commitment to break down the walls of sexism, which enclose and limit the potential of young people of either sex. Throughout the course of putting this book together, we exchanged ideas and materials.

We would like to express our gratitude to our editor, Louis Fischer, who conceived and understood the need for such a text and has never failed to make meaningful his belief in individual freedom, and to Florence Howe, whose critical and insightful reading was invaluable.

Many individuals have contributed their expertise and time to our efforts. Special thanks are extended to Shirley and Louis Pollack for all of their help and to Barbara Schimmel, whose assistance and friendship have been of benefit throughout.

Our sincere appreciation also to Leah Stern, Carol Ahlum, and Jackie Fralley, and to those who have read the manuscript and made important suggestions: Connie Gillen, Kathy Girard, Jane Gold, Jerry Gold, Sari Knopf, Debbie Link, Marcia Matz, Margaret Mehta, Lois Phillips, and Pat Sackery. Thanks also to Shelly Haugsby and to the library staff of the University of Wisconsin-Parkside for help with the research, and to Wilma Heser, Doris Holder, and Darlene May for typing the manuscript.

Above all, thanks to Jack Frazier, who has always understood what sharing responsibilities is all about and has never failed to give his support to this endeavor, and to David Sadker, who has demonstrated his concern about sexism in his teaching, in his life style, and in the help and encouragement he has given to this book. Also to our children, Leslie and David Frazier and Robin Sadker, who provide an immediate reason for working against the boundaries of sexism in school and society.

Nancy Frazier
Amherst, Massachusetts

Myra Sadker
Racine, Wisconsin

Introduction
The teacher
and the women's
movement

Like its nineteenth-century counterpart, the new feminism is a teaching movement. In addition to leaflets, pamphlets, magazines, newspapers, and a few books, the consciousness-raising group has made an impact on our lives and has begun to be felt in classrooms. But thus far at least, there have been few new textbooks, and none at all like this one.

In the course of the past decade, the movement pushed onto college and university campuses, demanding the revision of curriculum, as well as the examination of the status and treatment of women students, faculty, and administrators. Hundreds of studies of individual campuses, dozens of professional associations, and several of higher education in general have depicted identical pyramids: almost no women at the top, a few more women at each *descending* rank, and masses of secretaries, kitchen and cleaning workers, and female students at the bottom.

In 1970, I knew of 64 women's studies courses; in 1971, 610; by now, there are more than 1,200 in combined listings published by the Clearinghouse on Women's Studies, an educational project of The Feminist Press. Women's studies programs have grown at an equally prolific rate: fifty-two now have established themselves, six of which offer "minors" to students, and some dozen B.A.'s or M.A.'s. The Ford Foundation has just announced a program of awards for doctoral dissertations in women's studies to begin in the spring of 1973. Most important of all, there are signs that the feminist movement is now reaching out to the high schools and elementary schools.

Daily, the Clearinghouse on Women's Studies receives a dozen or more requests from high school and elementary school teachers for materials, syllabi, or even the names of other teachers who have begun to add women's history to their curriculum, for example, or to invent whole new courses on subjects such as sex-role stereotyping and women in mythology and early society. The Clearinghouse also receives from high school teachers interested in publishing in the *Women's Studies Newsletter* reports of their experiments with new courses. The excitement inherent in bringing a cultural revolution into classrooms regenerates teachers as well as students. For example, Lois F. Yatzeck, a history teacher at Kaukauna High School in Wisconsin, wrote to the Clearinghouse about her reasons for teaching a nine-week unit on "Women in History":

Being a woman has always been a problem to me. There was even a time when I felt I was the embodiment of the suffering of women during our time. Trained to achieve like a man, I was not accepted into a man's profession (the Christian ministry). Called to become an individual, I failed as a wife. I feel I spent most of my married life absolutely torn in two between my desires to be a good wife (and always failing) and my search for personal fulfillment in a profession (never achieving it). Now, two years after a divorce that I was reluctant to seek, I have a sense of personal peace and perspective that would make it possible to be a wife again, if that should ever come about, though it is not necessary. I don't blame my former husband nor my parents nor "society" for my past unhappiness. I was simply unable to define myself, make a harmony within myself. Now I can; and I feel I have much to give to my world, perhaps especially to other women.

I emphasize the teacher here, rather than her students, for several reasons. It is by now a truism in education that those who learn most in the classroom are teachers—that is, when anyone is learning anything at all. The energy that women's studies has unleashed on campuses is a function of that fact: the teacher of women's studies is typically converted by her own course, and if she is wise, she will understand the process, and learn quickly how to turn all her students into teachers—of each other and of those younger (or newer to the movement) than they.

My second reason for focussing on the teacher is more complex. Because most public school teachers are women, and because their numbers are so vast, I see them as key to changing the education of women (and men). But progress in this direction has been slow and markedly different from the patterns now discernible in higher education. For example, of the 1,200 women's studies courses, fewer than ten have been offered in education departments. Even the male-dominated professions of political science and economics have better records than education! I know of no school system or unit of a teachers' union, moreover, in which women teachers have voluntarily attempted studies of the status and treatment of women or of the curriculum comparable to those done on campuses all over the country.

There is nothing in public education thus far that resembles the pattern of change in progress on college campuses. There the swell has been *from the ground up:* that is, from teachers and students on a campus, who pursued studies of the treatment of women and of the curriculum, and who afterward pressed for women's studies courses and programs. The growth has often been, moreover, in vital relationship to a local women's movement. But of course campuses are smaller and neater entities—and there are fewer of them—than school systems. And while there are but fifty state education departments, compared to many of them, even the greatest multiversities grow diminutive.

It's not surprising, therefore, that the pattern of change emerging in public education is *from the top down.* There are stirrings in the American Federation of Teachers, and recently the National Education Association held the first national conference on sex stereotypes in the schools. Because of the energies of the women's movement, in three states—Pennsylvania, New York, and Massachusetts—new guidelines or laws were promulgated in 1972, calling for "equal opportunity for women" in educational institutions of all kinds. Such state-wide policies are potentially powerful, but only if parents, students, administrators, and teachers (a) know of their existence and (b) pressure for their implementation. Finally, the Higher Education Act of 1972 (Title IX) prohibits sex discrimination in education: "No person in the United States shall on the basis of sex be excluded from participation in, be denied the benefits of, or be subjected to discrimination under any education program or activity receiving Federal financial assistance." The guidelines written to enforce this law would make possible the revision of textbooks, counseling procedures, physical education, and the curriculum in general. But again, only if parents, students, administrators, and teachers know of the law, the reasons for its existence, and how to effect its implementation.

I expect that most people by now understand the limitations of movements for change that depend chiefly on directives from the top. And yet, of course, it is possible to put those directives to work, as it was after 1954 when the Supreme Court's decision in *Brown* v. *Board of Education* provided impetus to and an umbrella for vast social and educational change. Of all the means for implementing change, I would place priority on the education of teachers, both female and male. Women teachers who begin to understand their own lives in the context of sex-role stereotyping and sex bias are especially likely to be the most crucial agents for change. They are, indeed, closer to the ground than others in the system. Most important, the teacher is the single most powerful influence on children's school lives—more important, I believe, than textbooks or other curricular materials. When teachers "change," so does everything in their classrooms. When teachers begin to intervene in the rigid sex-typing of children in classrooms, when they begin to question the four-year-olds who are convinced that only boys can be sent into space, the eight-year-old girls who have already given up on math and science—only then will we have begun to create an atmosphere of equality and opportunity for our daughters and sons in schools.

The publication of this book should encourage schools and departments of education to inaugurate units or whole courses in which to examine the assumptions and studies, the questions, theories, and conclusions described by Sadker and Frazier. *Sexism in School and Society* summarizes clearly the failure of schools to offer equal opportunity to girls and women. And yet, the authors are never depressing. Teachers and would-be teachers will find the information they need and the energy and hope as well with which to turn to change.

In addition, this book should provide a useful text for in-service courses for teachers who need to become conscious of their roles in the socialization of girls and boys in their classrooms. Once aware, the next steps are not difficult: to prepare new courses and units for their own education and their own students. In New York City this year, in-service courses taught by staff members of The Feminist Press, offer teachers both compensatory education (in women's history, for example) and curriculum workshops. Teachers are participating with the aim of organizing usable curriculum units for their own students: they will, in the course of the year, try such units in their classrooms, and report back to the in-service course about their failures and successes. They will learn to find, develop, and share new materials and methods in women's history and in literature with other teachers in the group.

Teacher education and curriculum change will, if we are successful, occupy many of us for the whole decade of the seventies, and perhaps into the eighties as well. There are no short cuts. Social problems, as we all know by now, do not simply fade away. Even with the best of intentions they tend to persist and worsen, especially if they are ignored. To substitute in textbooks children colored brown or women at gas pumps is not to deal with the continued existence of racism or sexism. Instead of declaring sexism illegal or immoral and vowing never to look that way again, I would rather we work directly with its presence among us.

I should like to see the subject of this book, sex-role stereotyping, become openly a part of the curriculum at all levels of education—at least for the next decade. I think that where we have made strides against bigotry we have done so through its presence as a subject for analysis and discussion, even anger and confrontation, in the classroom. The feelings are there—among all of us. We live in a society that is both racist and sexist, and it is now permissible to say so, even at some of the highest levels of government. But to say so is not enough; even official statements are not enough. Nor is the consciousness of feminists enough. We need what someone once called "the entering wedge"—the crucial place in the system likely to respond significantly and productively to change.

If I am correct, and that wedge is teacher education and curricular reform, this book provides one useful beginning. It is written despite the knowledge that nearly two decades of efforts to improve the quality of education for blacks and poor people in this country, to combat racism, to expose (in order to eliminate) discriminatory tracking systems have produced painfully few fruits. It is written out of the buoyancy of the new feminism, the sanity and honesty of scholarship. And it dares to suggest that we have the energy and the audacity to build on those failures of the fifties and sixties, and to try once again to liberate ourselves and then our children.

Florence Howe
State University of New York
College at Old Westbury

Sexism in School
and Society

1
The possibility of change

Before one can begin to change a condition, one must believe in the possibility of change.

Paul Lauter and Florence Howe
The Conspiracy of the Young[1]

Several months ago I went to one of the fifteen-minute parent-teacher conferences regularly scheduled by the small elementary school that my daughter attends. The school had been making its cautious way toward innovation, and one of the steps had been to combine many of the activities of kindergarten through the second grade. A large space had been opened up by removing the conventional desks and installing a carpet, tables, and a flexible arrangement of partitions.

As we sat talking on the child-size chairs, the teacher repeated something that I had heard before about Leslie. She said that my daughter's major problem seemed to be an unwillingness to concentrate. For example, during a reading lesson, although she knew all the words, she simply would not pay attention to the text. The reading teacher, who was standing nearby, came over to add that she was handling this "problem" by having Leslie hold and move a piece of paper under the sentences as they went along, thus (in my words, not the teacher's) forcing Leslie to follow the text.

I simultaneously considered and answered the teachers' observations. I told them that I was reluctant to consider this a problem and that I felt it could be looked at in several ways. For one, it may simply be her age (eight), or it may be her personality, her indomitable style. On the other hand, I said, they had set before us a display of the new books that they were enthusiastic about—a set of colorful texts on explorers—and that they, no doubt rightly, believed would be more interesting than the traditional readers. But sitting there looking at those books, ranging in subject from Columbus to John Glenn, I was hard pressed to decide which man I would like to read about. "I wish there were at least one book about a woman," I said, "and I'll bet that if you had some texts describing the exploits of females, Leslie's interest would be better sustained."

Somewhat to my surprise and greatly to my delight, the teacher answered, "Yes, I think you're right." She said that she herself wondered why there couldn't be a book about Amelia Earhart, for example. In the few minutes that were left we talked about ordering other books that girls like Leslie might be anxious to read.

More recently, three women and I went to speak about sexism* in school with officials of a large school district representing about nine thousand students and nearly six hundred teachers. The men we spoke with, an assistant superintendent and the director of curriculum revision, were ready to listen to us because, owing to newspaper articles, educational journals, and more subtle pressures, they were becoming aware that discontent with sex-biased education was not only growing, but was perhaps valid. We were asked to write a proposal describing ways in which they might begin to overcome the perpetuation of sex bias in their schools.

Just today an associate and I were invited to speak to a class of future elementary school teachers. The invitation, which came from the professor in charge of elementary education, was phrased in this way: "I think it is important for these students to understand the feminist perspective on education."

These recent experiences, plus reports we get from around the

*Sexism—n. (1.) A belief that the human sexes have a distinctive makeup that determines their respective lives, usually involving the idea that one sex is superior and has the right to rule the other; (2.) a policy of enforcing such asserted right; (3.) a system of government and society based upon it. First defined by Kathleen Shortridge in "Women as University Nigger," University of Michigan *Daily Magazine*, Ann Arbor, 12 April 1970 country, show that educators are beginning to listen to what feminists are saying about the education of their children—of all children. And as our society and its institutions become aware of the necessity for change, we find ourselves believing enthusiastically in the possibility of change.

THE NEW FEMINIST: NOBODY'S PRINCESS

In 1970, Midge Decter, writing for *Commentary* magazine, presumed to define the new feminist in an article entitled "The Liberated Woman." Decter portrayed a very special, spoiled, upper-middle-class "princess" about whom she concluded, "The freedom she truly seeks is . . . a freedom demanded by children and enjoyed by no one: the freedom from all difficulty."[2]

Letters poured into the magazine in response to Decter's article. In fact, four months later the cover of *Commentary* listed: "Midge Decter and Critics: Women's Lib." (The term *women's lib* is rejected by many feminists because it has the sound of easy, glib dismissal.) This issue printed twenty-five letters from readers, a great many of which (and how many more not printed?) showed dissatisfaction, if not anger, with Decter's definition. Neither princesses nor hedonists, they bristled at her complete misunderstanding of the movement to which they are committed.[3]

By now it should be obvious that there is much more to feminism and feminists than can be sheltered under Midge Decter's plastic, see-through umbrella. When we try to describe who those women in the movement really are and what may have motivated them, we begin to recognize that there are as many reasons as there are women. Not only that, but there are as many reasons as there are women who have not yet "joined." For commitment means, essentially, that one has begun to see the extent to which our democracy has never truly served all people equally well and has never even anticipated serving females with the same freedoms of choice, opportunity, education, and reward as it has offered males. This recognition results in the realization that women are a deprived class. As a struggle, then, the women's movement is a class struggle.

Understood in this way, it should be realized that this class struggle can leave out no woman and must fight discrimination against any one of its members regardless of her race, religion, social or economic, professional, political, or educational status, or sexual preference. And it is also clear that the movement must challenge any institution that perpetuates discrimination against women and thus must challenge the practices, and often the very structure, of most institutions in America, including educational institutions.

"That the spearhead of the feminist movement has been middle-class in origin no one will deny," wrote sociologist Alice Rossi in reply to a distorted, backlash article by psychologist Joseph Adelson.[4] Adelson's article in the *New York Times Magazine,* entitled "Is Women's Lib a Passing Fad?," contended that the concerns of the women's movement were as "remote as the moon" to the average citizen.[5] Rossi countered, "A great deal of the real work of the women's movement is focused on bread-and-butter issues." She cited women's efforts in the repeal of state protective laws, in support of *amicus curiae* briefs to defend the rights of employed factory women, in the passage of the Equal Rights Amendment, and in the organization of countless thousands of women to assure their presence among the delegates to the national conventions. "And who does Professor Adelson think played a major part in the change in state abortion laws across the country during the last five years?" she asked. She pointed to the efforts of thousands of women who had campaigned against these laws, "seeking a right to control their reproductive lives—that is the very opposite of 'remote as the moon.' "[6] The aim and direction of the women's movement, then, is to cut across those traditional dividing lines that give separate sources of identity to women according to their traditional class, ethnic, or other affiliations. This is the meaning of "sisterhood."

To inveistgate the motivation of those women who, in the 1960s and early 1970s, first rejected institutionalized and personalized sexism, we must understand the contemporary situations to which they were reacting.

Many women during the 1950s were feeling bored, discontented, disenfranchised. During World War II their energies had been tapped for work outside the home, consisting of many varieties and of substantial importance. From factories to news magazines, women had done the jobs of men as part of the "war effort," taking seriously the pointing finger of the poster that read: "Uncle Sam Needs You." After the war, they quickly discovered that they had only been "filling in," because most of them were sent back home when returning soldiers reclaimed their jobs.

True, women of that era went home willingly, in the euphoria of postwar patriotism. But without being able to pinpoint its causes, they slowly became conscious of their growing discontent. It took Betty Friedan's book, *The Feminine Mystique,* published in 1963, to reveal their dissatisfaction as coming in great part from being outside of the mainstream.[7] She was able to show women, each one of whom had been inclined to think that her malaise was a personal problem, that many, many others were experiencing the same depression. Friedan's book led to the formation of NOW, the National Organization for Women, in 1966. The beginnings of the contemporary movement can be traced here, in a definition of the alienation of the American female.

During the mid-1960s, however, new commitment and direction were given by the insurgence of a younger generation of women. These women, together with young men, had, as Lauter and Howe define their activities, already devoted themselves to "service for change."[8] This kind of service contrasts with the traditional voluntary service that assumes the efficacy and justice of the social order and works for and within existing institutions. Instead, the new generation *joined* the opppressed to work with them against institutionalized oppression. They gave themselves to civil rights and anti-war activities, to working with the underprivileged in other countries, to changing the educational system. They were defiant and their defiance took many forms: a way of dressing or wearing their hair, using drugs, opting out of school, joining a commune, *protesting*; burning draft cards, marching for peace, desegregating buses, lunch counters, schools, and the polls; joining rock festivals, cleaning up the environment, *demonstrating*.

Yet as they protested and demonstrated against oppression, young women came to two realizations. That even as the current battles might be won, they themselves would still be effectively deprived of many basic freedoms, and that even this new counterculture movement, which challenged our society for all its other failures, failed to overcome discrimination against women within its own ranks. This seemed to be symbolized by the much-quoted statement of Stokely Carmichael, leader of the Student Nonviolent Coordinating Committee (SNCC): "The only position for women in SNCC is prone."

Within the youth movements women began to caucus, and to separate themselves. "We have met the enemy, and he is our friend," wrote Robin Morgan when she and others split from a radical movement, after concluding that they must first work for the liberation of women. In an article entitled "Goodbye to All That," she protested that the male-dominated left was "counterfeit."[9]

"Make policy, not coffee" became a slogan, and although it may sound facile, it shows that women resented that, despite the fact that their energy, education, and commitment were equal to their male counterparts', they were still doing the less important work, the housework of society and of the movement. This slogan had meaning for professional women, too, as the discrimination they experienced became increasingly distinct and tangible. Many of these apparently successful women admitted that they broke into professions during World War II. But as they examined "success," they saw that they were paid less than men. Whether teaching or sitting at a drafting table, they had little opportunity for advancement, either in terms of tenure or in moving from draftswoman to designer. And in all cases they still made and poured the coffee. Professional women also began to organize and to caucus, adding a third dimension to the impetus for the movement.

To these women might be added others with complaints of less specific sexism. Perhaps because of conditions during the 1960s and 1970s, they became aware, first emotionally and then more concretely, that they were effectively excluded from all the power and decision-making processes that were sending the country in directions that adversely affected women. The overwhelming concerns marking this era, above all war, pollution, and overpopulation, became, especially because of the media (live and in color), so close as to be virtually touchable. Certainly women had sent their sons and husbands to other wars, but never had it seemed so difficult to justify their loss. The discovery that air, food, and water were poisoned had the impact of a gigantic betrayal.

Betrayed and victimized especially were women who, as consumers, had accepted without question that which was stocked on the supermarket shelves, contaminated food and detergents that killed the fish not already tainted by industrial pollutants. There was also poison in the air, from radioactive fallout and industrial waste; poison that entered the food chain and showed up in surprising quantities when nursing mothers had their breast milk chemically analyzed. The visibly angry reaction of women provoked one automobile dealer to remark, "The consumer doesn't just want satisfaction today —she wants vengeance!"[10] He had caught the mood but not the substance of the reaction, for revenge can be an end in itself, but women wanted to go beyond that—they wanted change.

Women were also especially conscious of the awesome threats of overpopulation. The menace of an overcrowded world resonated in the minds of those who had been prepared to redeem themselves from the shame of being only female (a biblical convention supported by classical psychology) by propagating the species. And to the extent that their special role of nourishing and preserving life had

already been culturally ingrained, many women were shocked out of
their complacency by the unavoidable (21-inch and front-page) vision
of the destruction of living things by unjustifiable violence, con-
tamination, and by too many babies. All this could no longer be
ignored, nor accepted in the terms that those in authority might
insist on. And so many women who might not otherwise have been
touched also began to question and then to defy authority, especially
as it was vested in what was quickly recognized as the Establishment.

The above are some of the conditions that brought new social
and self-consciousness to women as the new feminism was coalescing
into a movement. The effect of women speaking out was to reach
others, so that more and more women became aware of the need for
change. Even the most superficial measures of women's opinions
began to show shifts in points of view. There was, for example, a
poll conducted by Lou Harris and Associates reported in March
1972. The survey, sponsored by Virginia Slims cigarettes (whose
advertising slogan was "You've come a long way, baby"), showed
that most of the 3,000 women polled then supported "efforts to
strengthen and change women's status in society." The figures (48
percent in favor, 36 percent opposed, the rest uncertain) were compared to a survey done the previous year that showed women opposing such efforts by 42 to 40 percent. "The news that just cries out
from this welter and mass of information about women's attitudes
and condition in 1972 is that women have sprung loose as an independent political force. . . . And once you let a force like that loose,
I would suggest that it can never be bottled up again," said pollster
Harris.[11]

We have to argue with his choice of words—the implication that
someone is letting women loose, and it must be men he is referring
to—because all of the evidence points to the truth that women are
not taking advantage of any weakness in the institutions of suppression, rather they are breaking through the walls of some very
solid structures. But Harris' statistics do acknowledge something very
significant: the growing inclusiveness of the women's movement,
which will end up by touching not only every member of the female
majority (51 percent of the population), but also every member of
the male minority.

BLACK LIBERATION (WOMEN'S)

As Pauli Murray has said, "Anything that affects women affects
everyone, and anything that affects society affects women." Dr.

Murray teaches American Studies at Brandeis University. She calls herself a Negro in reference to her age, because she was fighting for equality long before the word "black" gained its current meaning. In reference to the challenge of "exclusiveness" in either the black or the women's movement, Murray paraphrases a poem by Edwin Markham in these words, "If you draw a circle which excludes me, I will draw a larger circle which includes you."[12]

However, the initial reactions of many black women to the women's liberation movement were expressed by Toni Morrison: "What do Black women feel about Women's Lib?" she asked in the *New York Times Magazine* in 1971. She answered her own question with one word, "Distrust," and went on to explain, "It is white, therefore suspect. . . . Too many movements and organizations have made deliberate overtures to enroll blacks and have ended up by rolling them. They don't want to be used again to help somebody gain power—a power that is carefully kept out of their hands."[13]

The feeling that blacks who join the women's movement are diverting their energies away from the fight against racism to the fight against sexism discourages many blacks from supporting the new feminists. They feel strongly that the years of discrimination and humiliation they and their men have suffered together under the rule of white supremacy makes black liberation first in order of priority. These women are in fact often glad to put their men first and point out that white women too, not just white men, have been guilty of perpetuating the evils of racism. When Toni Cade, a black who edited the anthology *Black Woman*, spoke at the University of Massachusetts School of Education in 1971, many feminists came to listen and to applaud.[14] To the feminists' dismay, Cade's patience became strained as she was queried about the sexist attitudes of black males. Her real concern, she said, was with an alternative to the kind of school system that exists and that black children have little choice but to attend. Were not black women demeaned when black men called them "chick"?—seemed to Cade to overlook the complexities of black cultural interrelationships and was answered with an exasperated "that's not it."

In a way this is a problem that has other parallels, often expressed in terms of priorities. For example, the hypothetical extenuation of an old question: "Are you an American first, or a black first, a woman first, etc.?" The assumption is that each category has different ideals to fight for and different restrictions to fight against. One's first choice of definition often has to do with the individual's experience, and of course experience is not something that can be arbitrarily reordered, either for oneself or for someone else. Therefore, as we listen to Toni Morrison and Toni Cade's comments on the different emotional and cultural experiences of black and white women, we can see more clearly that what looks on the outside like a reordering of priorities is far more complex than that. And also depleting, for to face and fight discrimination against your people when you identify with one group hardly leaves abounding energy nor much incentive to step out of that group and into another equally oppressed group. Undeniably black women suffer the injustices and indignities of both racism and sexism. Both " 'isms" are scourges. But arguing that one is worse than the other is like arguing that death from cancer of the stomach is worse than death from cancer of the breast. And certainly when the facts of economic status are recounted (in spite of the observation that black women are employed more often than black men, usually at the most menial jobs), we find that black women are at the very bottom of the pay scale, well below white women, who are just below black men, who are far below white men.

Jo Ann E. Gardner, a physiological psychologist and one of the first national leaders of the new feminist movement, discussed with a black male psychologist, Charles W. Thomas, the question of diverting energies from battling racism to battling sexism:

Thomas: I would be less than candid, Jo Ann, if I did not say that the women's movement is a diversion in the same way that the environment movement is a diversion. Like the environmental thing that college kids are flocking into, feminism appeals to middle-class whites in part because it is an activist way to ignore racism. It is avoidance behavior.

Gardner: That's a lie, Tom, as far as the feminist movement is concerned. We're fighting the same thing the black movement is fighting—bigotry and the dehumanizing forces of this society. You've been put down by white supremacists while we've been brainwashed by male supremacists. Anybody in this white-male-dominated culture who is bad on race is likely to be bad on women—and the reverse is also true—a sexist is usually a racist at heart.[15]

The same thought was expressed and expanded by Shirley Chisholm, Congresswoman from New York, who had spent over twenty years in politics when she spoke at a conference in January, 1970:

I am, as it is obvious, both black and a woman. And that is a good vantage point from which to view at least two elements of what is becoming a social revolution: the American black revolution and the

*women's liberation movement. But it is also a horrible disadvantage
. . . because America as a nation is both racist and anti-feminist.
Racism and anti-feminism are two of the prime traditions of this
country.*

Then she went on to say what she felt must be done:

*In a speech made a few weeks ago to an audience that was pre-
dominantly white and all female, I suggested the following, if they
wanted to create change. You must start in your own homes, your
own schools, and your own churches. I don't want you to go home
and talk about integrated schools, churches or marriages if the kind
of integration you're talking about is black and white. I want you to
go home and work for, fight for, the integration of male and female
—human and human.*[16]

The message these women seem to be shouting over the com-
motion of others trying to decide who comes first, is that human
dignity comes first. Black liberation can, if it wishes, leave out
women's liberation, just as the youth movement can overlook discrimination against females within its midst. But the women's liberation movement can leave out no woman, and further, must draw a
circle that encompasses everyone.

LIBERATION AND FREEDOM

The concept of liberation, which is central to the women's movement,
is the principle that draws the ever-widening, finally all-inclusive
circle to which Dr. Murray referred. Because each person's liberation
is an individual process, we will speak of the meaning it holds for us.

We understand liberation as a prerequisite for the exercise of
specific freedoms. We believe it is an ongoing, continuous process
that resides in a state of becoming aware of the limitations placed
upon your rights and freedoms by others and then being able to
reject these limitations. As a heightened consciousness, liberation
allows an individual to consider herself (or himself) in relation to
dynamic and changing circumstances, both real and theoretical. Most
important, liberation becomes, as it proceeds, not only an individual
or personal benefit, but also a tool for assisting in the liberation of
others. For, in Walt Whitman's words, it is "indispensable to my
own rights that others possess the same."[17]

Liberation brings with it two kinds of freedom—freedom *from* physical oppression, convention, stereotype, the dictates of people or groups one no longer wishes to heed, and freedom *to* effect change, form new standards or values, in short to act toward self-determination.

Freedom, however, is an awesome thing. Contrary to Midge Decter's pronouncement that women are demanding the childlike wish for absolution from all difficulty, women are demanding liberation and a difficult freedom. The freedom to choose for oneself presents many more problems than does the relative comfort of having one's choices made by another. Discouraging is the fact that it is part of the human condition that subservience becomes internalized and so ingrained that, even when justice catches up and laws are made to remedy the infamy of any person or group holding any other person or group in bondage, the freed (or partially freed) slaves can hardly take advantage of their freedom because they have not endured or enjoyed the process of liberation.

We feel, and see among our contemporaries, both the pain and joy of freedoms becoming real. But whether painful or not, we see liberation and freedom as addictive. And the ability to *use* one's freedoms may be long and slow in coming, but that can never be an excuse for withholding them.

What we wish for children is that liberation from a sexist society will never be necessary and that they will be able, from their earliest education, to see themselves with unlimited potential and opportunity. That, of course, will be the millenium.

In the meantime there is much to understand and a great deal to do about the sexist ways our culture and its educational institutions operate. In the following chapters we hope to describe how sexism pervades society and schools in order that we might look finally toward the possibility and the reality of change.

NOTES

[1]Paul Lauter and Florence Howe, *The Conspiracy of the Young*, New York, World, 1970, p. 306.

[2]Midge Decter, "The Liberated Woman," *Commentary*, October 1970, pp. 33–44.

[3]Letters, *Commentary*, February 1971, pp. 12–36.

[4]Alice Rossi, letter in *New York Times Magazine*, 9 April 1972, pp. 6–18.

[5]Joseph Adelson, "Is Women's Lib a Passing Fad?" *New York Times Magazine*, 19 March 1972, pp. 26–98.

[6]Rossi, *op. cit.*

[7]Betty Friedan, *The Feminine Mystique*, New York, Norton, 1963.

[8]Lauter and Howe, *op. cit.*, pp. 3–24.

[9]Robin Morgan, "Goodby to All That," reprinted from the radical newspaper RAT by KNOW, Inc., Box 86031, Pittsburgh, Pa. 15221.

[10]Grace Lichtenstein, "Auto Dealers Bitterly Complain over 'Embezzling Consumers,'" *New York Times*, 11 September 1971.

[11]Judy Klemsrud, "Do Women Want Equality? A Poll Says Most Now Do," *New York Times*, 24 March 1972.

[12]The verse by Edwin Markham to which Pauli Murray was referring reads: "He drew a circle that shut me out—/Heretic, rebel, a thing to flout./But Love and I had the wit to win:/We drew a circle that took him in."

[13]Toni Morrison, "What the Black Woman Thinks About Women's Lib," *New York Times Magazine*, 22 August 1971, pp. 14–66.

[14]Toni Cade, ed. *Black Woman*, New York, Signet, 1970.

[15]Jo Ann E. Gardner and Charles W. Thomas in a conversation with T. George Harris, "Different Strokes for Different Folks," *Psychology Today*, September 1970. Reprinted from *Psychology Today*, September 1970. Copyright © by Communications/Research/Machines, Inc.

[16]Rep. Shirley Chisholm, "The 51% Minority," address delivered at The Conference on Women's Employment, Chicago, Illinois, 24 January 1970. Reprinted by KNOW, INC., Box 86031, Pittsburgh, Pa. 15221.

[17]Walt Whitman, "Thought," in *Leaves of Grass*.

2

Down with ladies, up with women, and off with the little white gloves[1]

A few years ago we all wanted our daughters to act like and grow up to be "ladies." Now that word is distasteful because it suggests a demure and passive female who accepts the conventions and proprieties of a society that treats her as a second class citizen. The little white gloves must come off because they are bound to get dirty in the fight against sexism.

A few years ago *sexism* was not a real word, and at this writing, it is still not in the dictionary. We anticipate that, as you read this book, it will have become as commonplace as the analagous word, racism. For a dictionarylike definition we have had to cite the interpretation put forth by a feminist who described what it means in the relationships of women and men.[2] Now we must ask, what is sexism all about in its visible, day to day manifestations? Where is it evident? When we say there are still the vestigial remnants of the concept of women as slaves or as property, what, specifically, are we talking about? What, in short, are some of the institutions and practices coming under attack from the women's movement?

MARRIAGE—RITES WITHOUT RIGHTS

Let us begin with one quite blatant example—the marriage ceremony and what it symbolizes. At a wedding the father *gives away* his daughter to her future husband and the latter takes over the responsibility of ownership that the father relinquishes. Or consider the dowry, the traditional gift brought by the female to her marriage, which served, at the least, to increase her value. Although a dowry is not usually proffered these days, we still see a father making a wedding as extravagant as possible, perhaps to signify his daughter's worth.

And on this "most beautiful day in a girl's life" there is another nicety which objectifies females and has become abject to the new feminists—the traditional white wedding gown. Apart from the idea that it represents wasteful economic exploitation of the female as a consumer—"Wedding dresses alone are estimated to have a $50 million market potential and the trousseau market is put at $162 million."[3]—and beyond the grating notion that brides are dressed up like dolls and put on a pedestal, is the insinuation that a white wedding dress symbolizes the purity of the bride. This insinuation piques irritation, if not anger, with one of the many double standards in operation for males and females. The white gown exemplifies the idea that, although men can be as promiscuous as they please, unmarried women must be virginal. Not only do feminists ask why this should be, they also point out that such double standards have the effect of victimizing the nonvirgin, attaching an unfair social stigma to her, and denigrating her character. Moreover, if she is unfortunate enough to become pregnant and have a child out of wedlock, her loss in social esteem is matched only by the amount of suffering she must endure.

For most women, marriage is the most important step taken in their lives. But it is a step that leads into a briar patch as often as into a rose garden. First consider why people marry. There is no way to trace accurately the primitive origins of marriage, although it is a subject of study in many scholarly disciplines. We do know that before the nineteenth century marriage was approached variously as a sensible economic step, a way to achieve status, a means of gaining prestige, or a union of family lines. Only within the last century has the marriage contract been made on the strength of love, but as it exists today, it is still entered upon like most business contracts, with the signatures of two willing individuals, or parties to the agreement. But the terms of the agreement are set not by the individuals, but by the state. And willing or not, "to reconcile marriage and love is such a tour de force that nothing less than divine intervention is required for success."[4]

A successful marriage can be seen from many perspectives, but for the moment let's just say that it means the husband and wife are satisfied with their union. Yet what sometimes stand in the way of the success of their marriage are the prejudicial terms of the contract that binds them. A recent survey of the laws that inhibit the freedom of a married woman came to the conclusion that, in most states, getting married is the most "sacrificial act a woman can perform. . . . More than 1,000 state laws . . . discriminate against married women's right to property, inheritance, guardianship, management of earnings, and the control of the family's wealth."[5]

Onerous too, and often stifling, is the male's part of the contract that obligates him to the financial, moral, and overall support of his dependent wife and children. In general, however, it is the privileges of self-determination, economic mobility, and independence that make a man's possibilities so much more appealing than the restrictions and impotence allocated to the woman. And when she sees, as many women do, that such privileges are symbols of freedom, what can be more demoralizing than the realization that a woman's closest associate (her husband) is enjoying many privileges that are denied her?

The first thing a woman gives up upon marrying is her name. "The probable effects of this unilateral name change upon the relations between the sexes . . . are profound. In a very real sense, the loss of a woman's surname represents the destruction of an important part of her personality and its submersion in that of the husband," wrote Leo Kanowitz in his exemplary study *Women and the Law*.[6] In twenty states, a recent count disclosed, it is actually illegal for her to use her maiden name.

Montgomery, Ala., Sept. 29—A three-judge Federal Court ruled here today that a married woman does not have a constitutional right to have her driver's license issued in her maiden name. . . . The court said, "The existing law in Alabama which requires a woman to assume her husband's surname upon marriage has a rational basis and seeks to control an area where the state has a legitimate interest."

The court said the state had a "considerable investment" in its driver's license control system and concluded that "the administrative inconvenience and cost of a change to the State of Alabama far outweighs the harm caused" to women who want their licenses in their maiden names.[7]

The next option a woman relinquishes, willingly or not, is the choice of domicile. For the marriage contract binds her, as it does her dependent child, to follow the "head of the household" wherever his business, profession, or fancy (if stated in reasonable terms) locates him. Yet many of the rights of a citizen in this country are based upon his or her domicile—the right to vote, to hold and run for public office, to receive welfare, to attend a state university tuition free, as well as the obligation to pay taxes.[8] There are some states in which a woman has more freedoms than others, but very few states, only four in 1963, allow her to have her own address unless she is separated from her husband "for cause."[9] And if a married woman chooses to live in a different state than her husband, she relinquishes many of the rightful privileges of a citizen. The legal options and responsibilities a woman has are confused by the inconsistency of the laws in the various states. It becomes difficult to determine the established rules even in one specific state, because these rules often evolve out of "case law," that is, the decision in one case establishes its own precedent, and the next case may vary so much in particulars that the precedent is not applicable.

The antifemale prejudice of the law inspired some thoughtful grooms of early feminists to sign statements renouncing the legal superiority to which their marriages could have entitled them. Robert Owen, son of the British social reformer and himself head of the Workingmen's Party in this country, did so when he married Mary Jane Robinson in 1832. He wrote a statement divesting himself of the unjust rights of matrimony as "the barbarous relics of a feudal, despotic system, . . . the existence of which is a tacit insult to the good sense and good feeling of this comparatively civilized age." Henry Blackwell, the husband of feminist Lucy Stone, signed a similar protest that concluded, "Thus reverencing law, we enter our protest against rules and customs which are unworthy of the name, since they violate justice, the essence of law."[10]

CONJUGAL CLIMATE

With all the legal inconsistencies within one state and among states, and even considering the reforms that are slowly coming about, often because of pressure from women's organizations, we must understand the foundation of these situations. It is British common law concept (the basis for common law in the United States) that defines the husband and wife as one—and that one is the husband.[11] In this respect the married woman has no legal existence at all. So it is that the law has created the atmospheric conditions, if not the actual climate, of the contractual marriage relationship. But this is just a small part of what happens after a wedding. Most women don't even collide with the legal restrictions imposed by marriage during the marriage; it is usually only upon the dissolution of the marriage, by death or divorce, that they have any encounter with their legal condition. (The unmarried woman is even today considered a social deviant and we can guess that, in the eyes of society the fact that she is fully responsible for herself is a disadvantage that she suffers as a result of being single. U. S. census statistics for 1969 show that only 5 percent of the women in this country over 45 years of age had never been married.)

Legalities aside, it is a woman's day to day experiences that are the barometer of her married existence.

Steve and Marge Everet were married with the regalia of a formal wedding—white lace and romance. Marge continued to teach for a year, and it took only that long for the joy of housework to wear off. But then, she was about to realize what she expected would be her "crowning achievement" as a woman—she quit her job and had her first child. By the time they had been married for six years and had their second child Marge was thoroughly dissatisfied with her life. The drudgery of housework exhausted her, but the most depressing part was the psychological isolation. "My world grew so small," she recalled. She found she was living vicariously, as something of a parasite. As for Steve, "I hated it," he admits.

Their marriage had reached a serious crisis, but they had a chance to recognize and do something about it. "I gradually woke up to the fact that Marjorie was my servant—that that's the role of women in general and I was doing my part to help keep women down," he said. Being a history teacher he felt especially guilty. "What does American history really mean," he asked, "if I go home to a wife who considers herself a slave?" By good fortune Steve was due for a year's sabbatical, so the Everets were able to switch roles. Marge went back to teaching and Steve stayed home. Predictably Steve gained new insight into what his wife's world was really like.

"The experiment was probably the most important thing that's happened to me in my life. But I was lucky—I knew it was coming to an end, and I had Marge's understanding of what life is like when you're confined to the house. I don't think a male can experience the hell a woman does."[12]

This true life story taken from *Woman's Day* magazine has several messages for its readers, and the choice of which lines to read and which to read between depends upon who is reading them. To most women, bondage would seem too harsh and strong a word to describe their condition. Those who deny categorically that the condition exists are likely to be the most enslaved; those who are open to examining the idea are most likely to profit from their investigation intellectually, emotionally, and legally.

It is the vision of relentless domestic misery, along with the complex legal situation, that leads many feminists to reject the idea of marriage under the conventional contract or licensing procedure. Some suggest that a couple intending to marry draw up their own personal marriage contracts. Trying to eliminate the loneliness and drudgery of housewifery was part of the impetus for some of the communes and collectives that grew up in the 1960s and 1970s. In many of them child rearing, domestic work, and other labor are shared. In those arrangements an underlying belief is often that love and trust in one another, as opposed to contracts, should be enough to bind people together. Such attempts to change "life styles" may be temporary, unworkable aberrations, and in fact, they do not often solve the problems of male and female inequity.

The kibbutz in Israel provides an illustration that is somewhat disheartening from a feminist point of view. "Whatever the reasons, kibbutz women are less active than men in fulfilling prestigious tasks, such as the central-managerial ones, and they are less vocal in the weekly general meeting, where many kibbutz problems are decided. Quite a few women in the kibbutz still struggle with traditional feelings of inferiority or dependence on male esteem. For most women in the kibbutz, then, it is not their work and social activity but their marriage and family that form the center of their lives," wrote Menachem Gerson, head of the Institute of Research on Kibbutz Education in Oranim, Israel.[13] Yet sexual equality was one of the main intentions when the kibbutzim were founded. We might wonder if one of the reasons their communal style fails to overcome sex typing is that the commune or kibbutz was fundamentally too reactionary. The inspiration for the kibbutz came, in great part, as a reaction to the middle-class industrial and intellectual situation in Europe in the early twentieth century. The work ethic and agricultural basis of the kibbutz was not only necessary to start a thriving nation, but was also idealized to the extent that there developed a "cult" of agricultural work. Although women shared field labor with men, the kitchen and the nursery were still female realms, though the kitchen was a common kitchen and the nursery was a "children's house" where everyone's children stayed for most of the day and slept during the night.

In a kibbutz or in a commune, women can share in the hard labor, as in fact they did in preindustrial, agricultural times. And men can, but most often don't, do an equal share of the housework and child care. However, such arrangements idealize a way of life that antedates the midtwentieth century. Even if kibbutzim and communes worked well, they would not solve the problems facing most of us today. For most women are not willing to give up their professional aspirations, even if they do appear to represent middle-class values or materialism. Whether equality does or does not work in a kibbutz has very limited applications to how equality should apply to a woman who, for example, is professionally employed in a firm that pays her less money and gives her less responsibility than a man in the same office or to a society that expects her to go home at night, cook dinner and put the children to bed. Nor could the shared responsibility of communal living mean very much to a woman who has spent her days as a domestic worker. Her priorities are more likely to include better wages, better job opportunities, or the option to stop tending other peoples' houses and children and stay home for a time in order to enjoy her own home and family.

What has not yet been successfully devised, either by the kibbutz in Israel or the commune in America, is a way for both men and women to pursue their intellectual, professional, or business inclinations in terms of the highly technological and "nuclear" family-oriented midtwentieth century. Equality should not require an a priori demise of the nuclear family (although communes or collectives or cooperatives should be an available option) or a rejection of what is euphemistically called progress. But it should mean that if a man and woman want to have children and live together with their children at home, the father should share equally in the childrearing and housekeeping and the wife should be able to share equally in the opportunity to work outside of the home. Such opportunities may well require a revolutionizing of the traditional workweek into something such as "sessional" work. Sessional work was conceived not for the benefit of male-female equality, but rather to solve some of the problems of an advanced industrial society. For example, to keep computers or industrial machinery working around the clock, a schedule of shifts is often arranged. And why not also to keep the full resources of our intellectual machinery in operation, if not around the clock, at least in some different, realizable increments?

There are many possible variations and combinations, and a large number of overall adjustments would have to be made. But this country, which has already been talking about the four-day-week as being inevitable, must be able to recognize that to use all of its work force efficiently is better than to use about half of it inefficiently. Many of our overcrowded schools have had to devise morning and afternoon sessions so that all the children in a town could be educated. Why could not Marge Everet have taught from, say, 8 A.M. to 1 P.M. and Steve from 1 P.M. to 6 P.M., or vice versa? Certainly these are oversimplifications of the possibilities, but the reason the problem is not solved is due to prejudice more than to the difficulty of solution. Consider this simple variation:

My husband and I were both teachers in secondary school, and we both wanted to continue our careers in education. We were anxious to take courses toward a higher degree. We wrote the board of education in our school district asking if we could talk to them about the possibility of our sharing a job, and it seemed to us that there were so many good points to credit such an argument. School officials would not even consider it, let alone grant us a hearing. The only response we had was: "If we let you do this, there will be no end to the people requesting part-time positions."

There should be such options, but there are not. The same night that I heard the above, I also heard a young woman express this typical dilemma: "I am at a terrible crossroads and I have to make a decision which seems almost impossible. I want to get married and have children, but I also want to continue my education and have a career. I don't seem able to choose one without sacrificing the other in some way. And I just don't know what to do." Of course without a higher education, she would probably never have such a difficult decision to make. But even as we realize that educating women gives them a thirst for more intellectual stimulation, which is difficult to quench in our society, we seem unable to open up our system so that women can appropriately use their education.

As we have noted, the reasons for marrying have changed over the last century. And it seems the closer the condition or education of women begins to approach that of equality with men, the greater the demands made by each party for personal satisfaction in a marriage. This satisfaction goes beyond physical and emotional comfort to that of self-esteem, which comes about with active realization of intellectual potential. When little in the way of personal satisfaction was expected, it was easy to consider most marriages adequate. Now we see divorce rates steadily increasing, and by 1971, at 3.7 per 1,000 population, they exceeded the highest rates ever before recorded in this country (1945.)[14] At the same time there has been a dramatic decrease in the numbers of young women marrying at what is considered their most marriagable ages. A survey in 1971 showed that 45 percent of women under 35 years of age were then single, compared to less than 38 percent in 1960; and most striking is the fact that at the age of 20 the proportion of single women rose in just ten years from 46 percent in 1960 to 58 percent in 1971. At age 21, during that same period, the proportion of single women rose from less than 35 percent to almost 47 percent.[15] Certainly these figures reflect many complex elements, but it cannot be denied that women's increasing dissatisfaction with the status quo is one of the most important factors.

"WHITE LADIES," "COLORED WOMEN"

If many women today refuse to be addressed as ladies, there are many others who never were. As Toni Morrison points out, this distinction has hardly been ambiguous to blacks:

More than those abrupt and discourteous signs one gets use to in this country—the door that says "Push," the towel dispenser that says "Press," the traffic light that says "No"—these signs were not just arrogant, they were malevolent: "White Only," "Colored Only," or perhaps just "Colored," permanently carved into the granite over a drinking fountain. But there was one set of signs that was not malevolent; it was in fact, rather reassuring in its accuracy and fine distinctions: the pair that said "White Ladies" and "Colored Women."[16]

The independence and autonomy now demanded by women of the middle class has long weighted down black women with less social and no economic status. For these women the varieties of legal discrimination against married women that we have just outlined are of no immediate importance. For them survival is in terms of food, clothing and shelter, getting and keeping a job to sustain themselves and their families, and not in the boredom and confinement of housewifery.

This black independence is not, however, a sign of liberation, "for they have been 'liberated' only from love, from family life, from meaningful work, and just as often from the basic comforts and necessities of an ordinary existence." Such liberation described by Eleanor Holmes Norton, a civil rights lawyer, has nothing to do with freedom.[17]

About 28 percent of all black families are headed by women, as opposed to 11 percent throughout the entire country. In the remaining 72 percent, for which a man is listed as head of the family, a large percentage of the wives must work to contribute to the family income. Unemployment is higher among black women than among black men and white women, although, as is often said, black women are traditionally more employable than black men—understandably so since few compete for the jobs they get as domestics and service workers. No other group in our society is so consistently paid so badly.[18]

What economic deprivation means in terms of family life must be distinguished from the overall pattern of the more comfortable population. This applies also to Puerto Ricans, Indians, Mexican Americans, and poor whites. And it must be understood in order to break the repetitive cycle under which the black woman is not so much oppressed by the institution of marriage as she is raped by every social and economic institution. If she marries she will probably have to work to help support her family. If and when her husband is unable to provide economic support (because black men have fewer job opportunities and fewer labor unions, or any other of the protective mechanisms available to working whites) he is quite likely to desert her because he cannot face the burden of having a family that he is unable to support or because if he leaves, the family will become eligible for welfare assistance. If she is alone, whether unmarried or deserted (divorce and alimony are hardly considerations), and she is able or chooses to work, her salary is unlikely to be much better than her welfare payments. And even worse, if her salary does go over the very low economic ceiling that allows her welfare assistance, she will receive no financial aid for the care of her children. Those children, with few opportunities to avoid the same experiences as their parents, are likely to continue the cycle.

No amount of explanation, and no accumulation of statistics, dispels the painful knowledge that the black woman has been used, not only badly, but by everyone. She is sexually abused by white men. She has been called the slave of a slave in reference to her treatment by black men who have taken out their humiliation and anger on her. This exponential slavery also describes her relationship to the white woman who, at her best, has been paternalistic toward her servants.

And paternalism, as we well know by now, is merely a sophisticated form of suppression.

In some ways black women have found dignity and have become strong in the process of coping with their oppression. Perhaps because the middle-class ethics of familial responsibility have not been deeply engraved in their consciousnesses, these women can begin on the road to female liberation more autonomously and independently than their middle-class sisters. Moreover, although we can rarely trust statistics as an accurate measure of people's feelings, there are some numbers that must be kept in mind when we go on to talk about education. In a study done by the Department of Labor's Manpower Research Administration on the educational and labor market experiences of young women, it was found that young black women, when asked how much education they would *like* to get, cite quantities that not only exceed the amount they *will* receive, but also the amount they *expect* to receive. These wishes, hopes, and expectations of young black women are even slightly more unrealistic than those of their young white counterparts from the same economic circumstances. And all young women have bigger wishes, along with smaller expectations and possibilities than young men from the same backgrounds.[19] Fortunately, or unfortunately, as these young women grow older their wishful thinking is pared down to meet a closer fit with reality. But at least these figures show that the brainwashing of women is not effective quite as early in their lives as we might have thought.

Nor is it finally quite as thorough as we may have guessed. This is borne out in another way by a labor department study at Ohio State University. This study, as reported in the *New York Times*, indicated that "black women are more favorably inclined toward the idea of mothers working," and even when they do not need the money, black women want paid employment more than do white women with the same economic comfort.[20] This seems to reinforce the idea that they do not accept middle-class dependency as desirable.

These studies show that black women reject both the system that limits their education as well as the system that delineates a dependent role for women. The latter point is made by black women who are sensitized to the paranoia of the white middle class. Eleanor Holmes Norton goes on to say:

> But our problems only begin with the reconstruction of the black family. As black men begin to find dignified work after so many generations, what roles will their women seek? Are black people to

reject so many of white society's values only to accept its view of woman and of the family? At the moment when the white family is caught in a maze of neurotic contradictions and white women are supremely frustrated with their roles, are black women to take up such troubled models? Shall black women exchange their ancient insecurity for the white woman's familial cocoon? Can it serve us any better than it has served them? And how will it serve black men? There is no reason to repeat bad history.[21] (Emphasis added)

None whatsoever. And this is what the women's movement would like to make clear. But to do so, they must demand some immediate changes in the oppressive social structures and systems that form physical and psychological ghetto walls around all women.

CHILD CARE

There may be no law that says outright, "Jane Doe, when you have children you must stay home and care for them," but the notion that woman's place is in the home is culturally sanctioned at the very least. For the mother who takes a job, whether it is because she *wants* to work or because she *has* to work, the problems she encounters make it exceedingly difficult. To put it mildly there is little incentive offered. To put it less mildly, the situation is intolerable.

Consider that in 1971 there were 12.2 million mothers among the 31.7 million women in the labor force, representing a total of 25.7 million children, 5.6 million of whom were under 6 years of age, and the question of whether mothers should or should not be working is entirely irrelevant. Less academic is the question of how, where, and by whom their children are being cared for. The first answer is that most small children are cared for, often in their own homes, by relatives—an older child, an unemployed father, grandparents, or more distant relatives. The smallest number of these children, only about 6 percent, are cared for in an organized setting such as a nursery school or a day care center.[22] And most of those day care centers, for a number of reasons, including insufficient funding, are inadequately staffed, supplied, and managed. These simple answers reflect an obvious conclusion that should be more startling than it is: *Our society has made no satisfactory commitment to the care of the children of working women.*

It is not that our government is totally unaware of the need for some commitment, for the morass of federal and state restrictions that govern the size, shape, stairs, exits, materials, windows, and bathrooms, among other things, in the physical construction of day care centers is impressive, if not overwhelming. More indicative of the premise on which these concerns rest is the fact that, in thirty-six states, it is the welfare departments that license these centers, and in only one state is licensing up to the department of education. The premise is, it seems, that custodial day care must, as a community burden, be made available to mothers who are unable to take care of their own children. Bettye Caldwell points out that this vision of the principle of day care comes from the idea that the children involved are from "families with some type of social pathology."[23]

Feminists do, and everyone should, categorically reject the social pathology premise of child care. Quality child care (as opposed to merely custodial) must become a commitment of our society, and it must be available to all. Probably there should be no charge, or at the most cost should be on a sliding scale. The social objectives of child care need long and hard consideration, but not so long nor so hard that a program never gets started. What will be the role of the family and the community in the running of these programs? And how can the rights as well as the needs of the child be observed? How are the children to be amused and/or educated, and what individual attention will be paid to their developing intellects? How will their social and emotional needs be tended to? Who will control, license, and monitor the centers to make sure that standards are being met? We do not know the answers to those questions, but we do know that many concerned feminists, mothers, fathers, and educators are trying to work them out.

We also know that providing funds to care for children is not outside the realm of government support, not, at least, when the government recognizes that providing such aid is to some important advantage. For during World War II, when women were needed to work in war production, the Lanham Act was passed to make federal money available to support nurseries for children of those working mothers. After the war federal support was withdrawn, and women (and their children) were sent back home.

Similarly, industries have at times shown an interest in providing child care facilities for their employees, but not often enough, and their interest in day care has been "translated into actual programs only in a limited number of instances," according to a survey done by the Women's Bureau.[24]

As one of its political platforms, the women's movement is working hard for the establishment of state or federally supported child care to free mothers for work, as well as to help working parents—a distinction based upon the assumption that child care is the responsibility of both parents. In 1971 the federal government did take steps toward making money available to very low income families. It also moved toward providing working wives some tax relief for child care, which they are denied under a ludicrous tax setup in which a man can deduct huge expenses for entertaining business associates while his working wife, who cannot even go out the door without paying a baby sitter, is allowed no valid claim to a deduction.

There was, however, a serious setback to progress late in 1971 when President Nixon vetoed the Comprehensive Child Development Bill that would have provided some help to mothers in low economic brackets. The President, as part of his rationale for withholding support for child care, cited the "family weakening tendencies" of the bill. Elinor C. Guggenheimer, as founder and honory president of the New York City Day Care Council, wrote to the President via the editorial page of the *New York Times*:

Unless he is preparing legislation to bar mothers from the labor force, women will continue to be absent from the home for a substantial portion of the day whether we provide care for their children or not. The President's vision of Mom in the kitchen putting up the conserves, fruit and vegetable is almost antediluvian. Take a good look, Mr. President. Mom—almost twelve million Moms of children under eighteen—has moved out of the kitchen and into the canning factory on the edge of town. We continue to allow more than two million preschool children to receive less than adequate care, because legislation has been based on a vision instead of reality.[25]

In rebuttal to protests that children suffer when their mothers are not their constant attendants, one hardly needs a full-fledged study to show that it is not the quantity but the quality of nurturing, whether by a man or a woman, that counts.[26] For this reason it is important that the quality of child care reflect a nonsexist bias. It is imperative that child care centers do not begin the system of tracking, that is, guiding children along narrow, predetermined paths, by sex stereotyping, but rather that they encourage girls and boys to feel comfortable investigating and doing a variety of things that might interest them. A small girl can be encouraged to develop strength and dexterity by hammering nails. A small boy can learn a great deal by playing with dolls—imagining and projecting into fantasy situations with dolls that represent people he is likely to meet and would do well to understand as he grows up. Also, it is important that men participate in caring for and teaching young children. It will help children learn that it is not only women who are responsible for and to children. And a man (or a woman) in a child care program should not be the kind of person who admonishes a weeping child, "Come on now, boys don't cry." For boys do cry, and we would go so far as to insist that they should not only feel free to cry but should find sympathy in tearful situations. Breaking the system of sex stereotyping in early childhood could accomplish wonders in eradicating the discriminatory stereotyping and tracking of children in their later education.

Certainly many women derive their satisfaction from using and developing the skills of homemaking, and they also enjoy the rewards of full-time mothering. The women's movement should in no way intimidate anyone who has such inclinations—male or female. It insists only that all people be given a real choice.

> *I've always been good about standing by the front door at 2:30 when my kids get home from school, but I've always resented it. It got worse when I found out it wasn't for the kids, it was for the front door.*[27]

A woman who wants to work full time, part time, occasionally, or when her children are grown up, needs a social structure that provides these options, without any negative moral judgments implied. And a woman who considers being a mother and a wife her most important vocation should be free to do so but should also recognize that one who has some intellectual stimulation outside the home may come back to that home with more to offer a family. Simply, if a person is happier, he or she has a greater capacity to give happiness.

JOBS

Sometimes the fight for child care centers hardly seems worth the effort (except, of course, that for many it is a financial necessity) since most employed women have such unrewarding jobs. As reported to Congress in 1971, women make up more than 75 percent of the total employed in the following fields: bookkeepers; cashiers; dressmakers, seamstresses; housekeepers, private household; nurses, professional; office machine operators; operatives, apparel and accessories; operatives, knitting mills; practical nurses; elementary school teachers; stenographers, typists and secretaries; telephone operators; waitresses. Women are exploited by being funneled into the lowest paying, most menial jobs of our society. Most of those listed will sound familiar to the high school or college student who has done part-time or summer work; and that those jobs are part-time, en route to better things, is often the only rationale for doing them. But it is full-time for the women who do 75 percent of that work. In fact, women head 6 million families, 25 percent of them in the poverty area; 1.4 million working women have unemployed husbands (disabled or retired), and 7.2 million working women are single.[28]

There are some jobs in which women, often unwittingly, compete with men. When women argue that protective legislation is really discriminatory what they mean is this: A law states that Jane Doe, because she is a woman, cannot lift more than thirty-five pounds (despite the fact that the toddler she carries around all day may weigh that much) or that she cannot work at night. In effect, whatever the original intention might have been, the employer or the union favors the male who might want the same job or may be seeking overtime pay. During World War II when she was needed in defense plants, Jane Doe became known as Rosie the Riveter. Often a wife and a mother, Rosie was not considered too frail for men's work. It is a special pragmatism that dictates the role women are allowed to play, and it is not based upon women's desires or their capabilities. The question is: protecting *whom*? There are signs of change:

Savannah, Ga., April 24 (1971) AP—Mrs. William B. Weeks of Swainsboro has been awarded nearly $31,000 in back pay by a Federal judge in her suit against the Southern Bell Telephone Company, charging job discrimination. The company had refused to give Mrs. Weeks a job as a switchman because of a Georgia Labor Commission regulation that says a woman may not be required to lift more than 30 pounds on her job. The job involves the maintenance and testing of switching equipment.[29]

"Women are getting smart on filing complaints, and they are learning how to do it," Dorothy Haener of the United Automobile Workers told members of business and industry at a national conference. She was backed up by statistics from the Department of Labor that described some results of legal actions taken under the Fair Labor Standards Act. From 1964 to 1971 $30 million was found due to almost eighty thousand employees, almost all of them women, and complaints have doubled over the last two years. Among the 234 lawsuits filed for equal pay (more than 95 percent of equal pay cases are settled without litigation) there were decisions resulting in payment of more than $900,000 plus $100,000 in interest to two thousand women employees in one case, and in another case, $126,000 plus $24,000 in interest was awarded to 176 women and 26 men.[30]

If protective laws are needed, which they may well be, they should be equally protective. If it is unhealthy for a person to work more than twelve hours in twenty-four, or if it is unwise for a 130 pound person to lift more than 60 pounds, and if these are not arbitrary standards (although in our example they are hypothetical), then they should apply to both males and females. A 180 pound woman should have the same opportunty as a 180 pound man to make an extra $1,000 per year by lifting an extra 15 pounds (when that is the criterion), hernias not withstanding.

What we will call the credibility gap in the employment of females is reinforced at every turn. Across the board, women are hired last, paid less, promoted more slowly if at all. The statistics in Table 1 tell the story.

One last statistic from the National Science Foundation: The soaring unemployment rate in 1971 showed that among unemployed scientists there were more than twice as many women as men, 5.2 percent women compared to 2.3 percent men.[31]

And one more story that symbolizes the blindness of all profes-

TABLE 1.   Median Wage or Salary Income of Full-Time Year Round Workers, by Sex and Selected Major Occupation Group, 1970

Major Occupation Group	Median wage or salary income		Women's median wage or salary income as percent of men's
	Women	Men	
Professional and technical workers	$7,878	$11,806	66.7
Non-farm-managers, officials, and proprietors	6,834	12,117	56.4
Clerical workers	5,551	8,617	64.4
Sales workers	4,188	9,790	42.8
Operatives	4,510	7,623	59.2
Service workers (except private household)	3,953	6,955	56.8

SOURCE: U.S. Department of Commerce, Bureau of The Census, Current Population Reports, p. 60, No. 80.

sions toward women. It was recounted to me by a friend who started her premedical studies when her third child was eighteen months old:

> When I began my residency, several of us were being clued in on hospital policy and procedures by the chief of residents. One of the things he told us was this: When you have a patient with a terminal illness, if he is a man, you should tell him that he is dying since he will probably have some business affairs that he must set in order. If the patient is a woman, you should not tell her she is dying, first because she will have no affairs to take care of and second because she will not be able to cope emotionally with the knowledge of her death.

ACADEMIC ANEMIA

As discrimination pervades other social and professional realms, so it infests educational institutions, in concept and in practice, from nursery school right up through the postgraduate level and into academic professions. Teaching children started out with an onus similar to that of midwifery. Midwives plodded along delivering babies to the degree and the ability the technique, if not the technology, was available for doing so. As soon as medicine came up with a science of obstetrics male doctors took over, the trade became a profession, and women were excluded.

Teaching young children has been considered work for women, the aged, the lame, or the otherwise socially useless. In Greece, where the word "pedagoge" joined the vocabulary and was defined "to lead a child," the job was assigned to slaves. The instruction of "adults" was left in the hands of important men—Socrates, Plato, Aristotle, for example. "Apparently, recognition was accorded teachers in direct ratio to the age group they taught."[32]

Stages in the course of history—the advent of Christianity, the colonization of America, the independence of the United States, and the institution of mass public school education—witnessed the development of different theories and realities of early childhood education. Yet one kernel of truth remains. The occupation of teaching the very young is still a career without status, and it is now overwhelmingly staffed by females in this country. It is also still true that as the age of the student increases, so does the prestige and the salary of his or her teacher.

Joe Porter went to Harvard and his future wife, Mary, to Radcliffe. They met, dated, studied, and graduated together, both cum laude. They went to graduate school together, took the same courses, both got their Ph.D.'s in the same field of study, and then they got married. Together they sent off job applications to one hundred colleges. The only difference in their academic records was that Mary's was slightly better. After a flock of preliminary inquiries Joe was given a choice of eight teaching positions. Mary did not receive a single job offer.[33]

This will not surprise many women who have had ambitions in the academic realm. "Women are the drones in the academic hive. They are taken for granted, subjected to subtle exclusion, refused tenure or promotion, judged expendable and let go," according to sociologist Alice Rossi. Although women comprise about one-fifth of the faculties of the nation's 2,600 colleges and universities (all that is left after the vigorous weeding out that tries in every way to discourage women from getting that far), they are bunched at the lowest rungs of the academic ladder. Usually they are accepted in the least prestigious institutions, and even there they are relegated to the lowest ranking positions, untenured instructors and teaching assistants. Moreover, they are channeled into the "feminine" areas such as education, library science, nursing, and social work.[34]

But again women are getting smart, and hundreds of discrimination charges are being filed against various schools. In 1971 in response to charges of discrimination, Harvard was forced to open its files to the federal government upon the threat that if they did not show themselves unprejudiced their federal funding would be withdrawn. Columbia University was threatened with similar withdrawal if they failed to establish a program of equality in hiring. Still, the first woman in the nation who actually tried to force a university to take action on the principle of equal pay for equal work lost her case at the University of Michigan in June of 1971.

POLITICAL ACTION

Taking offenders to court is a way of remedying a specific injustice. Each case won helps to break the system, but it does not cure a basic deficiency. Because of this, women's groups tried for almost fifty years to get their own Equal Rights Amendment to the Constitution. Its passage in 1972 should establish as federal policy that equality of rights under the law shall not be denied or abridged by the United States or by any state according to sex. The legal status of women, which is otherwise undefined by the Constitution, should no longer be left to the vicissitudes of the various states. This amendment makes it possible to enforce Title VII of the Civil Rights Act, which prohibits job discrimination on the grounds of race, color, religion, or sex. And it should also wipe out the British common law evaluation of women, which, as we have noted, gave married women no legal value.

In order to win the passage of the Equal Rights Amendment as well as to abolish all of the discriminatory practices that undermine the operation of a just democracy in this country, women have formed new political action groups. In the summer of 1971 more than 300 women with a variety of political backgrounds met in Washington to organize the National Women's Political Caucus. One of the main purposes of the caucus is to reach out to women across the country in all social, economic, and racial classes and to heighten their political awareness. For it is undeniable that if 53 percent of the voting population are rallied, the political influence they can exert will be phenomenal. In its statement of purpose the caucus expressed the intention to "rally national and local support for the campaigns of women candidates—federal, state, and local—who declare themselves ready to fight for the rights and needs of women, and of all under-represented groups."

The national caucus stimulated the formation of state caucuses, and they broke into regional groups in order to operate more efficiently at local levels. The Massachusetts Women's Political Caucus, in its plenary sessions, made a point of incorporating into its platform a statement condemning the practice of discriminatory tracking of children in educational institutions. The members showed an interest in watching local elections for positions taken by candidates for school committees or school boards.

The political caucuses also expressed their intention to monitor and protest against the sexist habits of the mass media. Much of education of children takes place outside schoolhouse doors, and these days the television set is one of the strongest forces in educating young people. Television can be, and in some ways is, a fine resource. But, unfortunately, even when it is at its best, it can be doing its worst. The educational program "Sesame Street" for example, was developed for the specific purpose of helping ghetto children to learn to read. It is an ingenious and delightful program in many ways. But, it has also been guilty of typically sexist attitudes in the way it portrays male and female roles. There were usually few if any females playing major parts, and when women were presented in the show, they tended to provide the least admirable of all the possible "role models" for girls.[35] So in many ways, a program such as "Sesame Street," which has done wonders in raising the reading readiness and ability of young children, can be as harmful as "The Flintstones," a despicable cartoon program that polarizes males and females into dumb, selfish men and conniving, cunning women. Equally counterproductive are the many advertisements that show women with their aprons on praising a superb product that will allow them to be out of the house in no time flat (adding fuel to the argument that no one in her right mind would *want* to stay home and that "women's work" lacks interest). Other ads that show women devoutly grooming themselves for the purpose of attracting men (and men being smug about finding the hair oil, deodorant, or shave cream that will make the women flock to them) can teach children many unnecessary lessons. There are too many examples of television programs and commercials that lock children into visions of males and females in stereotyped roles. They educate these children to reproduce the stereotypes as though they had to take up parts in a television script. The system can't be broken without approaching it at many difficult levels, from many different angles, and if mobilized to political action, as through the caucuses, women will begin to be able to use power as a lobbying and legislative tool for renovating an out of date structure.

The potential strength of the women's political caucus became tangible during the course of the political campaigns and conventions preceding the presidential election of 1972. Early in his campaign for the Democratic nomination Senator George McGovern announced that, were he to become president, he would use the first opportunity to appoint a woman to the Supreme Court. He also said that he would name a woman ambassador to the United Nations and would be sure that women would be present in the cabinet as well as in the National Security Council. Moreover, during the process of selection of delegates to the political nominating conventions it was established as policy for the first time that women be present at state delegations in reasonable ratio to their presence in the population.

RESPONSIBILITY

Taking political action will do much to make women active subjects rather than passive objects in the decisions and arrangements governing their lives, and this leads to another dimension of resentment against the treatment of women as objects. Women today want the choice to control their own bodies. In Massachusetts, for example, there is still at this writing a law that makes it a crime to distribute birth control information or contraceptives to unmarried people. Abortion is still illegal in most states, whereas on the other hand minority women have been pressured, forced, or deceived into sterilization!

Perhaps the governing moral value has been that marriage is the license that allows men the opportunity and gives women the responsibility to procreate and that once procreation has begun, it is an irreversible moral commitment. But taking today's realities and more contemporary morality in hand, plus the advanced technology that makes birth control and abortion safe and feasible, feminists are fighting for the free dissemination of birth control information and repeal of abortion laws. Their feeling is that what a woman does with her life and her body should be left to her discretion. This idea presents a multitude of moral, spiritual, and religious dilemmas among a people that has been ambivalent about birth control and has long believed that abortion is evil. It is a difficult reconciliation to make for many. President Nixon stated publicly, "From personal and religious beliefs, I consider abortions an unacceptable form of population control. Further, unrestricted abortion policies, or abortion on demand, I cannot square with my personal belief in the sanctity of human life—including the life of the yet unborn."[36]

Yet liberalized abortion laws are slowly becoming an accepted social reform. According to one doctor, legal abortion is the fastest growing social revolution in the United States. So far, New York, Alaska, Hawaii, and Washington have gone farthest in legislation that, in effect, allows abortion on demand. One already obvious positive result is a significant decline in maternal deaths that resulted from women resorting to dangerous, illegal, or self-induced abortions. Infant mortality has also declined enough to indicate that many defective babies, who might have died at birth, were not born as a consequence of women being able to terminate pregnancy early. Even more persuasive are statistics showing that, after legal abortion was made available in New York City, the births of illegitimate children, which had been rising steadily, declined for the first time in ten years.[37] Finally, a survey published toward the end of 1971 demonstrated an amazing shift in public opinion regarding abortion policy. Although surveys done in 1965 showed that 91 percent of the population disapproved of liberalized abortion policies, just six years later a study made by the Federal Commission on Population Growth and the American Future disclosed that 50 percent of the population favored liberalizing the restrictions on abortion. Ironically, it was President Nixon who proposed the establishment of that commission.[38]

There are many other areas in which discrimination against women operates as though by divine mandate. The mandate, which turns out not to have been divine anyway, is being strenuously challenged, and the system is slowly relently to reform. But "the conviction of male authority is so deeply imbedded in the present collective consciousness and integrated so cunningly, with social norms that it operates almost by blind axiom, even, to be sure, with the consent of the dominated. Sexual inequity functions insidiously, through habit, as a divine mandate—rather like a religion in its own right. The liberation movement is naturally, then, an act of heresy, for its members refuse to be bound any longer by the patriarchal faith and are casting aside every scrap of its dogma."[39]

NOTES

[1]The title of this chapter is taken from an advertisement run in the *New York Times*.

[2]See footnote p. 2, Chapter 1.

[3]From Brides Showcase, International Press Kit, New York Bridal Fair, New York, 1969, as quoted by Robin Morgan, ed., *Sisterhood is Powerful*, New York, Random House (Vintage), 1970, p. 558. Reprinted by permission.

[4]Simone de Beauvoir, interpreting Kierkegaard in *The Second Sex*, New York, Knopf, 1953, p. 438.

[5]"The Geography of Inequality," A *McCall's* Survey, February 1971, p. 90. Reprinted by permission of the publisher.

[6]Leo Kanowitz, *Women and the Law, The Unfinished Revolution*, Albuquerque, University of New Mexico Press, 1969, p. 41. Reprinted by permission.

[7]"Maiden Name Barred For a Driver's License," *New York Times*, 30 September 1971.

[8]Kanowitz, *op. cit.*, p. 47.

[9]*Ibid.*, p. 48.

[10]Owen and Blackwell's statements are quoted by Aileen Kraditor, ed., *Up from the Pedestal*, Chicago, Quadrangle Books, 1968, pp. 148–150. Reprinted by permission of the publisher.

[11]"The theoretical basis for the married woman's loss of legal rights was the feudal doctrine of coverture. Based in part upon biblical notions of the unity of flesh of husband and wife, described by Blackstone. . . . In modern times the doctrine has been described with greater candor as rest-

ing 'on the old common-law fiction that the husband and wife are one . . . [which] has worked out in reality to mean . . . the one is the husband.' " Kanowitz, *op. cit.*, pp. 35–36.

[12]"Mother Went to Work . . . and Father Stayed Home," Jorie Lueloff *Woman's Day*, August 1971, p. 52. Reprinted by permission.

[13]Menachem Gerson, "Women in the Kibbutz," *American Journal of Orthopsychiatry*, July 1971, p. 567. Reprinted by permission.

[14]*Monthly Vital Statistics Report, Annual Summary for the United States, 1971,* Department of Health, Education and Welfare, National Center for Health Statistics, Rockville, Md. 20852.

[15]Jack Rosenthal, "Population Growth Rate in U. S. Found Sharply Off," *New York Times*, 5 November 1971.

[16]Toni Morrison, "What the Black Woman Thinks About Women's Lib," *New York Times Magazine*, 22 August 1971, p. 14.

[17]Eleanor Holmes Norton, "For Sadie and Maude," Morgan, *op. cit.*, p. 355.

[18]See Sonia Pressman's "Job Discrimination and the Black Woman," *Crisis*, March 1970, p. 103.

[19]See Frederick A. Zeller and John R. Shea, "Educational Aspirations," *Years For Decision*, vol. 1, monograph no. 24 of the Manpower Administration of the U. S. Department of Labor, 1971, p. 153.

[20]"Women's Attitudes on Working Studied," *New York Times*, 25 April 1971.

[21]Norton, *op. cit.*, pp. 355–356.

[22]"Who Are The Working Mothers?" leaflet 37 (rev.) 1972, Women's Bureau, Employment Standards Administration, U.S. Department of Labor.

[23]Bettye M. Caldwell, "A Timid Giant Grows Bolder," *Saturday Review*, 20 February 1971, p. 47.

[24]"Day Care Services: Industry's Involvement," bulletin 296, Women's Bureau, U. S. Department of Labor, p. 31. See also Caroline Bird, *Born Female*, rev. ed., New York, Simon and Schuster (Pocket Books), 1971.

[25]Elinor C. Guggenheimer, "Look Here, Mr. Nixon!" *New York Times*, 21 December 1971.

[26]An important discussion of these points can be found in Alice S. Rossi, "Equality Between the Sexes: An Immodest Proposal," in Robert J. Lifton, ed., *The Woman in America*, Boston, Beacon Press (Daedalus Library), 1967, pp. 98–143.

[27]Carol Kleiman of *The Chicago Tribune* as quoted in *The Spokeswoman*, an independent monthly newsletter of women's news, Chicago, Vol. 2, 15, September 1971.

[28]Material presented by Susan Deller Ross for the record to the Committee on the Judiciary, House of Representatives, 92nd cong., Hearings on Equal Rights for Men and Women, 1971, p. 179. And "Why Women Work" Women's Bureau, Employment Standards Administration, U.S. Department of Labor, July, 1972 (rev.)

[29]"Woman Wins Job Suit," *New York Times*, 25 April 1971.

[30]Enid Nemy, "Toting Up Dollars-and-Cents Cost of Sex Discrimination," *New York Times*, 14 May 1971.

[31]Gerd Wilcke, "The Highly Educated Jobless," *New York Times*, 18 July 1971.

[32]Louis Fischer and Donald R. Thomas, *Social Foundations of Educational Decisions*, Belmont, Calif., Wadsworth, 1965, p. 282.

[33]"Women Profs Fight Back," *Newsweek*, 17 May 1971, pp. 99–100. Reprinted by permission of the publisher.

[34]*Ibid.*

[35]See, for example, Jane Bergman, "Are Little Girls Being Harmed by 'Sesame Street'?" *New York Times*, 2 January 1972.

[36]"Text of President's Abortion Statements," *New York Times*, 4 April 1971.

[37]"Abortion: How It's Working," *Newsweek*, 19 July 1971, pp. 50–52. Reprinted by permission of the publisher.

[38]"Survey Finds 50% Back Liberalization of Abortion Policy" *New York Times*, 28 October 1971.

[39]Muriel Haynes, "Fettered and Stunted by Patriarchy," *Saturday Review*, 29 August 1970, p. 27.

3

Who is silvia?
What is she?

On Tuesday mornings the eleven-year-old girls and boys
at Finchley County High School assembled for music.
Schubert was a favorite and Shakespeare provided the words for
one of the first songs we learned. It was about a woman named
Silvia:

Who is Silvia? What is she,
  That all our swains commend her?
Holy, fair, and wise is she:
  The heavens such grace did lend her,
That she might admired be.[1]

The melody was tricky, but that's not why the first verse of
the song has been haunting me through the years. Rather, it is
the vision of womanhood, the idealized, mythical version that
has survived the centuries. Holy, fair, wise and graceful—these
were the attributes loaned to Silvia (not innately hers) for
the purpose of pleasing men. Consider her, in our twentieth-
century jargon, a role model for girls and a sex symbol for
boys, but realize that, in both cases her existence is a male's
definition or fantasy of the female, and one that is now
vigorously challenged.

There is another Sylvia who draws our attention away from the mythical woman and causes us to think twice and three times about all definitions of females up to the present. Sylvia Plath was a poet and novelist whose life became so intolerable that she ended it by suicide in her thirty-first year. When she died in 1963 there was not a forceful movement for the liberation of women, but since her death she has become a symbol of the suffocation of the female spirit. In her work Sylvia Plath described the circumscribed existence of a woman whose role is so closely defined by society that she feels unable to breathe. The title of her novel, *The Bell Jar*, is an analogy for the way her heroine was destroyed—in a vacuum.[2] The formidable demand of the women's liberation movement is that women start to breathe freely and to redefine themselves.

What happens to a woman who refuses the circumscribed definition of a female and deviates from socially prescribed norms? She is considered a social deviant and is not usually rewarded with approval, nor is she easily accomodated in the culture or society that she persists in defying.

For when it really means business, a culture solidifies its expectations (and limitations) with unequivocal rules and regulations. We recognized some of them in Chapter 2 where we saw them crystallized into laws that inhibit freedom and equality. Yet there are discriminations that cannot be legislated—the discriminations implicit in stereotyping or setting up norms for behavior based, not on an individual's potential, but on society's presumptions. Thus, for example, there can be no law that decrees that females must be nurturant. However, since this is a value that is culturally sanctioned, such a gap in the law is solidly bridged by very strong assumptions; in this example the assumption might be that a woman's role in life is to raise a family. So it is that assumptions are meant to close and complete the system. But it doesn't always work, and as long as there are loopholes, there will be people to find their way through them. When one of these women who wants something for herself that the culture has not appropriated to her, will not give up going after it, she is punished. When her misdeed is illegal, it is a misdemeanor, and she is punished under the law. When her misdeed is not necessarily illegal but is anticultural, the punishment is emotional and psychological. A woman who would not give up or let go described, at a much later date, the emotional toll her persistence had taken:

The passionate desire of the women of my generation for higher education was accompanied throughout its course by the awful doubt, felt by women themselves as well as men, as to whether women as a sex were physically and mentally fit for it. . . . I cannot remember the time when I was not sure that studying and going to college were the things above all others which I wished to do. I was always wondering whether it could really be true, as everyone thought, that boys were cleverer than girls. Indeed, I cared so much that I never dared ask any grown up person the direct question, not even my father or mother, because I feared to hear the reply. I remember often praying about it, and begging God that if it were true that because I was a girl I could not successfully master Greek and go to college and understand things to kill me at once, as I could not bear to live in such an unjust world.[3]

M. Carey Thomas, who told of her prayers in a speech given to the Association of Collegiate Alumnae in 1907, lived well beyond the shadow of her doubts to become a leader in the fight for women's higher education. She battled the assumptions about female physical and intellectual inferiority and triumphed. But nine out of ten females don't fight; they don't even question the assumptions.

How can such festering stereotypes, expectations, and assumptions be exorcised? Sometimes by providing an example, so that to deviate as an individual, as Carey Thomas did and as many other women have done, helps to clear the path for others. Not only is the personal strain great, but the barriers are nearly insurmountable. This is another reason why not enough women can successfully deviate to prove what an irrational sham the stereotypes are. Moreover, to approach an even footing with men, women often have to be, not just as "good" (i.e., as qualified) as men, but even better:

For this year we believe that any girl who ranks in the top fifteen percent with mid-500 boards who is recommended by you and in a good solid college program undoubtedly will be admitted. For the males drop in down to the top twenty-five percent with low 500's with the same characteristics and they should make it.[4]

This letter was sent by an associate dean of admissions at a large eastern state university to the high schools that he had visited. This is not atypical.

If categorizing and limiting people is bad, if it represents an undemocratic and immoral limitation upon the freedom of the individual, and there can be no doubt that it does, then how might we be able to effectively discredit such activities? We might hope to do it by systematically finding material that refutes all of the assumptions that differentiate male and female and so devolve a sexist culture. Thus we might look to the academic disciplines for objective research to show conclusively that sexism rests upon unfounded myths.

But trying to do this what often happens is that, when we look to "science," we also see sophistry and when we listen to "learned men," we also hear lies in the language of anthropology, sociology, psychology. The sophistry and lies wind in and out of fantasy and fact, and the research tends to become useless, for we still end up asking ourselves, does anyone know anything useful about the differences between male and female? We find the answers always depend on who has posed the original question about sex differences and why, how the question has been framed, who has done the research, what has been left out, and to what extent the answer has been shaped by the framing of the question. And not the least of variables is the very sex of the scholar. But in spite of all, we must pursue this research because it is our responsibility, and on top of that, it is fascinating and informative. When it is neither of these, however, it is frustrating.

In *The Golden Notebook* Doris Lessing describes a scene in which a renowned professor is about to lecture the staff of a hospital on the orgasm in the female swan. All of the women doctors in the audience walk out on him when he says that he has "conclusively proved that female swans do not have orgasm," and that "he would use this useful scientific discovery as a basis for a short discussion on the nature of the female orgasm in general." One of the women is asked why she left. She answers, "But my dear . . . women of any sense know better, after all these centuries, than to interrupt when men start telling them how they feel about sex."[5]

As we now, figuratively, step back into the lecture hall, we might consider ourselves participants in a marathon program under the heading "Who Thinks What About The Differences Between Male and Female," and the question that should haunt all present is a whispered, "And why?" So in this context, we will first listen to an introductory series of interpretations of the female and her role that range from frivolous to perilous. Each in its own way distorts information to fit the inclinations of the man at the podium. Next we will consider the interpretation of woman's role from an historic-evolutionary point of view, one that also depends upon the philosophies and circumstances surrounding the individual describing the situation. Then we will consider a newer theory of human behavioral evolution derived from research into the neurological basis of behavior. From there we will step into the areas where biology and sociology encounter one another, where geneticists and environmentalists argue, where physiologists and psychologists match wits, and where sometimes the dividing lines are taken away and we hear environmental geneticists and physiological psychologists try to answer our questions. We will hear about, and we will comment upon, the stereotypically male characteristic, aggression. We will lend an ear to the father of clinical psychology and to his disciple, the popular father of practical child-rearing, in order to see the effect of theory on widespread practices. And we will end up by refining the question with which we began: Who and what is Silvia?

SCIENCE AND NONSENSE

Generalities about women range from tongue in cheek such as this: *London, (AP)—A Royal Navy expert says that the extra layer of fatty tissue a woman has equips her to better survive in a cold sea and therefore, "technically speaking, the lifeboat drill should be men and children first."*[6]

To tragicomedy such as this:

Would any of you trust any of the so called free and equal females to pilot you in a jet liner across an ocean? No. And neither does any airline in the world. . . . I think that the average woman, led by her own instinct, knows she is limited in capacity, in responsibility, and in stability, if not by ability, by being rendered thus by the very essence of her cyclic nature. From pubesence to senescense, this creature is riven monthly by uncontrolled physical and mental gyrations. . . . But change her if you will—and can.[7]

And even as we move along into the realm of responsible scientific investigation, which the above can in no way claim to be, we can be misled into interpretive conclusions. Here it is that we encounter Ashley Montagu, a well-known anthropologist, self-styled supporter of the female sex, and author of *The Natural Superiority of Women*. Dr. Montagu draws information about chromosomes and hormones into his thesis that insists that females are naturally superior to males. We can detect the direction of his argument from the way he describes the Y (male) chromosome, "[It] is among the smallest of the forty-six chromosomes. It may have the shape of a comma, the

merest remnant, a sad-looking affair compared with the well-uphol-
stered other chromosomes. As we shall soon see, the Y-chromosome
really is a sad affair." And it doesn't get any better, for the significance of his paltry endowment of chromosomes is, according to
Montagu reflected in the male's biological inferiority to the female
—he is less resistent to certain specific conditions and diseases, from
dense hairy growth on the ears (*ichtyosis bystrix gravor*), to hemo-
philia (bleeder's disease). Physically also the male is no match for
the female in strength, for hers is constitutional rather than simply
muscular; and finally, "with respect to psychological and social qualities, the facts again, it seems to me," says Montagu, "prove that
women are superior to men."

All of this has a deeper purpose, Dr. Montagu insists, than to
make us pity men in their weakness for which, he says, they have a
tendency to overcompensate. Rather Montagu wants us to understand
that the superiority of women is arranged so that they may be the
bearers of children, and that they, by their knowledge of maternal
love, can teach men the way of that love: "Woman must stand firm
and be true to her own inner nature; . . . Were women to fail in this
task, all hope for the future of humanity would depart from the
world."[8]

Could this be considered science in the cause of humanity? If so,
it has a missionary zeal. But such zeal is equalled by an opposing
point of view that claims Montagu is completely misled and that "it
never occurred to women that men's superior social position was
bought and paid for by performance; in a way, this blind spot con-
stitutes a tribute to how well men have done their job of creating a
sheltered place for woman to live in." This was written by David
Allen, who is not a scientist, in a book called *The Price of Women*.
Allen is the author of another book, *The Nature of Gambling*, which
provokes the misanthropic thought that it seems we place our bets
as we see the game; that is, it is the point of view of the observer
that determines what he sees.[9] This seems to be a means by which
the shadows lengthen over and distort scientific observation, the lay-
man takes up arms, and the true battle of the sexes is joined. In most
cases, the ranks of both armies are filled by men rather than women,
enlistees rather than draftees, at that!

The above are examples of nonsense and vulgarity and show how
objective information can be bent beyond any recognition of objec-
tivity. This is a perennial problem, it is a human problem. The
examples we have used are meant to serve as a red flag that says:

Danger! Beware Conclusions. Now we will reflect on another aspect of attempts to uncover the roots of the current cultural differentiation of the roles of male and female.

THE MATRIARCHY MYSTERY

The most obvious, superficially damning, and often perplexing riposte to challenge concerning woman's nature and position is this: If women are and always have been the potential equals of men, how is it that they have been so successfully dominated by male-established values and orientation? The most common answer is that women, simply because they bear and nurture infants, are forced, at least for certain periods of time, to stand on the sidelines. Tangent to this answer is a reference to women's lesser physical strength (although it is questionable whether this is culturally or physiologically dictated) that has also kept them out of the action while the shape of our culture was being moulded.

These are not quite satisfying explanations, too much seems to be left out, and there are other interesting and curious speculations that have tried to throw a different light on the subject. There are suggestions that we step back and consider the possibility that women were not always secondary creatures, rather that they were once autonomous at the least and perhaps the dominant group.

The first man to describe the idea of female cultural dominance was a Swiss anthropologist and cultural historian of the nineteenth century. Johann Jakob Bachofen was an early evolutionist who, by examining the writings of the ancients, felt that the concept of patriarchy came about after two earlier stages of development.

The initial stage, he believed, was an era in which there existed a state of public and promiscuous sexuality. This era was so abusive to females that they took matters into their own hands, rejected promiscuity, and insisted upon matrimony. This institution of marriage brought along with it the period he describes as matriarchy, (which literally means rule by the mother), women then being the central and important purveyors of progress. "Man's abuse of woman leads to conjugal matriarchy," Bachofen wrote. "For in all things it is abuse and perversion that provide the greatest stimulus to development." In his line of argument, the next stage, that of patriarchy, Bachofen considered an even higher step on the evolutionary ladder, for in his terms, "the realm of the idea belongs to man, the realm of material life to the woman."[10]

Bachofen's concept of matriarchial societies out of which patri-
archies grew was honored by sociologists until the beginning of the
twentieth century, but his thesis if not his insights are currently
discredited. There are now very different approaches to theorizing
about cultural development. Setting Bachofen and his contemporaries
in historical context, however, we note that they were writing during
the post French revolutionary period, a time when disillusionment
with mankind was deep and disturbing. It had seemed that so much
good should have come out of the revolution, but after witnessing the
chaotic failure of noble intentions, philosophers like Bachofen tended
to believe it was foolish, after all, to work toward justice—perhaps
progress was foreordained. These historical circumstances surrounding Bachofen's work are described because a recent attempt to understand women's position in categories that depend upon cultural evolution will soon be described, and the question will be raised whether
this also is a result of disillusionment due to the failure of democracy
in our more recent experience.

Bachofen's ideas were adopted and given new direction by Frederick Engels (and later, Karl Marx), who saw the subjugation of
women as a stage through which a capitalistically oriented society
must necessarily pass. For Engels the notion of paternity led to the
establishment of property rights. (The "discovery" of paternity assumes that it took time and certain sophistication before our ancestors came to recognize that the male contributed something to the
conception, by a female, of a child. The discovery has been described
by Gloria Steinem as a giant light bulb turning on above someone's
head, and he says, "Oh *that's* why!") For female monogamy had to
be decreed in order for men to make sure that their rights to their
property, children, and wives, were satisfactorily established.

There are other variations of these scenarios that seek to put
women in different historical perspectives. In the 1930s Robert Briffault examined social relations among animals and preliterate people
and described the shift from matrilocal to patrilocal societies. (Societies in which the line of descent is traced through the mother are
"matrilocal" as are cultures in which the family lives with or near the
mother's ancestors.) He felt able to write, "Definite economic power
was first placed in the hands of the men by the domestication of
animals, which are always regarded as appertaining to the province
of the hunter, and by the development of pastoral societies," and, he
concluded, "In the end, no economic change established male
supremacy more firmly.[11]

Some forty years later (i.e., the 1970s), departing from current
information that challenges a few entrenched myths about female
sexuality, there were outlines for a new plot with a new heroine and
perhaps even her vindication in the last, as yet unwritten, chapter.
Drawing upon the scientific findings of Doctors William Masters and
Virginia Johnson, one of these novel speculations insists that we
take account of two important, experimentally derived facts about
female physiology. Masters and Johnson discovered that females
have a biologically insatiable sexual appetite. In this female sexuality
differs from that of the male, for the male finds satiation after one
orgasmic ejaculation. A female, they have reported, could theoretically continue having orgasms indefinitely, to the point of physical
exhaustion. This, together with the discovery that women are not
sexually passive but, on the contrary, have a "biologically determined, inordinately high, cyclic sexual drive," has led Dr. Mary
Jane Sherfey to propose that in prehistoric, prepatriarchial civilization—a hunting, fishing, and gathering nomadic society—woman's
sexuality had free reign. Female eroticism, far from being conducive
to monogamy and family life, was rather too demanding to be
allowed to continue, it interfered drastically with maternal responsibilities and was certainly detrimental to progress toward the agricultural revolution. Sherfey says, "It is conceivable that the *forceful*
suppression of women's inordinate sexual demands was a prerequisite
to the dawn of every modern civilization and almost every living
culture." She notes that with the suppression of their primary sexual
drive necessarily came the subjugation of woman's entire emotional
and intellectual life. This suppression was "neither man's sadistic,
selfish infliction of servitude upon helpless women nor women's
weakness or inborn masochism," but was rather a simple prerequisite
for moving from a nomadic existence to a settled, agricultural civilization, which was in turn, of course, the precursor for the industrial
revolution.[12] In a way, Sherfey sees preagricultural times in much the
way Bachofen viewed the era of promiscuity, but she reverses the
roles, for she describes something more like females abusing males as
the intolerable situation if progress was to be realized.

And if we now put this evolutionary drama into the context of
midtwentieth century history and understand that women are as
disillusioned by the current failure of democracy as Bachofen was
in his time, we might find that Sherfey's theories can be projected
into a futuristic scenario showing the downfall of the western world,
including, in the last act, or chapter, the vindication of the heroine.

For we are now in what is very often called the "postindustrial era." Much of our population has become the "new nomads," a term used to describe their mobility, and sexual mores are widely reported to be breaking down. If we take all this a step further and consider that the circle, or more accurately the vertical spiral in time, is closing, we might envision a posthistoric scene: a cavewoman with a leopard skin costume dragging her mate behind her, avenged at last.

HORMONES AND
THE PLEASURE PRINCIPLE

Whereas the preceding discussions have provided us with an overall evolutionary view of how current social arrangements may have come about, there are other routes for making some sense out of the behavior of humans. One of the most interesting current theories is being developed by neurophysiologist, H. J. Campbell of the Institute of Psychiatry in London.[13] In his research Dr. Campbell has been studying animals' devotion to pleasure seeking. He has devised an experimental situation in which animals can take advantage of external stimuli that give them pleasure. For his first test he set up two goal posts in a fish tank with a mild current traveling from pole to pole. The sensation the fish must have experienced Campbell describes as probably similar to "stroking." From fish to crocodile to squirrel monkey, the subjects, in Dr. Campbell's experiments sought sensory stimulation avidly until they reached a point of satiation. This, he says, is equivalent to the way we are likely to find our pleasures from day to day. "When we are given a large bowl of strawberries we think at first: 'This is wonderful!' But after a certain number of mouthfuls we decide that we have had enough strawberries. So we put the bowl aside and do something else."

As the result of his observations of this process of seeking and satisfying one's need for pleasure Dr. Campbell has developed a new theory for the neurological basis of behavior. Building upon the "fundamental requirement of all vertebrate nervous systems . . . that the pleasure areas of the brain must be kept constantly activated" and understanding that it is a property of peripheral (external) receptors that they adapt and no longer respond to a continuing stimulus, then we can conclude that the pleasure seeking drive will start off in another direction, scanning the environment for another source of sensory stimulation. In this construction we can envision the progress of our civilization being set by humans seeking new forms of stimulation to keep the pleasure areas activated.

With respect to our examination of male and female behavior, Dr. Campbell has found that when he administers male hormones to his animals their pleasure seeking increases, and it decreases with the administration of female hormones. Must we anticipate that new generalities and theories about the roles of men and women will be drawn from Dr. Campbell's work associating sex-linked hormones with pleasure seeking? Are we likely to hear such questions as this: Since men more consistently seek pleasure and since that quest is a determinant of progress, can this information be used as evidence to explain men's leadership roles throughout history? Fortunately we can defray such useless speculation (and the discussions that would accompany it asking, for example, whether progress in a male-led culture is good or bad). For exactly what this hormone information means in terms of specific behavior is still very nebulous. And certainly Campbell himself is not taking up that speculation or argument. He points out that he was experimentally raising the hormone levels far above the normal limits. "All this shows is that [some] hormones play a part in pleasure seeking. *What* part they play, in detail, remains to be discovered."

However Dr. Campbell does mention that there seems enough evidence to speculate that the hormonal changes that take place during pregnancy might well account for the "sense of contentment [due] at least in part . . . to the action of progesterone [a female hormone] on their pleasure areas." But we might also point out that other factors might also be in operation that would lead to a decrease in pleasure seeking. For example, it could be caused by the great fatigue that is experienced by many pregnant women. And shouldn't we also consider the idea that pregnant women derive sufficient pleasure from the knowledge that they are fulfilling their culturally designated role by becoming a mother?

When he distinguishes modes of intellectual pleasure seeking, Campbell sees absolutely no differences related to gender. However, when he goes on to discuss from a personal viewpoint, in his correspondence with the authors, the different means by which males and females seek sensory pleasure, he is dismayed by those women who tend to find their satisfaction in very self-oriented ways. He describes women primping and preening, putting on too much perfume, makeup, and baubles, "living in a hall of mirrors," whereas men tend to search for sensory pleasure in ways external to themselves, such as engaging and competing in sports and other physical activities. Excessiveness in both kinds of activities Campbell believes is stupid, but he does go on to say, "If women continue to place so much energy, time, money, and thought at the disposal of their external shell, it is unlikely that men will look any deeper, and the arguments of women will be treated with the contempt they do *not* deserve."

Dr. Campbell is making an interesting and rather curious point. We might offer this observation by way of reply: Perhaps the adult female's excessive self-adornment comes about because girls are taught at a very early age that they have little intrinsic value other than to be as pleasing as possible to the opposite sex. If they grow up with a lack of self esteem perhaps this makes them feel compelled, as they grow older, to disguise themselves, to ornament the shell. And certainly this underlying insecurity that well might lead to excess is pandered by perfume, jewelry, and cosmetics manufacturers, most of whom are men. Women who have become aware of this, especially women in the liberation movement, are not inclined to wear much makeup themselves. Also curious as a contemporary phenomenon and an amusing aside, during recent years while young women in this country have tended to use less makeup, men have shown a tendency to cover their faces with luxuriant beards and audacious moustaches!

Having investigated some theories about how sex role socialization might have come about in evolutionary schemes, we now ask, is there any evidence that the way sex roles are distributed derives from any *necessary* circumstances? What can we find out about arguments stating that these roles are determined by inherent, biological characteristics?

GENETICS (AND HORMONES)
VS. ENVIRONMENTICS[14]

Taking our investigation of scientific evidence that explores biological differences between male and female into the realm of genetics and endocrinology requires recognition that there are, here too, various interpretations of factual information. Often the variation is due to the emphasis different investigators put upon the same basic elements of information. We have already made a hasty survey of the obstacle course that a woman must negotiate if she wants to run the race in her own way, whether competing with men or not. If we pretend that all the obstacles are taken away, we find the judges are still arguing about the rules. Keeping in mind that what we hear is taking place in our culture (as opposed, for example, to the Tchambuli tribe in New Guinea where the social if not biological roles of male and female appear to be reversed), let us listen to the dispute.

On the one hand, it goes, you cannot deny that there is an enormous difference between male and female, from their characteristics of sex (breasts, genitals, body hair and body fat, etc.), right on to structural and chemical differences in their brains. Further, all these *inherent* differences serve to predispose if not limit males and females to certain specific behavior and roles. These roles we see realized in what we have come to recognize as masculine and feminine. We might call the disputants in this camp the *predestinarians* in that they lean toward a genetically prescribed stress on predestiny.

On the other hand is the position taken by a group we might call the *environmental determinists*, since their conclusions actually imply not so much self-determination as social and cultural determinism. They argue that the differences between male and female are exaggerated and hardly meaningful. For deeper and more important than differences in sex are similarities between people as human beings. They are likely to say, further, that when you do cross-gender studies (male-female) you will probably find that as many females are similar to males, and males similar to females, as females are like females, or males like males. The contingent on this side holds that the most salient differences are caused by social and cultural pressures rather than genetic and biological determinants.

This is a simplification of a dizzying discussion that has antecedents in and parallels with theological arguments opposing predestination and free will. Much experimentation and thought is gathered for evidence of what can and cannot be pinpointed as male or female. Well over a thousand studies have been done to describe the sex differences in the mental functions of human beings.

If we were to ask ourselves what it might take to prove to us irrevocably that sex difference, in terms of behavior, is a functional rather than a social or cultural reality, we would probably concede that if a female brain and central nervous system were substantially different from that of a male, we might be led to believe that there was a functional differentiation.

There have in the past been mistaken evaluations of the importance of the size and weight of a brain in relation to the intelligence of the creature who was carrying that brain in its skull. There was a time, as you might expect, when "evidence" that the male brain was larger than that of the female seemed to reinforce the belief that the male's mind was better, that he was more intelligent. It was subsquently discovered that brain size has little relationship to the intelligence quotient, and it was also discovered that, as a matter of fact, considering the ratio of body weight to brain dimension, the female brain was proportionately just as considerable as that of the male.

There is currently another approach to *hypothesizing* whence the brain-mind-behavior relationship might derive. It has to do with the effect hormones may have on the early development of the brain. In order to understand this approach, we must first refresh and revise some of our background knowledge of genetics. Then we may gain perspective on the fascinating discoveries that provide information for this hypothesis.

New findings in genetics and endocrinology (the study of glandular secretions, hormones), have a good measure of shock value. For example, believe it or not, if a genetic male or female embryo in the womb is castrated, then the baby is born with female morphology! What does this startling announcement really mean?

We know that a person's sex is determined by the chromosomal makeup of his or her cells and that this is originally established by whether the father's sperm contributed a Y- or X-bearing chromosome to combine with the X chromosome in the mother's ovum. (Mothers carry no sex determining Y's; fathers carry X or Y.) If the father donates a Y, the XY combination determines that the baby will be male, if he donates an X, it will be female.

Father	Mother	Child
X	X	XX female
Y	X	XY male

These genetic prescriptions, until recently, seemed finite. Newer research shows that during the first six weeks of development, an embryo is of indeterminate sex, regardless of the genetic combination. (After about six weeks the embryo is called a fetus.) It is not until a male sex hormone, an androgen, intervenes that male anatomy will begin to follow the basic XY blueprint, or code, that the chromosomal pattern predicted. Even when the blueprint specifies an XX makeup, a female, if androgen is added at a critical moment the embryo will differentiate with male physical characteristics. If no androgen is released, then in spite of an XY blueprint, a physiological female will be born.

Father	Mother		Child
X	X	androgen	XX male
X	X	—	XX female
Y	X	androgen	XY male
Y	X	—	XY female

"In other words," wrote Dr. John Money, a medical psychologist of Johns Hopkins University School of Medicine, "without androgen, nature's primary impulse is to make a female—morphologically speaking, at least."[15]

This knowledge is taken a step farther with the conjecture that, as the androgen is released into the system during the later stage of embryonic development it causes the establishment, by the brain, of a pattern of sensitivity. This pattern determines how hormones shall be received by the brain in the future. In this way, as the hypothesis expands, we see that the initial action of androgen affects the brain and even discriminates into the part or parts of the central nervous system that will become either "masculine or feminine," leading finally to the concept of predetermined psychosexuality.

We might think about this graphically by drawing the analogy of a pinball machine. Once the machine is on, the game has started. A lever is pulled and the first ball is sent on its way. The ball hits a post, a light turns on, and the first score and probably the direction of the game has been set. What the next balls can accomplish depends to a great extent upon the pattern that the first ball established. But keep in mind that you can change the whole game by tilting the machine.

Before we see how the machine can be tilted, we will consider how the end result of the action of androgen is being interpreted in terms of predetermining psychosexual behavior. In order to recognize and pinpoint this process of hormonal intervention, scientists have been experimenting with animals and changing the course of the animal's physical development by the addition or subtraction of hormones during various critical stages of development. Dr. Seymour J. Levine of Stanford University School of Medicine, after conducting experiments of this kind on rats, was led to speculate, "If the brain differentiates into male and female types, may not the difference be reflected in fields of behavior other than sexual (i.e., mating)?" For by removing the ovaries or testes of rats before the critical stage of development in the womb, then injecting male or female hormones, he could change the postnatal physiology and behavior of his maturing animals. Levine believes his findings "invite a full exploration of the extent to which behavior, nonsexual as well as sexual, can be masculinized by testosterone (a specific male hormone) treatment or feminized by castration at the critical stage of sexual differentiation. . . . The artificially masculinized female rat and the feminized male have opened a wide new field for speculation and research."[16]

Indeed they have. This type of research and its possible applications causes many humanists to tremble as they haven't since the discovery of nuclear fission. The idea of sex determination during the embryonic stage, the possibility that parents (or the state) can determine in advance whether they will have a girl or a boy is a frightening prospect. The idea of hormonally engineering and manipulating behavior—let's make that one more "aggressive" and this one more "passive"—hints at a totalitarianism beyond any yet imagined. Add to these the development of cloning, a technique that may permit individuals to make biological replicas of themselves by using the nucleus of their own cells that will grow new organisms with the same genetic characteristics as their donors, and it is only at its outermost fringes that our imaginations can begin to grasp what the world might become. Even one of the most straightforward pragmatists of the twentieth century, Herman Kahn, author of *On Thermonuclear War*, who has been called the midcentury Machiavelli, told an interviewer in 1971:

Now this is a very hard thing for me to say—ten years ago I couldn't have said it, five years ago I began to think it—but the knowledge and technology that are now becoming available are very hard for society to absorb, so we may well need an index of forbidden knowledge. . . . You will be able to design your children in the next twenty–twenty-five years; I doubt that that will increase human happiness, and there are many other examples of dysfunctional knowledge that seems likely to be available. . . . Whatever the intellectual dangers of an index [of forbidden knowledge], they pall in comparison with the danger of not having one.[17]

These speculations take us beyond our current look at physical and psychosexual differences between males and females. Besides, a giant step, or leap is still required to make the transition from rats to humans, and of course you cannot yet experiment on healthy people by castrating them or by injecting them with large doses of hormones in order to see what will happen.

ENVIRONMENTICS VS. GENETICS (AND HORMONES)

Having followed a train of thought that could lead us to conclude that there is a great deal to be said for predestination in psychosexual behavior and roles, we are fortunate to be able to present a point of view that takes into account the same basic genetic and hormonal in-

SEXUAL DIFFERENTIATION IN THE HUMAN FETUS

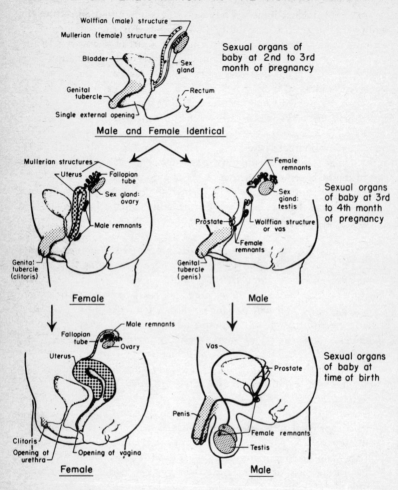

SOURCE: Courtesy of Dr. John Money.

formation but stresses a more generous conclusion. The evaluations by Dr. John Money attribute greater influence to the social and cultural environment, which is, after all, a condition that can be changed for the better without resorting to Kahn's index of forbidden knowledge.

EXTERNAL GENITAL DIFFERENTIATION IN THE HUMAN FETUS

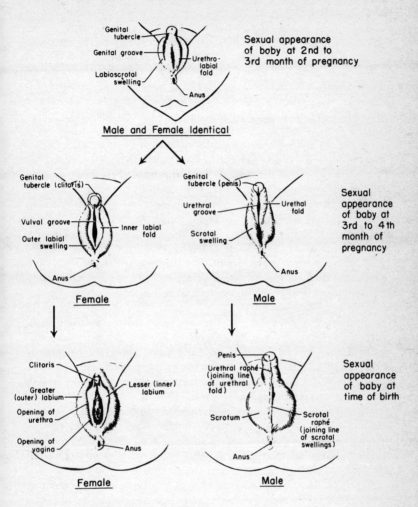

SOURCE: Courtesy of Dr. John Money.

Dr. Money insists that we totally revise our understanding of the means by which gender (male-female) identity ("identity is the subjective experience of role, and role is the enactment of identity") is achieved. He sees gender identity as an ongoing process with various stages at which identity goes critical, so to speak. These stages are the moments that we mentioned earlier at which the pinball machine may be tilted. In diagrams on pages 54–55. Dr. Money gives us a graphic description of the bipotentiality of sex determination in the fetus. An embryo becomes a fetus between two and three months, and there is only a short period of time during which a fertilized egg can be interfered with and made to reverse the physiological program for which it was genetically coded.

It is not known exactly which chemicals control the development of the primitive gonads (sexual glands) into either an ovary or a testis. But Dr. Money's drawings do make clear what he calls the bipotentiality of dimorphic selection. This means that at *each stage* of the physiological sex determination of the fetus there are *two possibilities* (direction male or direction female) and that selection and development in one direction at one stage does not preclude selection or development in the other direction during the next stage. Nor are the alternatives quite so bipolar as they are often assumed to be. This evidence seems to indicate that physiological differences are no more (perhaps even less) clearcut than are similarities, and it would follow that they are not necessarily clear cut in those areas related to physiology, such as individual hormonal release and its effect on behavior.

In what we understand and conventionally accept as the normal course of events, however, this bipotentiality and range of ambiguities in developmental selection do not become apparent. For once a child is born, the child is assigned a sex based upon the most obvious external physical appearances. After that no ambivalence is allowed, by parents or society, and a "normal" child is channeled along the straight path of psychosexual gender identity—polarized at this point into typically masculine or typically feminine behavior. Yet the essential bipotentiality still exists. In studying a number of hermaphrodites who have had a variety of genetic, hormonal, and environmental influences on their lives, together with experimental work, Dr. Money has come to the conclusion that biological or genetic programs can be overridden, not only by "abnormal" occurrences during the formation of the fetus but by postnatal influences.

For just as the dimorphic selection process occurs before birth, as illustrated on the chart, it begins again after the baby is born, but in terms of gender identity. It is then that environmental influences can intervene in the direction of psychosexual development. Such influences might include insufficient tactile or emotional stimulation of the infant, or on the other hand, too much stimulation. Influences or stimuli specifically related to sex that could cause divergencies might include an unusually early exposure of the child to excessive and dramatic sexual activity, not enough opportunity for normal sexual play and investigation, or uncertainty on the parents' part regarding expectations for "masculinity" or "femininity" of their children. These are just a few of the environmental and emotional events that could "disrupt" gender identity during late infancy and early childhood. Others have been observed and more have yet to be identified. And we might add that a disruption of this traditional gender identity can also be considered in positive terms, an observation that we will consider later in this chapter.

Gender identity, and subsequent behavior, when seen in this way is a "differentiation process [that] would appear to be a rather delicate one, rather easily subject to disruption." In Money's analysis, we are brought up to believe in and to thoroughly commit ourselves to our "gender identity." That is, we are not allowed and do not allow ourselves any ambivalence when we think of ourselves as boy or girl, man or woman; rather we feel compelled to act according to the rules of masculine and feminine behavior. We believe our genders so irreversible that it has become part of "popular and scientific folklore that something so intensely and personally unnegatible as one's own sense of gender identity must, in some way, be preordained in the genes." But, he concludes, "All the experimental evidence . . . from sex-reversed fish to human hermaphrodites shows that such a simple minded theory is untenable." On the contrary, "The program in the genetic code spells out only a readiness to differentiate gender identity and role," and all specifics, refinements, and details are "programmed into the social code of interaction and learning." And finally, "It is a feature of man's phyletic heritage that environmental influences [on] the genetics of our behavior are vast in scope—more vast than in any other species."[18]

AGGRESSION

Having touched on a number of discussions related to masculine and feminine behavior, the stereotypes, expectations, and assumptions that define them, and the biology to which they may be attributed, let us concentrate on a specific sex-based characteristic. Male aggressiveness is so much taken for granted that if we were to hear a teacher remark, "That boy is aggressive," we would understand immediately what he meant and consider the boy's behavior quite normal, whereas if the teacher were to say, "That girl is aggressive," we would almost instinctively feel that the girl was rather abnormal. One of the most disparaging remarks made to professional women is, "The trouble with you is that you are an aggressive woman." An aggressive man, on the other hand, we are apt to anticipate will be the president of his company.

When we think of aggression in its least derogatory connotation we can define it as an expenditure of energy, and this energy is spent on or toward another person or object. In this context an aggressive tennis player or an aggressive playwright can be an admirable person; his or her aggression is directed toward success in acceptable ways.

Aggression becomes problematic when its intent is hostile. *Webster's Collegiate Dictionary* defines aggression as an "unprovoked attack or act of hostility," and offers for synonyms "attack," and "offensive." In his article "Sexual Differentiation and the Evolution of Aggressive Behavior in Primates," David Hamburg says, "By 'aggressive behavior' I mean behavior in which an animal inflicts, or tries or threatens to inflict, damage on another animal. We are, in other words, concerned with threat and attack patterns."[19]

In either case (that is, in its least or most socially desirable form), aggression is expected of a male and not expected of a female. And because society rarely accepts aggressiveness as an outlet for their hostility, whatever hostility females experience and need to express is most likely directed inward. Or perhaps this hostility manifests itself verbally in "cattiness" or is suppressed and swallowed in "docility."

The nature of violence and aggression in animals and in man is the subject of study and controversy. To what extent can recognition of the patterns of aggression in monkeys, apes, and chimpanzees be considered applicable to aggressive behavior in human beings? By studying mankind's closest living relatives, some suggest we might uncover the "evolutionary roots of human aggressive tendencies."[20] Others believe that humankind has its own unique evolutionary story.

"One focus of the controversy is whether violence in man is an inherited trait derived from carnivorous ape ancestors or an acquired behavior pattern invented by modern man as a response to the stresses of civilization."[21] Archeologist Louis B. Leaky took the position that there is evidence that during the first two million years of human evolution there was no incentive and no need for violence. "Then, about 40,000 years ago everything changed" [with the invention of man-made fire and the discovery of leisure.] "Fire gave us leisure, leisure to think, leisure to invent abstract words like love, hate and jealousy. With the development of abstract thought, man took his last step toward you and me today. But it ended up with an ever-growing aggression."[22]

The controversy is not likely to be resolved very soon. Nor is this question: To what extent is aggression in the eyes of the beholder? Here is a description of aggression via a report of a probably un-precedented achievement—breeding the rare peregrine falcon in captivity. Dr. Heinz Meng designed the special setting in which the feat occurred by, as he described it, "thinking like a bird." The news story reporting the event reads:

During the mating season [Dr. Meng] would cower away from the cage after feeding when the assertive male wailed and clawed at him as a suspected intruder on the nest. This [Dr. Meng] said helped the tiercel (male falcon) feel more assertive and "masculine" during this period.[23]

That is one interpretive illustration of male aggression seen in the drama of sexual behavior. But consider this description:

"Look out!" At Arthur Bowaland's warning, I instinctively ducked and waited for the familiar sound of wind whistling through feathers, the electrifying scream of an attacking eagle, and the blur of a black projectile hurtling past my head. Month after month we had clam-bered over this cliffside, high on an 8,000-foot spur of South Africa's Drakensberg Range, to observe a family of three black eagles. And time after time, the mother eagle had attacked, as if trying to knock me over the precipice. Once, diving steeply from the sky, she raked the back of my sweater with her out-stretched talons, ripping it from waist to neck. . . .

Now . . . the mother eagle had momentarily put me out of her mind while a jackal buzzard challenged her for possession of a hyrak —a mammal the size of a rabbit.

Locked in savage conflict, these two giants—an eagle with a seven-foot wingspan, a buzzard with a five-foot span—tumbled toward the plateau 200 feet below."[24]

This second illustration (written by a woman, incidentally), shows as much aggressive ferocity as the first, but the latter we would be likely to dismiss as the aberrant result of maternal instinct, whereas the first would be considered a normal display of male aggression.

Is our very recognition of aggression so frought with social prejudices and assumptions that the very same behavior has different connotations when seen by (or in) different people? Dr. Vincent Nowlis, a psychologist who participated in early sex research has commented, "The Kinsey series of histories suggested that scientists who engage in sex research on any species are no more free of anxieties and conflicts about sex than are other individuals." (True, Nowlis is talking about primate sex behavior rather than aggression per se, but the point still holds because one of the most consistently noted forms of sexual behavior is the aggressive role played by the male.) He illustrated his point with a personal reminiscence:

I recall a leisurely visit in 1946 to the Primate Section of the St. Louis Zoo with Alfred Kinsey and Robert Yerkes. Both had been studying primate sex behavior for years and had communicated with each other many times, but this was the first time they had had an opportunity to discuss their observations at the moment they made them. Each observer noted as sex behavior many items which the other had either ignored or categorized differently.[25]

For another perspective on aggression, there is an interesting view of male (monkey) aggressive behavior in Dr. Paul D. MacLean's article entitled "New Findings Relevant to the Evolution of Psychosexual Functions of the Brain." MacLean finds a similarity, almost an interchangeability, in the physically expressed characteristics of sexual aggression, dominance aggression, and fear. All these reactions are accompanied by penile erection,[26] and all result from stimulation of areas of the brain that are in close proximity. Dr. MacLean has composed his observations into a theory that might have sociological implications, for he suggests that we might finally understand how the loincloth came to be used. "Is it not possible," writes MacLean, "that man with his superior intelligence discovered that by assuming the fig leaf, and later the loin cloth, he was able to reduce the unpleasant social tensions created by the show of these aggressive impulses? Perhaps this had facilitated acculturation on the long hard road to civilization."[27] Well, it is possible, one must suppose. It is also possible, if we accept Dr. Sherfey's explanation of evolution, that the loincloth came to be used by males as a necessary part of their suppression of the female's inordinate sexual appetite!

Aggression is a complex phenomenon and an ambiguous term. There is little agreement on its behavioral roots or in descriptions of its manifestations. We tend to use the term because we haven't another suitable expression. The controversy over and fascination of the subject far outreaches the dimensions of this book. But we are in a position to make a value judgment. Rather than accepting hostile aggression as an inevitable male (or female) trait, we would prefer to see the energy behind it diverted and redirected. Since we really do not know otherwise, we might assume that both boys and girls have about the same aggressive potential and if both are encouraged to express it constructively (e.g., physical education, especially noncompetitive), rather than destructively (e.g., fighting in the schoolyard), and not to inhibit it (e.g., sitting passively at a desk) we are working in the right direction.

WOUNDED WOMEN

Sigmund Freud, whose turn of the century work has had major and enduring effects on all psychological thought and practice, made incorrect assessments of females in his theories of the libido. The libido is basically hedonistic, that is, pleasure seeking, and triggers action toward its own gratification. Sexual gratification is probably the strongest libidinous drive. When Freud discussed the libido, he never recognized the female's libido as much other than a variation of the male's.

The problem with theories, especially those derived from erroneous assumptions, is that their practical application is either useless or harmful. Freud believed, erroneously, that "anatomy is destiny." And the female anatomy, ergo the female destiny, he saw as missing something, namely, a penis. Included in his perception of female and male psychosexual makeup were the ideas of penis envy (girls want to have one) and castration complex (boys fear losing theirs). In the psychological development of a young girl there had to come a time when she discovered that in place of a penis she had a "woundlike aperture." The idea of the female as mutilated male (and the fear of the male that he might be mutilated) becomes a real and severe problem to overcome in the freudian vision of human development.

Further, Freud outlines two specific phases of development of sexuality for the female. In his description, the erotic pleasure moves from the clitoris to the vagina as the female progresses from infantile subjective eroticism to adult objective eroticism. Because she must pass through two distinct phases, he believed she was more in danger than the male, whose eroticism never leaves the penis, of not reaching the end of her full sexual evolution. She may get bogged down more easily in the infantile stage and consequently develop neurosis. Before we consider why this is no longer (in fact never was) accurate, it is interesting to recall another perception of John Money: "In view of the alleged higher incidence of psychosexual pathologies in males it is conceivable that masculine psychosexual differentiation is more difficult to achieve than feminine, and is more vulnerable to error and failure."[28]

Freud's idea about the two stages of female sexuality in the satisfaction of the libido has been discounted by the clinical work of Masters and Johnson. They have shown that the clitoris is and remains the only female organ specific to sexual pleasure (in fact the only human organ with no other function, for the penis serves both for elimination and eroticism); that the vaginal tissue has for the most part no sentience; and that, in short, orgasm could not be caused solely by vaginal stimulation, except to the extent the clitoris is affected. This does not contradict the obvious fact that females reach orgasm via coitis, or that there is an experiential difference between orgasm reached by intercourse as opposed to purely clitoral stimulation, but it states that in either case the sensitive and receptive organ that triggers an orgasm is the clitoris.

Apart from this error in his physiological rationale for female psychosexuality, and without going into the specifics of his theory, Freud's essential mistake, as far as women are concerned, was the typical construction of basing the female libido on male evaluation. "The libido is constantly and regularly male in essence, whether it appears in man or in woman." He declines to regard the feminine libido as having its own original nature, and therefore it will necessarily seem to him like a complex deviation from the human libido in general.[29]

Whether we go on to understand Freud in terms of the Victorian atmosphere in which he lived or in terms of his own personal dispositions has little relevance to practical, every day dissemination of his ideas and theories into the climate of our culture. Many of his successors have modified his ideas in specifics, some with intentions of remedying obvious errors. Sometimes they do not go far enough, and other times they go too far, but the problem as far as women are concerned is that they are almost always going in the wrong direction. Erik Erikson, for example, devised a theory of femaleness being an expression of "inner space."[30] That is, because females carry most of their reproductive organs inside their body, their characteristic behavior, based on the groundplan of their personal knowledge of the human body, results in inward or inner-directed thoughts and activity. This is opposed to the "outer space" orientation of the male. Although Erikson is taking steps to counterbalance Freud's idea with the concept that females derive great and satisfactory identity from what they have themselves, practically speaking, one idea is hardly more useful than the other in terms of experiencing generalized personhood. Nor is the idea of Karen Horney, who proposes womb envy as the alternative to penis envy, that is, that men suffer regret because they cannot bear and nurture children.

It is a temptation to reject all psychological theory. In an article by one dismayed psychologist, Naomi Weisstein, a study is cited that surveyed the results of analysis and therapy. She writes:

Some might argue that while clinical theory may be scientifically unsound, it at least cures people. There is no evidence that it does. In 1952 Hans Eysenck of the University of London reported the results of an "outcome of therapy" study of neurotics that showed that 44 percent of the patients who received psychoanalysis improved; 64 percent of the patients who received psychotherapy improved; and 72 percent of the patients who received no treatment at all improved. These findings have never been refuted, and later studies have confirmed their negative results, no matter what type of therapy was used.[31]

More recent approaches to therapy that are behavior-oriented, that is, that deal with observable individual behavior, and theoretically disregard the sex of the client, could be more successful. And the attitude of feminists toward psychology is usually more revisionist than abolitionist (there are many feminist psychologists). That something needs to be done is evident. In an important study, Inge and Donald Broverman *et al.* looked at the standards of clinically trained psychologists, psychiatrists, and psychiatric social workers of different schools of thought, and established that to these practitioners "healthy" women differ from "healthy" men, and further, that what they considered healthy for men was synonomous with healthy human beings. Their conclusions, in their own words, need special attention:

Thus, for a woman to be healthy from an adjustment viewpoint, she must adjust to and accept the behavioral norms for her sex, even though these behaviors are generally less socially desirable and considered to be less healthy for the generalized competent, mature adult.

By way of analogy, one could argue that a black person who conformed to the "pre-civil rights" Southern Negro stereotype, that is a

*docile, unambitious, childlike, etc. person, was well adjusted to his
environment and, therefore, a healthy and mature adult. Our recent
history testifies to the bankruptcy of this concept. . . .*

*We are not suggesting that it is the clinicians who pose this di-
lemma for women. Rather, we see the judgements of our sample of
clinicians as merely reflecting the sex role stereotypes, and the differing valuations of these stereotypes prevalent in our society.*[32]

Evaluating this study a concerned psychologist remarked, "This research supplies empirical support for what feminists have long suspected: that therapy is bad for women."[33]

Perhaps therapy will be able to help women when psychology,
psychologists, analysts, and therapists change their sexist attitudes.
Perhaps many women wouldn't need help if the sexist attitudes of
society were changed. Moreover, men need just as much to be seen
in a new frame of reference, for nervous disorders in males are often
traceable to a masculine mystique, something now being called the
machismo factor. Our civilization is well beyond the era when men
needed the kind of physical strength required to hunt animals for
survival. Even for the sophisticated warfare carried out today, long
range weapons can take the place of direct physical combat. So many
of the stereotypes based on the assumption of the need for male
physical aggressiveness are outdated, and yet they still pervade our
expectations of gender identity. So we look not only for the tall, dark,
handsome syndrome, but we expect a deep voice, physical hardness, a
competitive and aggressive nature.

It reminds me of a strange story I covered several years ago when
I was working as a reporter. I was sent to investigate a report that
came out of a health clinic in New York City. According to the press
release, the doctors claimed a spectacular success in restoring the
sense of manhood to adult males who were frought with concern because their voices were high-pitched and "effeminate." Social esteem
and self-respect were in the offing. The means? Showing these men
how, by pressing down on their voice boxes with two fingers while
they spoke, they could in no time at all change their speaking voices
to a masculine baritone. Another nicety of securing gender identity?

If a new attitude in psychology can do some good, that would be
useful. Especially if the effects are as pervasive as the original con-
structions managed to become. For while it may be true that only a
small percentage of the population seek therapy, the dissemination of
Freudian and neoFreudian ideas throughout American culture is incredible. Consider the case of Dr. Benjamin M. Spock. There is

hardly anyone who has had an equal effect on childrearing during the middle part of the twentieth century. His book, *Baby and Child Care*, rivals the Bible in sales and has been persistently used for direction when questions about child care arise. Dr. Spock subscribes to the freudian formulations leading to definition of differences in the behavior of girls and boys, and he also considers differences in temperament innate. In his books he stresses these differences and "hoped that parents would bring up their children to be enthusiastic about, rather than minimize their maleness or femaleness."[34] A quick look through the "bible" turns up a section called "managing young children":

A boy doesn't grow spiritually to be a man just because he's born with a male body. The thing that makes him feel and act like a man is being able to copy, to pattern himself after, men and older boys with whom he feels friendly. . . . If a father is always impatient or irritated with him, the boy is likely to feel uncomfortable not only when he's around his father, but when he's around other men and boys, too. He is apt to draw closer to his mother and take on her manner and interests. . . .

A girl needs a friendly father, too. It's easy to see that a boy needs a father to pattern himself after, but many people don't realize that a friendly father plays a different but equally important part in the development of a girl. She doesn't exactly pattern herself after him, but she gains confidence in herself as a girl and a woman from feeling his approval. I'm thinking of little things he can do, like complimenting her on her dress, or hair-do, or the cookies she's made.[35]

After many years and much thought, Dr. Spock came around to revising his ideas a little. "Some of these opinions are embarrassing for me to acknowledge now," he wrote in 1971. "It is obvious that I, like most men up to a couple of years ago, harbored an underlying sexism . . . in some matters. . . . There was at least a trace of male insecurity and chauvinism in my assumption that men and women should be conscious of distinctly different sexual identities and that parents need to emphasize these during childhood." But Dr. Spock does not recant all the way. His article concludes, "Realizing that in all probability the trend for a long period will be to minimize differences, I'll no longer recommend arbitrarily to parents that they treat their sons and daughters differently. I'll define aspects of the issue and leave the decision up to the parents."[36]

What aspects of the differences need definition? And why does

Dr. Spock step back from arbitrariness to ambivalence? But most of all, what is so frightening about not knowing immediately whether a person is a boy or a girl? Why in the late sixties and early seventies was it a subject of such distress to onlookers when, from the back and often from the front, they could not tell male from female? Why is it the first thing a mother hears in the delivery room is either, "You have a bouncing baby boy," or a "beautiful baby girl?" Why does gender identification seem so overwhelmingly important? Why does it even seem we must know a person's gender before we know how to react, how to judge, or what to expect of that person? What is Sylvia? What for that matter is Sam?

In schools, we shall see, many differences between girls and boys are relentlessly documented. Yet over the gulf of definitions the bridges from masculinity to feminity crisscross each other. The definitions of male and female we accept or reject depend quite heavily upon our own level of consciousness, and as that consciousness rises we seem to come to the point where we insist that the only definition that matters is the one that a woman (or man) uses to define herself, according to those standards that she herself sets. Then the most persuasive description of what woman (and man) can become will not be sex-related at all, but rather arrived at by an understanding of *humanness*—as seen by Abraham Maslow—as healthy, self-actualizing human beings.[37]

NOTES

[1]William Shakespeare, *Two Gentlemen of Verona*, Act IV, Scene II.

[2]Sylvia Plath, *The Bell Jar*, London, Faber and Faber, 1966.

[3]Quoted in Aileen S. Kraditor, ed., *Up From the Pedestal*, Chicago, Quadrangle Books, 1968, p. 90. Reprinted by permission of the publisher.

[4]*The Phoenix*, Cambridge, Mass. Reprinted in the University of Massachusetts *Daily Collegian*, 14 April 1971.

[5]Doris Lessing, *The Golden Notebook*, New York, Simon and Schuster, pp. 187–188.

[6]"Navy Expert Calls Women More Fit for Dip in Cold Sea," *New York Times*, 18 July 1971.

[7]Eugene Berman in Martha Stuart and William T. Liu, eds., *The Emerging Woman, The Impact of Family Planning*, Boston, Little, Brown, 1970, pp. 57–66.

[8]Ashley Montagu, *The Natural Superiority of Women*, New York, Macmillan, 1968.

[9]David Allen, *The Price of Women*, New York, Jarrow Press, 1971, and *The Nature of Gambling*, New York, Coward-McCann, 1952.

[10]Johann Jakob Bachofen, *Myth, Religion and Mother Right*, Princeton, Princeton University Press, 1967, p. 150.

[11]Robert Briffault, *The Mothers*, New York, Macmillan, 1931, pp. 245, 248.

[12]Mary Jane Sherfey, "A Theory on Female Sexuality," in Robin Morgan, ed., *Sisterhood is Powerful*, New York, Random House (Vintage), 1970, pp. 220–230. Reprinted by permission.

[13]Information about Dr. Campbell's work can be found in his book entitled *The Pleasure Areas*, scheduled for publication by Dell in 1973. Dr. Campbell was kind enough to supply much of this information in this section by personal communication.

[14]This phrase taken from John Money, "Sexually Dimorphic Behavior, Normal and Abnormal," in Kretchmer and Walcher, eds., *Environmental Influences on Genetic Expression: Biological and Behavioral Aspects of Sexual Differentiation*. Available from Superintendent of Documents, U. S. Government Printing Office.

[15]John Money, "Psychosexual Differentiation," in John Money, ed., *Sex Research, New Developments*, New York, Holt, Rinehart and Winston, 1965. Also see John Money and Anke Ehrhardt, *Man and Woman, Boy and Girl*, Baltimore, Johns Hopkins, 1972.

[16]Seymour Levine, "Sex Differences in the Brain," *Scientific American*, April 1966, pp. 89–90. Reprinted by permission.

[17]"Herman Kahn Thinks About the Thinkable—Most of the Traditional Causes of War Have Disappeared," interview with G. R. Urban in *New York Times Magazine*, 20 June 1971, pp. 12–24.

[18]This information on Dr. Money's work can be found in Money, *Sex Research, New Developments, op. cit.*, as well as his new book with Anke Ehrhardt, *Man and Woman, Boy and Girl, op. cit.*

[19]David Hamburg, "Sexual Differentiation and the Evolution of Aggressive Behavior in Primates," in Kretchmer and Walcher, *Environmental Influences on Genetic Expression, op. cit.*, p. 143.

[20]*Ibid.*, p. 142.

[21]Boyce Rensenberger "Behavior is Described in Philadelphia Report," *New York Times*, 29 December 1971.

[22]*Ibid.*

[23]Nancy Hicks, "Upstate Biology Professor, 'Thinking Like a Bird,' Breeds the Rare Peregrine Falcon in Captivity," *New York Times*, 10 June 1971.

[24]Jeanne Cowden, "Adventures with South Africa's Black Eagles," *National Geographic*, October 1969, p. 553. Reprinted by permission.

[25]Vincent Nowlis in Money, ed., *Sex Research, New Developments, op. cit.*, p. 149.

[26]I also enjoyed Dr. MacLean's description: "Caspar, the animal which proved to be the dominant male in the colony, displayed (his erect penis) to all the other males but none in turn displayed to him. In contrast, Edgar, the male lowest in rank, displayed to none of the other males, but all displayed to him. Edgar displayed only to humans!"

[27]Paul D. MacLean in Money, ed., *Sex Research, New Developments*, *op. cit.*

[28]John Money, "Psychosexual Differentiation," in Money, ed., *Sex Research, New Developments, op. cit.*

[29]A feminist discussion of Freud is found in a variety of works. We suggest the interpretations of Simon de Beauvoir in *The Second Sex*, New York, Knopf, 1952, especially Chapter II, and Shulamith Firestone, *The Dialectic of Sex: The Case for Feminist Revolution*, New York, William Morrow, 1970, especially Chapter 3.

[30]Erik H. Erikson, "Inner and Outer Space: Reflections on Womanhood," in Robert J. Lifton, ed., *The Woman in America*, Boston, Beacon Press, Daedalus Library, 1967, pp. 1–26.

[31]Naomi Weisstein, "Woman as Nigger," *Psychology Today*, October 1969, p. 22.

[32]Broverman *et al.*, "Sex-Role Stereotypes and Clinical Judgments of Mental Health," *Journal of Consulting and Clinical Psychology*, 34 (1970), pp. 1–7.

[33]Jo Ann Gardner, "Sexist Counseling Must STOP," *Personnnel and Guidance Journal*, 49 (May 1971), p. 712.

[34]Benjamin M. Spock, "Male Chavinist Spock Recants—Well, Almost," *New York Times Magazine*, 12 September 1971, pp. 98–102.

[35]Dr. Benjamin Spock, *Baby and Child Care*, New York, Simon and Schuster (Giant Cardinal Edition), pp. 314–315. Copyright © 1945, 1946, 1957, 1958 by Benjamin Spock, M.D. Reprinted by permission of Pocket Books, division of Simon and Schuster, Inc.

[36]Spock, "Male Chauvinist Spock Recants—Well, Almost," *op. cit.*

[37]Abraham H. Maslow, *Toward a Psychology of Being*, New York, Van Nostrand Reinhold, 1968.

4

The final report card

In comments made by renowned educators, in goals and philosophies drawn up by various educational commissions, in lists of school objectives stored in forgotten corners of principals' files, a common theme reverberates—one of the most important purposes of education is to put all children in complete possession of their abilities and talents. It is reflected in goals that have been set forth by the Committee on Concepts and Values of the National Council of Social Studies: "Recognition of the dignity and worth of the individual" and "widening and deepening the ability to live more richly." There is an overwhelming verbal agreement that education is concerned with the sacredness of each individual and that one of its prime mandates is to encourage each child to grow and to develop to his or her fullest potential.

In my personal experience as a university faculty member and as a supervisor of student teachers, I see examples of sexism daily at all ages and grade levels that belie these educational goals. This week I spent some time at an elementary school, at a junior high school, and at the university. I would like to relate some of the sexist practices I observed during these seven days, not because they are dramatic or outstanding, but simply because they provide an indicator of how casually and frequently sex bias occurs in schools.

In a fifth-grade classroom, a popular male teacher was about to collect money for a charitable cause. "Now what shall I collect the money in?" he mused half aloud. The students began calling out suggestions. "I've got it," he said. "Let's take this small pencil case and put the girls' money in it, and then we'll take this big, tall pencil case for the boy's money because the boys in this class are big and tall."

At a junior high school an enthusiastic student-teacher was working with a ninth-grade class, trying to illustrate the different kinds of conflict one might find in a novel: "You might read about a soldier who has a conflict with the enemy or about a boy whose dreams of becoming President are in conflict with his poverty and lack of education." Suddenly the teacher stopped short. "But I guess you girls wouldn't read those stories. What do you read? Love stories and books about *Marsha Blaine, Angel Nurse* and stuff like that?" Some of the girls looked down or twisted in their chairs with obvious discomfort. A few, more outspoken, shot back, "We do not. That's so dumb."

This week I had a conference with a university senior who was about to begin looking for a teaching job. Uneasy over the way the phrase teacher shortage was turning into teacher surplus, he said, "I went to an interview yesterday—an eighth-grade opening—and I think I stand a good chance to get it. The job description said 'male preferred' and in the interview they said they were really looking for a man."

Toward the end of the week I attended a dinner party with faculty members from various universities. At one point during the evening I became involved in a conversation with a professor who stated that he had never discriminated against a woman in his life. Later, when this professor became aware that I was carrying a full teaching load and had a baby, he reproached me for not remaining at home full time as my "biological responsibility dictates."

Most of these people are concerned—some even dedicated—educators. All would be appalled to think that they might be teaching inferiority to female students or limiting their potential in any way. In their practice of sex discrimination these educators are in no way atypical. When I now look back on my own career in public school teaching, I am uncomfortably conscious that I too was guilty of many of the sexist practices that I now watch others perform.

Keeping in mind the educational goal of each individual's growing to his or her fullest potential, let us now complete in some detail the picture of what the female student is like after her trip through the educational process. To create this portrait, we will draw boundaries that are somewhat forced and artificial. Two areas to be looked at, cognitive development and emotional development, come directly within the purview of the school; the third area, that of developing occupational potential, is related to the school, but more indirectly. Some of the key studies will be drawn together in a list, meant to be representative rather than inclusive, to gain some sense of the growth that has been stunted and of the promise that has been denied.

Loss of academic potential

1. Intellectually, girls start off ahead of boys. They begin speaking, reading, and counting sooner; in the early grades they are even better in math. However, during the high school years, a different pattern emerges and girls' performance on ability tests begins to decline. Indeed, male students exhibit significantly more IQ gain from adolescence to adulthood than do their female counterparts.[1]
2. Although women make much better high school grades than do men, they are less likely to believe that they have the ability to do college work.[2]
3. Of the brightest high school graduates who do not go to college, 75–90 percent are women[3]
4. In 1900, women earned 6 percent of all doctoral degrees, in 1920, 15 percent, and by 1968, only 13 percent. In short, the percentage of doctorates earned by women has actually descreased since the 1920s.[4]

Loss of self-esteem

1. As boys and girls progress through school, their opinions of boys grow increasingly more positive and their opinions of girls increasingly more negative. Both sexes are learning that boys are worth more.[5]
2. Fewer high school women than men rated themselves above average on leadership, popularity in general, popularity with the opposite sex, and intellectual as well as social self-confidence.[6]
3. On the Bernreuter personality inventory, norms show that women are more neurotic and less self-sufficient, more introverted and less dominant than men.[7]
4. College women believe that men desire a woman who is extremely passive and who places wifely and familial duties above her own personal and professional development.[8]
5. College women respond negatively to women who have achieved high academic or vocational success, and at times display an actual desire to avoid success.[9]

6. Fifty-five percent of a group of women at Stanford and forty percent at Berkeley agreed with the following sentence: "There is a time when I wished I had been born a member of the opposite sex." Only one in seven male students would endorse such a statement.[10]

7. Both male and female college students feel the characteristics associated with masculinity are more valuable and more socially desirable than those associated with femininity.[11]

*Loss of occupational potential**

1. By the time they are in the fourth grade, girls' visions of occupations open to them are limited to four: teacher, nurse, secretary, or mother. Boys of the same age do not view their occupational potential through such restricting glasses.[13]

2. By the ninth grade 25 percent of boys and only 3 percent of girls are considering careers in science or engineering.[14]

3. Decline in career commitment has been found in girls of high school age. This decline was related to their feelings that male classmates disapproved of a woman's using her intelligence.[15]

4. In a survey conducted in 1966 throughout the state of Washington, 66.7 percent of boys and 59 percent of girls stated that they wished to have a career in professional occupations. However, 57 percent of the boys and *only 31.9 percent of the girls stated that they actually expected to be working in such an occupation.*[16]

5. College women become increasingly interested in being housewives from their freshman to their senior year in college. This is at the expense of academic and vocational goals.[17]

6. In 1967, the median income for a white man was $7,396; for a nonwhite man $4,777; for a white woman $4,279, and for a nonwhite woman $3,194.[18]

7. The gap between men's and women's income is widening. In 1955, the median wage of women working full time was 64 percent of what men earned. In 1968 it had decreased to 58 percent.[19]

8. Fewer than 1 percent of working women earned more than

*The attitude and competencies with which a young woman enters the labor market will become of increasing importance. It has been estimated that nine out of ten females will be working on a full-time basis at some point in their lives. Between 1968 and 1980, the Department of Labor estimates that the total number of women in the labor force will increase by 27 percent, whereas the total number of men will increase by only 20 percent.[12]

$10,000. The proportion of men earning that much is 20 times higher.[20]

Behind these statistics and surveys and facts and figures are individuals who, during the school years, have suffered a devastating loss. This "report card" is a cynical testament to the failure of school to encourage, indeed, even to allow female students to achieve their full potential. And now with freshly awakened consciousnesses, concerned feminists are beginning to look at the school environment where their sons and daughters spend so much time. With increasing awareness and anger they are learning to hold the magnifying glass up to school life in order to ferret out and to expose each sexist practice, and they are beginning to despair over the harmful lessons their daughters are learning there.

As one of these feminists, I have my own vested interest in eliminating sex bias from schools and exploding the myths about appropriate male and female roles. My daughter Robin is two years old. I try to picture what she will be like as she goes to school, and I am concerned about what she will learn there.

When she is in the early grades, will she be told by boys in the schoolyard, "You're only a girl. Girls are sissies. You can't play"? And will supervising adults, who would be angered to action at "wop," "yid," or "nigger," take little notice of these comments?

In the middle grades, will she learn in school like a little lady, obediently, submissively, thoughtlessly, making pretty papers out of the teacher's directives?

In junior high school, will she scour the school library shelves for books about wise, proud women, powerful and charismatic, only to find one or two and then stop looking?

In high school, will she look down in class, answering questions softly and uncertainly? Will she turn to male students for ideas and solutions, having lost all faith that she has any of her own?

And when she leaves school, will she be working at a job that makes a mockery of her potential and pays her a fraction of what she's worth? Or will she be settled into the routine of housewife and mother, surrounded by dishes and diapers, wondering if there isn't something more?

Obviously, it would be an exercise in senseless scapegoating to lay the full blame on the schools. Sexist attitudes are woven throughout the whole fabric of society: They are in the mass media bombardment that depicts enamored housewives extolling the hygenic cleanliness of their bathroom bowls; in religious institutions that allow only male spokesmen to lead congregations in prayer to a male God; in the more than one thousand state laws that restrict a married woman's property rights; in the marriage ceremony where the wife gives up her father's name only to assume that of her husband, never having a name to call her own; in the very nature of language where the universal pronoun is "he" and all humanity is subsumed in the word "mankind." No, the schools cannot be singled out when they are surrounded by mass societal participation operating to keep women in their place. However, our system of education, as perhaps the most organized and systematic agent of socialization, must assume a heavy share of the responsibility and of the blame.

Education does not have to be this way. Boys and girls do not have to be channeled into separate activities and courses and schools. There do not have to be discriminatory admissions policies and discriminatory hiring practices. There does not have to be a biased and prejudicial curriculum. Girls and young women do not have to learn in school to become less than their promise and their potential. There can and must be changes in staffing patterns, in curricular materials, in the way teachers are trained, in the very nature of instruction itself. Schooling must no longer be a sexist activity.

NOTES

[1]Eleanor Maccoby, "Sex Differences in Intellectual Functioning," in Eleanor Maccoby, ed., *The Development of Sex Differences*, Stanford, Stanford University Press, 1966.

[2]Patricia Cross, "College Women: A Research Description," *Journal of National Association of Women Deans and Counselors, 32,* no. 1 (Autumn 1968), 12–21.

[3]*Facts About Women in Education*, prepared by the Women's Equity Action League. Can be obtained from WEAL, 1253 4th St., S.W., Washington, D.C.

[4]Edith Painter, "Women: The Last of the Discriminated," *Journal of National Association of Women Deans and Counselors, 34,* no. 2 (Winter 1971), 59–62.

[5]S. Smith, "Age and Sex Differences in Children's Opinions Concerning Sex Differences," *Journal of Genetic Psychology, 54,* no. 1 (March 1939), 17–25.

[6]Cross, *op. cit.*

[7]R. G. Bernreuter, "The Theory and Construction of the Personality Inventory," *Journal of Social Psychology, 4,* no. 4 (November 1932), 387–405.

[8]Anne Steinman, Joseph Levi, and David Fox, "Self Concept of College Women Compared with Their Concept of Ideal Women and Men's Ideal

Woman," *Journal of Counseling Psychology*, *11*, no. 4 (Winter 1964), 27–33.

[9]Matina Horner, "Woman's Will to Fail," *Psychology Today*, *3*, no. 6 (November 1969), 36–38. Reprinted from *Psychology Today*. Copyright © by Communications/Research/Machines, Inc.

[10]Joseph Katz, *No Time For Youth*, San Francisco, Josey Bass, 1968.

[11]John McKee and Alex Sheriffs, "The Differential Education of Males and Females," *Journal of Personality*, *35*, no. 3 (September 1957), 356–371.

[12]Jeanne Holm, "Employment and Women: Cinderella is Dead," *Journal of National Association of Women Deans and Counselors*, *34*, no. 1 (Autumn 1970), 6–13.

[13]Robert O'Hara, "The Roots of Careers," *Elementary School Journal*, *62*, no. 5 (February 1962), 277–280.

[14]Daryl Bem and Sandra Bem, "We're All Nonconscious Sexists," in Daryl J. Bem, *Beliefs, Attitudes, and Human Affairs*, Monterey, Calif., Brooks/Cole. Copyright 1970 by Wadsworth Publishing Co.

[15]Peggy Hawley, "What Women Think Men Think," *Journal of Counseling Psychology*, *18*, no. 3 (Autumn 1971), 193–194.

[16]Walter Slocum and Roy Boles, "Attractiveness of Occupations to High School Students," *Personnel and Guidance Journal*, *46*, no. 8 (April 1968), 754–761.

[17]Linda Bruemmer, "The Condition of Women in Society Today: A Review—Part 1," *Journal of National Association of Women Deans and Counselors*, *33*, no. 1, (Autumn 1969), 18–22.

[18]U. S. Department of Labor Statistics, 1970, quoted in JoAnn Gardner, "Sexist Counseling Must STOP," *The Personnel and Guidance Journal*, *49*, no. 9 (May 1971), 705–714.

[19]*Ibid.*

[20]*Ibid.*

Sex bias: the hidden curriculum in the elementary school

ducators are enthusiastic about a new teaching concept. It is one that has revolutionary implications for the future of education. Here is a descriptive report of the innovation as excerpted from a prominent educational journal.

Farrington Elementary School is a source of great pride to the Southern California children who go to school there. The modern school building has large glass windows, carpeted floors, and sliding walls that turn small rooms into large lecture halls and back again at the press of a button. There is no lack of the most current educational technology, and each room can boast of its own 16 mm. projector and videotape recorder.

This fall, when students returned to Farrington after summer vacation, they met with an interesting new concept in education. The school was beginning the Program for Educational and Occupational Needs (PEON). PEON is based on a study of occupational patterns of previous Farrington graduates. The study shows that future occupational status appears to be closely tied to student ethnic background. Consequently, PEON operates on the premise that separate and different training should be given to children of different ethnic backgrounds so as to provide their best possible adjustment to future occupational life. At the heart of the program is the concept of the segregated class.

Two ethnic groups—white Americans and Mexican Americans—are participating in this intriguing and promising method of instruction.

Research makes clear that while white students choose the professions, Mexican Americans are drawn into the field of agricultural labor. Therefore, the white students are taught with more academic curricular materials, and in Mexican American classes there is heavy emphasis on physical activity—exercises in crouching, bending at the waist, and stretching to increase the agility so necessary for the successful harvest of agricultural crops.

The occupational study has also shown that Mexican Americans who leave Farrington Elementary School do not often rise to positions of leadership. Consequently, games stressing docility and submissiveness are a popular aspect of course work. Follow the leader, Simple Simon Says, and May I? have proven to be particular favorites.

These Mexican American children will be subjected to more frequent change of locale and living conditions than will their more affluent classmates. Therefore, the curriculum has been designed to help them cope with shifting locations and a generally impoverished environment. Here are some of PEON's objectives designed to be most meaningful to the needs of the Mexican Amercan child:

1. *the ability to adjust to a changing environment*
2. *the ability to maintain cleanliness when plumbing facilities are not available*
3. *knowledge of foods that are cheap yet filling*

The staff has been extremely enthusiastc about the success of PEON. In fact, results of an extensive program evaluation were so promising that Mr. Togib, the district superintendent, announced that PEON has received increased government funding for the following year.

Shocking? Of course. Absurd? Of course. And, of course entirely fictional. Fortunately, in the United States today there is no room for an educational program that flaunts such overt ethnic discrimination. Unfortunately, however, there appears to be much more than elbow room for discrimination of another kind. Although just as shocking and absurd, the following account of a pilot program in segregated education is true.

In 1966, an article appeared in the widely read and highly respected *National Elementary Principal* describing a new program in instructional grouping by sex that was taking place in Wakefield Elementary School, Fairfax County, Virginia. The separate class concept was instituted in order to lessen the difficulties that boys face in school. At the time the article was written, 310 elementary students were receiving their instruction in separated classes. The author of the article was delighted about the possibilities of classes separated by sex. He outlined some teaching methods that were being used or that could be used in single sex classrooms. (*Italics mine*)

1. *In working with boys, we employ more science materials and experiments. There is more emphasis on building things and on studies of transportation.* As a result, we can create and maintain a high level of interest.

2. We have found it well to let the interests of the classes guide the teacher in areas such as science and social studies. Depending on the sex of the group, this sometimes results in quite different activities. *From studying the atom, for example, a boy's class moved easily into a study of nuclear fission. It is unlikely that girls would respond this way. Or another example, mold can be studied from a medical standpoint by boys and in terms of cooking by girls.*

3. In all-boy and all-girl classes, we have used different songs and rhythms. *For girls we use quieter games, fairy stories, and games and songs which emphasize activities such as sewing and housekeeping. For boys, we use more active physical games which involve noise and muscle movement and are based on a transportation theme.*

4. *Different reading stories are also used. Girls enjoy all stories in readers, even those about boys, but boys do not like stories about girls.* Boys prefer tales and stories about industry, transportation, and vocations. The same differentiation applies to creative writing.

The Wakefield Forest Elementary School reports successful results for its sexually segregated classes: (1.) Boys in the sexually segregated classes make better progress in language arts and math than do boys in mixed classes. (2.) A second year in the same sex class is more beneficial to boys than to girls. (3.) Boys want to continue in separate classes more than do girls.[1]

A 1969 article in *Nation's Schools* reports that Greely, Colorado, has also had great success with an all male kindergarten and an all male first grade. In Greely's all male classes, teachers try to bring the boys' first two years of school "more in line with their more active and aggressive natures."[2] In all the male classrooms, quiet and order are replaced with increased action and horseplay. There are fewer assignments to be completed at the students' seats, and more work takes place at five interest areas. There is an abundant supply of science equipment, and live animals are brought into the boys' classrooms. To stimulate writing, the boys use typewriters to prepare compositions.

While all these innovative practices were being introduced into male classrooms, the article makes no mention of what the girls were doing. Perhaps, like their sisters in Fairfax County, they were playing "games which emphasize feminine activities such as sewing and housekeeping." Or perhaps the author did not believe that describing the girls' curriculum was worth the effort. The discriminatory tone of the article becomes most overt in its title, "No Girls (or Lady Teachers) Please." This warning has a disturbingly familiar ring to it. It raises memories of other no trespassing signs such as "Whites Only" and "No Irish Need Apply." The one discordant note is the "please" tacked on to the end. Evidently one must be polite when discriminating against the ladies.

It is appalling that such sexist arrangements could be lauded approximately fifteen years after the Supreme Court ruled, in another context, that separate is not equal, and during a time when racism is a loudly rattling skeleton in the educational closet. Ironically, although racial segregation and stereotyping are now anathema, sex segregation and stereotyping are still acceptable in schools.

We have looked briefly at two examples of overt sexism in the elementary school, but discrimination is whispered as well as shouted. In the major part of this chapter, we will listen to this whispering and try to decipher the message it conveys. First, it would be helpful to consider the impact elementary school has on children and to draw a picture of what young boys and girls are like before they step through its portals.

THE HIDDEN CURRICULUM

One of the rather remarkable things about elementary school is that children spend so much time there. In most states, school time amounts to 6 hours a day for 180 days a year. This means that, if a student is in regular attendance, (s)he is immersed in the elementary school environment for a little more than a thousand hours a year. By the time (s)he departs for junior high school, (s)he has spent approximately 7,000 hours under the supervision of teachers. Phil Jackson, in *Life in Classrooms*, underscores how great an influence, in terms of time, the elementary school actually has: ". . . Aside from sleeping, and perhaps playing, there is no other activity that occupies as much of the child's time as that involved in attending school. Apart from the bedroom (where he has his eyes closed most of the time) there is no single enclosure in which he spends a longer time than he does in the classroom. From the age of six onward, he is a more familiar sight to his teacher than to his father, and possibly even to his mother."[3]

Another remarkable thing about elementary school is that children are forced to be there. Only two other institutions—prisons and mental hospitals—are so thoroughly compulsory in nature. Of course, this is not to suggest that conditions in schools are similar to those in prisons and mental hospitals. The authors, however, do mean to point out the one factor the three have in common: in each, human beings are forcefully institutionalized.

The elementary school is a place where many child-hours are spent. It is a place where children are exposed to a variety of stimuli, and it is a place where they can't escape from these stimuli—no matter how much they may want to.

Fortunately, there is much about the environment in an elementary school that is delightful. There may be boldly colorful bulletin boards, arrangements of autumn leaves in the fall, vases of flowers in the spring, pine cone, pipe cleaner turkeys at Thanksgiving, and countless variations of the Santa Claus theme at Christmas. If the school is affluent and somewhat progressive, there may be cooking supplies and an oven that warns of about-to-burn brownies. Perhaps there is a large tank where phosphorescent fish flash through the water in a medley of exotic colors, and a box where children gather in awe around a new litter of gerbils. And the room may be permeated with the work-and-play sound of a dedicated teacher and some twenty children.

To find out what happens to students in this elementary school classroom a visitor could consult the official curriculum, the one that is set down on paper and lists the class schedule, the lesson plans, and maybe even the behavioral objectives. (S)he might find that students are taught arithmetic, English, social studies, reading, science, gym, and perhaps even a foreign language. However, this official curriculum tells only a small part of what will happen to students in the classroom. From peer interaction patterns that develop, from the teacher's use of power as he or she offers and withdraws praise and reprimand, from the children's conflicts with school rules and rituals, from reading between the lines in textbooks, and in short, from an incredible variety of incidental contacts with the environment, a hidden curriculum emerges that has a powerful impact on its young students.

The workings of this hidden curriculum have been studied and analyzed by prominent educators, sociologists, and anthropologists. For example, Phil Jackson discusses it in his perceptive analysis, *Life in Classrooms*.[4] Melvin Silberman, in his book, *The Experience of Schooling*[5] ties several articles together in this theme. In *Clinical Supervision*, Robert Goldhammer refers to this hidden curriculum as "incidental learning,"[6] and George Spindler, in *Education and Culture*, indicates that "unintended goals are often transmitted along with those that are intended."[7]

What is this hidden curriculum, these "incidental learnings," that you will not find listed in the teacher's plan book? Here are a few examples of how the ubiquitous hidden curriculum operates.

1. From 8:30 to 9:15, the class studies English; from 9:15 to 10:00, science; from 10:00 to 10:45, social studies. Between 10:45 and 11:15, there is a recess break. As a student in this class, you may learn that English has nothing to do with science; neither one has anything to do with social studies; and play time is totally unrelated to all three. Moreover, you may learn that all children learn the same thing at the same time and it takes forty-five minutes to do this learning.

2. In your class texts, there is only one picture of a black person. It is of a porter lugging baggage in a railway station. As a student in this class you may learn that black people do not fill many important roles in society.

3. Whenever your class elects officers, you are never nominated. When the teacher assigns work to be done by partners, it seems that nobody wants to work with you. When teams are chosen on the playground at recess, you are often the last one to be selected. In these situations you may learn that you are not a very likeable or worthwhile person.

4. In your class, the teacher gets very angry and yells at students when they don't know the right answer. You may learn that being unaware of knowledge is equivalent to being bad or naughty. You may also learn that being wrong is frightening and humiliating and that learning can be a pretty miserable affair.

It is the total and constant immersion in the hidden curriculum—the repetitious and continual incidental contacts students have with one another, with the teacher, with the rituals and rules of the school, with subtle meanings in textbooks—that have an intensely pervasive and critical impact. Marshall McLuhan's popular slogan that applies to so many environments also fits education: In the schoolroom, the medium is the message. Students may be learning more from the complex social environment in which they are immersed than from the content matter that is officially taught them.

Thus, when the casual visitor enters an elementary school classroom, (s)he may be told that, according to the official curriculum, (s)he will be observing children learning to read. However, (s)he might as accurately be informed that (s)he will be seeing children learning lessons in how to get around school rules, in how to steal attention away from thirty classmates, in what it is like to be a member of a minority group, in how to make friends, and in what it feels like not to have any. (S)he may also see children learning that different kinds of behaviors are expected from girls than are expected from boys, that each sex is entitled to a different set of rewards, privileges, and punishments. Every day that girls and boys attend elementary school, the hidden curriculum functions as a subtle forge in which awareness of the male role and female role is shaped.

SEX TYPING IN
CHILDREN'S HOMES

This molding does not begin in the elementary classroom. It has been taking place for five or six years in the homes of preschool boys and girls. Before we examine what happens in schools, it is important to recognize the sex typing that has gone on before children get there.

To begin at the beginning, let us visit the maternity ward of a hospital. If we travel the hospital corridors until we arrive at the nursery, we find the newborn infants, sleeping, howling, making their first instinctive explorations into their new surroundings. Swaddled in receiving blankets with only their wrinkled, prune-like faces visible, they hardly seem such formidable creatures. Yet their parents can already be heard speculating about what their young son will become—a chemist, a doctor, a newspaper editor, an artist—indeed, the myth that anybody can become president still leaves that job as a potential. He can choose the career that will best meet his individual needs and abilities. This is his birthright.

On the other hand, when the birth certificate reads female, parents don't bother to do much guessing. In twenty-five or thirty years it is highly likely that, no matter what individual abilities or needs each female may have, most will be channeled into one activity—that of housewife. When the child is female, individuality becomes irrelevant.[8] And children pick up these expectations. As parents first speculate, or don't bother to, the channeling process begins.

Soon the newborn infants are taken home, and the sex typing continues in earnest. The infant boy finds himself in a blue world, and around the baby girl everything is pink—from ribbons, to stuffed animals, to the clothes she wears. These colors serve as announcements to the outside world of how the young child should be treated. The baby boy, gender indistinguishable except for the blue jumpsuit he sports, brings exclamations like: "My what a husky fellow. Looks like you've got a football player on your hands." The baby girl, gender equally indistinguishable, tips off visitors by her pink outfit, and the cooing begins: "Isn't she adorable. How sweet." The channeling process is furthered.

At first there are many toys that are considered neuter, from rattles to colorful mobiles. As children begin to grow the toys start to differentiate between the sexes. For boys there are trucks and cars, bats and balls, guns and a wide variety of science equipment. Girls are offered an incredible array of dolls that walk, that say "mama," and come with luxurious fashion wardrobes. Later they graduate to paper dolls, cooking supplies "just like mom's," sewing and jewelry making kits. Whenever a child rummages through his or her toy box, a great deal about "appropriate" sex role behavior is learned.

Because girls dream about being a ballerina, Mattel makes Dancerina . . . a pink confection in a silken blouse and ruffled tutu. . . . Wishing you were older is part of growing up. . . . Barbie, a young fashion model, and her friends do the "in" things girls should do—talk about new places to visit, new clothes to wear and new friends to meet. . . .

Because boys were born to build and learn, Mattel makes Tog'l [a set of building blocks] for creative play. . . . Because boys are curious about things big and small, Mattel makes Super-Eyes, a telescope that boys can have in one ingenious set of optically engineered lenses and scope . . . that . . . create dozens of viewing devices—all for science or all for fun.

Reported in "The Image of Woman in Advertising" by Lucy Komisar.

As we mentioned previously, the television set, in many homes a constant companion to family activity, makes its own commentary about what men should do and where women belong. As children sit transfixed before the T.V., they see males reporting the important news of the world—news that seems to be almost entirely about more males. They see talk shows hosted by males (except for Dinah Shore who cooks with her guests in the kitchen). They watch the violent machismo shows about cowboys and cops and robbers. When they do see women, too often it is as absurd caricatures in commercials; they clean their toilet bowls and dust their furniture; they primp before mirrors, dye their hair, camouflage their faces with the latest cosmetic; or they retreat to the medicine cabinet seeking pills because they cannot cope with their world.

Even as children watch shows designed especially for them, the lessons they learn are just as clear and just as unfortunate. When the much publicized "Sesame Street" parades its personality-plus gallery of puppets across the screen—once again children learn that the important gender is male. For children, watching television is like taking lessons in male violence and female unimportance and invisibility.

The way parents treat their children may be the most important factor of all in the creation of sex stereotypes. When one compares the life of the young girl to that of the young boy, a critical difference emerges: She is treated more protectively and she is subjected to more restrictions and controls; he receives greater achievement demands and higher expectations.

Failing to receive sufficient "independence and mastery training" throughout the infant and early childhood years, girls are allowed and at times even encouraged to exhibit dependency, passivity, and conformity.[9] In one study it was found that six-month-old girls were spoken to and fondled more frequently than were baby boys of the same age. When they were thirteen months old, these same girls were more reluctant than the boys to leave their mothers, and they remained closer to them throughout the play period. When a barrier was placed between mother and child, the girls tended to cry helplessly, but the boys actively tried to get around it.[10] It is small wonder that at all ages there are more studies reporting dependency, passivity, and conformity for females than for males.[11]

In contrast, parents more often and consistently disapprove of passivity and docility in their sons, and they encourage the active display of his aggression. (As has been noted previously, aggression is an ambiguous term with highly connotative meanings. For purposes of this discussion, it will be considered as the expenditure of energy toward another person or object, an expenditure that, in its negative sense, involves overtones of hostility.) For example, one mother of a kindergarten child was interviewed with the question, "How important do you think it is for a boy of Ted's age to act like a real boy?" She answered: "Very important, very important—I will repeat that. By a real boy, I mean not being a sissy; it is very important. I wouldn't want him otherwise—I would give him boxing lessons if I had to."[12]

This mother was one of 379 interviewed. Although her attitude was a bit stronger than most, it is generally reflective of how parents expected their sons to behave. In contrast, parents punish such aggression in their daughters. The results of these child rearing practices are documented in empirical research, and it is difficult to find a sound study of preschool or school age children in which aggressive behavior was not more frequent among boys than among girls.[13] "Such findings indicate that the differential treatment of the two sexes reflects in part a difference in goals. With sons, socialization seems to focus primarily on directing and constraining the boys' impact on the environment. With daughters, the aim is to protect the girl from the impact of environment. The boy is being prepared to mold his world, the girl to be molded by it."[14]

So on that first day of the first grade, the experienced teacher will be ready for more active, rambunctious behavior from her young male charges and will expect quieter compliance from the young girls. Are these sex-typed behaviors that children bring to school with them reinforced there? Are they in any way attenuated? Does exaggeration of sex-typed behaviors ever take place? We are now ready to explore the different effects the elementary school environment has on its young students.

SCHOOLING AS A
SEXIST ACTIVITY

There is no course in the official curriculum called "Male Role Development," or "Learning How to be a Girl," but such learning takes place incidentally, and a variety of signals—some obvious, some hidden—insure that sex typing will be reinforced.

One obvious way sex typing occurs is by dress code regulations that many schools still maintain. Regulations that insist that girls wear skirts or dresses rather than slacks have a much deeper impact than on mere appearance. When a girl complies with such regulations she relinquishes freedom—freedom to run as fast as she is able, freedom to sit in complete comfort, and freedom to turn a somersault at recess on the play yard. Because of the clothes she is forced to wear, her physical mobility is hampered and restrained. It is a symbolic confinement.

Recently dress codes have been widely challenged as is illustrated by the following memo sent out by a Massachusetts principal to his faculty:

I am being beseiged by 6th grade girls who want to wear slacks to school. May I have your opinions?

Do you think we ought to permit slacks? In cold weather only?—In any weather?—any slacks (dungarees, chinos, etc?)

Any other comments about dress?

This will be one topic of discussion for Friday.

This memo is not only indicative of a few cracks beginning to appear in the sartorial armor; it is also indicative of how basically solid the armor still is.

Another distinction children learn, and we are still dealing with the obvious examples, is that boys are supposed to be stronger than girls. When school maintenance chores are assigned, boys draw those tasks requiring heavier manual labor whereas girls are asked to help in quieter, more sedentary ways. This separation of tasks is often inappropriate and forced since some girls mature faster than boys, and in the early grades, are frequently as big and as strong. However, if stacks of heavy texts are to be moved from one room to another, a small boy may be found struggling under their weight, while a girl—perhaps larger and stronger—sits and watches.

School against boys

There are many learnings about sex role behavior that are less obvious. To begin with, we will concentrate on the incidental learnings that are reserved for the elementary school boy. One of his early unhappy learnings may be that he and school don't get along very well. Let's look at an active 6-year old's first encounter with school.

It is Tommy's first day in the first grade. With a sense of bewilderment, he surveys the unknown faces, the shelves of books, the collage of bulletin board pictures, the rows of desks that comprise the classroom. Despite his confusion, he does receive certain definite impressions.

First of all, he finds that the person in charge of his new life is a woman. She seems annoyed whenever he leaves his desk, or talks to the boy in front of him, or spills his crayons on the floor.

He particularly hates following directions and being neat about it. In the arithmetic lesson, the teacher instructs the class to divide their papers into three boxes and to draw one lollipop in the first, two flags in the second, and three ice cream cones in the third. Tommy begins drawing the objects before the instructions are completed. Consequently, he mixes up the number of lollipops and ice cream cones, and since he has forgotten to bring an eraser, he desparately tries to rub the error out with spit. When the teacher stops by his desk to check his work, she reprimands him for the messy hole that has emerged in the middle of his lollipops.

Obviously not a very pleasant or rewarding encounter for Tommy. It is a beginning attempt to check the independence and mastery training that he has profited from in his home environment—one that, along with numerous variations, will occur again and again throughout the early grades.

Many educators feel that the cards are stacked against the elementary school boy. At age 6 when he enters the first grade, he may be twelve months behind his female classmate in developmental age, and by nine this discrepancy has increased to eighteen months.[15] Thus he is working side by side with a female who may be not only bigger than he, but who seems able, as we shall see, to handle school more competently and more comfortably. Added to this handicap is the fact that the elementary school boy must function in an environment that is antithetical to the independent life style he has been encouraged to develop up until then. He is in a situation where neatness, good manners, and docility appear to be keys to success. Writers and cartoonists often depict him as a male misfit in a female world, a young bull whose every move seems to disrupt the delicate balance of the china shop.

Patricia Sexton is one educator who has frequently expressed concern for the development of the young boy in the "feminine" elementary school. In a *Saturday Review* article titled "Are Schools Emasculating Our Boys?" she has stated:

Boys and the schools seem locked in a deadly and ancient conflict that may eventually inflict mortal wounds on both. . . . The problem is not just that teachers are too often women. It is that the school is too much a woman's world, governed by women's rules and stand-

*ards. The school code is that of propriety, obedience, decorum, cleanli-
ness, physical and, too often, mental passivity.*[16]

She is not alone in her analysis. A review of the recent educational
literature discloses a number of articles with titles that reflect similar
concern: "Males: A Minority Group in the Classroom" (*Journal of
Learning Disabilities*),[17] "Are Girls Really Smarter?" (*Elementary
School Journal*),[18] "For Johnny's Reading Sake," (*Reading Teacher*),[19]
"Elementary Education—A Man's World," (*Instructor*).[20] Numerous
other articles with titles less explicit deal with problems young boys
experience in their encounter with the elementary school. No corresponding concern anywhere near such magnitude can be found for
the elementary school girl.

The conflict between boy and school has also provided a fertile
source of material for humorists. One of the major themes of school
cartoons has been that of the mischievous boy doing battle with the
weary and rattled female teacher—chuckling with anticipation as he
places a thumbtack on her chair, subdued as he trudges home with her
retaliation in hand, a report card of Ds and Fs. Cartoonists also draw
these rebellious young boys conspiring together with advice such as,
"Play it dumb for the first few weeks, then start producing. The
teacher will think she's doing wonders with you." They are also pic-
tured as continually trying to explain the bad grades they get to their
parents: "You can see she's against me—she has me even dumber
than I was last month, and you know that's impossible," or, "I'm
saving my brains for real life."[21]

What does the young boy learn from this feminine environment
that stresses passivity, neatness, and docility? For one thing, he may
learn how to be more quiet, neat, and docile—although for many
this is not likely. He may instead learn—that school is a girl's
world, one that has little appeal, meaning, or pertinence for him. In
fact, one study has shown that elementary school children, both boys
and girls, labeled school objects such as blackboard, book, page of
arithmetic, and school desk as feminine rather than neuter or masculine.[22]

In a sense the femininity of the school is paralleled by the femininity of the home. The home, like the classroom, is usually organized by
a woman, and we can safely guess that, if a similar study were done
and children were asked to label home objects such as sink and
table, they would label them feminine also. However, in each situation the young boy is treated quite differently. The woman in the

home is more likely to foster her son's independence so that he will develop the appropriate "manly" qualities. The woman who runs the classroom, with thirty children on her hands, may fear that unless independence and activity are checked, her room will explode and she will lose control.

Thus, the young boy must spend approximately a thousand hours a year at an institution that restrains and checks him. This lack of comfortable fit between the more active behavior allowed at home and the passivity demanded in school may force young boys into open rebellion. We can see how this happens as we take another look at boys in the elementary school.

The scene is a restless and unruly afternoon in Miss Hodgkins' fifth-grade class. She has issued warning after warning trying to get the class to quiet down, but she has little success. Finally she explodes, "I've had just all I'm going to take! As usual, the boys are causing all the trouble, so, as usual, all the boys will stay after school. If only you boys could be nice and quiet like the girls, what a pleasure teaching would be."

How likely is it that this scene (or some reasonable facsimile) will occur in an elementary school? Educational research suggests that it is quite likely indeed. Those who study what goes on in classrooms have focused much attention on classroom interaction patterns, who talks with whom, how much of a lesson is teacher talk, who is criticized, who is praised and how often. One finding of these studies is that a different pattern of interaction emerges for boys than for girls.

Researchers studied how teachers dispensed reward and disapproval in three sixth-grade classrooms. Children in these classes were asked to nominate those classmates who received the teacher's approval and those who received her disapproval. Both classroom observers and the children themselves noted that the teachers expressed greater approval of girls and greater disapproval of boys.[23] In another study it was found that boys receive eight to ten times as many prohibitory control messages (warnings like: "That's enough talking Bill. Put that comic book away, Joe.) as their female classmates. Moreover, this same researcher has also found that when teachers criticize boys, they are more likely to use harsh or angry tones than when talking with girls about an equivalent misdemeanor.[24]

However, it has been found that teachers not only disapprove of

Boys are doctors.

SOURCE: Whitney Darrow, Jr., *I'm Glad I'm a Boy! I'm Glad I'm a Girl!*
New York, Simon and Schuster, 1970. Reprinted by permission of Windmill Books/Simon and Schuster.

boys more, but also interact with them more in general. In a large study involving twenty-one fourth- and sixth-grade classes (thirteen taught by male teachers and eight by female teachers) it was found that teachers interacted more with boys in four major categories of teaching behavior: approval, instruction, listening to the child, and disapproval.[25] So it seems that teachers not only reprimand boys more, but also talk with them about subject matter more frequently and listen to what they have to say more often. In short, boys are receiving more than their share of the teacher's active attention.

Although it is difficult to assess the impact of all this attention,

Girls are nurses.

SOURCE: Whitney Darrow, Jr., *I'm Glad I'm a Boy! I'm Glad I'm a Girl!* New York, Simon and Schuster, 1970. Reprinted by permission of Windmill Books/Simon and Schuster.

including negative attention, on boys, one researcher suggests the following result: "One consequence might be a cumulative increase in independent, autonomous behavior by boys as they are disapproved, praised, listened to, and taught more actively by the teacher."[26]

We have been discussing school as a feminine environment in which boys rebel against the network of restrictions imposed upon them. It also appears that boys view this feminine environment as an inappropriate arena for combat and achievement. They are consistent losers when school laurels in the form of grades are given out.

The teacher has just handed back a major unit test to her third grade class. She states that she has stars to put on the papers of

*those who received A's and B's, and she requests that children with
the appropriate grade come up to her desk to claim their reward. The
line that circles her desk is overwhelmingly female.*

Elementary school boys appear to be quite unsuccessful when it comes
to winning good grades. Among boys and girls of comparable IQ,
girls are more likely to receive higher grades than boys. Also, boys
who do equally as well as girls on achievement tests get lower grades
in school. In fact, throughout elementary school two-thirds of all
grade repeaters are boys.[27] Within this general pattern of low achievement, one subject is singled out for particularly poor performance.

*It is ten o'clock. A glance at the daily lesson plan shows that read-
ing is scheduled, and if one steps inside the classroom, (s)he will find
the teacher calling upon Johnny to read a selection in the basal reader.
Johnny stumbles his way through the passage—his reversals and
omissions turning the printed word into a tortured garble. The teacher
sighs with impatience and then calls on Loretta who reads the section
fluently.*

Reading is a subject that seems to be a good deal more difficult for
boys than for girls. In a study of one thousand first graders in Mary-
land, it was found that for every girl with a reading problem, there
were about two boys.[28] Other researchers have found that three
times more boys than girls have trouble with reading.[29]

There is evidence that shows that this difficulty is not something
inherently male, but rather one of the more pernicious examples of
incidental learning. John McNeil studied seventy-two kindergarten
boys and sixty kindergarten girls who were enrolled in a reading
program that consisted of programmed instruction. In this program,
the children sat in individual cubicles; they were presented identical
segments of reading material at a common pace, and they received
the same number of taped comments of encouragement. The boys
and girls were given equal opportunity to respond, and the same
number of responses were demanded daily from all learners. On a
word recognition test administered after the program had been in
operation for four months, boys made significantly higher scores
than girls did. After completing this program, the children were
placed in a regular classroom situation where they received their
reading instruction from female teachers. After four months of classroom reading, a similar test was administered. This time the boys did
not do as well as the girls.

In an attempt to figure out reasons for the shift in test scores, McNeil asked the children to nominate those in their reading group who received negative comments from the teacher such as "Sit Up!" "Pay attention." The nominations indicated that boys not only received more negative admonitions, but also were given less opportunity to read.[30] Thus it appears that boys may be taught reading in a more punitive manner, and these negative contacts may be associated with difficulties boys have in beginning reading.

A cross-cultural study also makes the point that the young boy's trouble with reading is a socially learned disability. Reading achievement levels of over a thousand students in Germany and over a thousand students in the United States were analyzed. In the United States, mean scores for girls were higher than mean scores for boys. In Germany, however, the opposite was true; boys had the higher scores. It was noted in the study that teachers in Germany are primarily male, and this may have contributed to the boys' superior reading scores.[31] It appears that reading disability in either sex can be attributed to cultural factors. However, one cannot assume that male teachers will necessarily result in higher reading performance by male students. Other studies report no difference in reading gains made by students with teachers of either sex.[32]

In many ways the experience of schooling reinforces the already partially formed sex role stereotypes that boys bring to it. Often the nuclear family environment is a feminine one from which the father departs early in the morning and does not return until evening, possibly even after the youngster has gone to bed. Mother and child spend long unbroken hours in one another's company. Typically, the elementary school classroom is also a "feminine" environment organized and administered by a woman. A difference emerges in the way the young boy is treated in these two environments. At home an independent life style is fostered. In the classroom, where approximately thirty individuals are packed into close quarters, activity and independence are frowned upon. There, docility is the message of the hidden curriculum. Often boys rebel. This rebellion brings increased teacher disapproval, but also increased teacher attention in general. As they refuse to buy this message of docility, as they interact more directly and actively with teachers, their approach to learning becomes increasingly independent and autonomous.

That is a positive result of the boy's conflict with school. There are negative effects, too. School may become so distasteful that he drops out. He may do this literally, but he can also drop out in a less concrete fashion. Although he may remain a firmly entrenched figure in the second seat, fourth row, his thoughts and energy are everywhere but in the classroom. This kind of dropping out can be seen in high male failure rates, in bad grades, and in the expressed hatred of school.

School against girls

Educators have not spent as much time worrying about what happens to girls in elementary school. A review of the educational literature does not disclose numerous articles pleading, "Let's Give the Girls a Break" or asking, "Is School Destroying our Daughters?" Until very recently, that is. The women's liberation movement has caused increased awareness and indignation at unequal treatment of females in all institutions of society, and as one of these institutions, attention is focused on the school. Most frequently, discrimination is being examined at the university level. However, girls learn harmful lessons at all rungs of the educational ladder, and the groundwork for future discrimination is established early.

If the young girl has experienced sex typing at home, it is likely she will enter school already somewhat compliant and passive. These characteristics are well in line with the norms of the elementary school; it seems that the young female student should feel very much at home there. In order to see if the sex typing is reinforced, let's visit the classroom again. Let's join Mary-Alice as she experiences her first day at school and the arithmetic lesson that went so unhappily for Tommy.

Amid the noise and confusion of thirty five- and six-year-olds settling into their desks, Mary-Alice was led to her seat. The busy turmoil of the classroom confused her and a hundred different vignettes competed for her attention: mothers waving goodbye, colorful pictures on the bulletin board, a cage with a hamster, bookcases lined with picture books, children whispering together in the corridor. She was puzzled and anxious about her new surroundings, and she waited cautiously at her seat to see what would happen.

After introducing herself to the class, the teacher gave instructions for a lesson in arithmetic. Mary-Alice listened very carefully, and then working slowly and methodically, she took her ruler and divided her paper into three equal compartments. In the first box she drew one lollipop, in the second, two flags, and in the third, three ice cream cones. When the teacher stopped by her desk to check her work she was delighted: "This is the most attractive paper in the class. I'm going to put it on the bulletin board so that everyone can see it." Mary-Alice smiled and silently vowed that tomorrow she would try to make her paper even neater and prettier.

Mary-Alice does indeed feel at home in elementary school—and therein lies the problem. Jerome Bruner summarizes the result of this too comfortable fit:

> *Observant anthropologists have suggested that the basic values of the early grades are a stylized version of the feminine role in society, cautious rather than daring, governed by a lady-like politeness. . . . Girls in the early grades who learn to control their fidgeting earlier are rewarded for excelling in their feminine values. The reward can be almost too successful in that in later years it is difficult to move girls beyond the orderly virtues they learned in their first school encounters. The boys, more fidgety in the first grades get no such reward, and as a consequence may be freer in their approach to learning in the later grades.*[33]

> A girl whose spirits have not been dampened by inactivity, or innocence tainted by false shame, will always be a romp. . . .
>
> Mary Wollstonecraft
> *A Vindication of the Rights of Women,* 1792

Girls are reinforced for silence, for neatness, for conformity—and in this dispensation of rewards, the process of learning is thwarted. One study, concerned with fifth-grade children, points up the unhappy effects that reward-seeking can have on intellectual curiosity. It shows that when students are anxious to receive good grades and teacher praise, they hide their academic weaknesses from the teacher and avoid situations of intellectual challenge.[34] Thus the young girl, programmed into dependency on rewards, will be more likely to avoid the academically challenging problem wherein lies the possibility of failure and loss of teacher approval but also the potential for greater academic growth and stimulation.

In fact it has been shown that grade school girls are more likely to avoid possible failure than are boys of a corresponding age. One very interesting study was concerned with nursery and elementary school children. Each child was given two seven-piece wooden puzzles and was told that (s)he had one and a half minutes to complete each. The experimenter, however, only pretended to time the children's performances, and in actuality manipulated success and failure. The children were allowed to complete only one of the puzzles. The other was removed after five pieces had been connected, even if the time limit had not been reached. After the children had attempted to complete both puzzles, the experimenter announced that there was a little extra time to work on one of them again. The children were asked to choose the puzzle they wished to work on a second time. For the nursery school group, no significant difference was found between the repetition choices of boys and girls. For the grade school group, however, a telling pattern emerged. Boys more often chose to return to the puzzle they had failed to complete. In contrast, *girls more often repeated the puzzle that they had put together successfully*. They avoided the failure situation.[35]

Owing to the teachers' bestowal and withdrawal of rewards and an environment that stresses docility, the elementary school directly reinforces the passivity that the young female student may bring with her from home. The result is a bizarre distortion of the learning process. Neatness, conformity, docility, these qualities for which the young girl receives good grades and teacher's praise have little to do with active intellectual curiosity, analytical problem solving, and the ability to cope with challenging material. For good grades and teachers' praise, the grade school girl relinquishes the courage that it takes to grapple with difficult material. This naive young bargainer of seven or eight has made an exchange that will cost her dearly.

This passive approach to learning, this avoidance of the challenging situation, this fear of failure are obviously unfortunate, detrimental attitudes. What is even more disturbing is the fact that they can literally be translated into a decline of ability. It has been found that during the formative childhood years some children's IQs increase, some remain constant, and some decline. Eleanor Maccoby depicts the children at age six whose IQs will be likely to increase by the time they reach age ten. They are "competitive, self-assertive, independent, and dominant in interaction with other children. The children who show declining IQs during the next four years are children who are passive, shy, and dependent."[36] These are attitudes that tend to differentiate boys and girls. In effect, a devastating paradoxical theft has been committed. By effectively reinforcing a passive approach to learning, the school runs the risk of decreasing the female student's ability. Ironically, while attempting to increase student potential, the school, in reality, may be likely to limit it.

As was mentioned earlier, boys look around the elementary school and find that the school is staffed by female teachers; the result may be a conflict between their active life style and the school environment. Girls, however, experience their own difficulties with the staffing patterns of the elementary school.

Joanne is in the sixth grade at Barnes Elementary School. She has gone there all her life, and all her teachers have been women. Joanne has seen that sometimes students get fresh and hard to handle, and then the teacher sends these students to the principal's office. She has also noted that whenever the teacher doesn't know the answer to a question about school rules and regulations, the teacher says that she will find out the answer from the principal. All her teachers have taken their orders from the principal and have gone to him when they need help. And the principal is a man. Joanne wonders if, in every profession, women always get directions and orders from men.

It may be that elementary school is a woman's world, but a male captain heads the ship. Futhermore, the trend is toward replacing more and more of these principalships with men. According to a 1928 National Education Association report, 55 percent of elementary school principals were women.[37] In 1966, men out-numbered women in these principalships by a ratio of three to two.[38] In 1971, although women comprised 88 percent of elementary school teachers, they were only 22 percent of elementary school principals.[39]

The woman principal is a vanishing breed, and apparently her extinction is not coming about because men are better at the job. In a 1955 study, which has since been replicated, it was found that female principals were more democratic and were more concerned with the objectives of teaching, with pupil participation, and with the evaluation of learning.[40] This indication of the superiority of the female principal is not necessarily a sign that women are more capable administrators. Rather it points up the far richer female talent pool that is available to begin with. Not only do more women than men go into elementary education, but there is also evidence that women who choose education for a profession are brighter than men who choose this field. In 1968, 268 male and 811 female merit scholarship finalists and semifinalists chose secondary education for a career, and for elementary education, the figures were two men and 146 women.[41] Evidently, when administrative talent is selected, the brightest is not the best.

As one climbs higher on the administrative ladder, there are fewer

Boys invent things.

SOURCE: Whitney Darrow, Jr., *I'm Glad I'm a Boy! I'm Glad I'm a Girl!* New York, Simon and Schuster, 1970. Reprinted by permission of Windmill Books/Simon and Schuster.

and fewer women to be found. In 1971, there were only two women among the thirteen thousand district superintendents in the United States.[42] Moreover, as of 1960 more than one-half of all school boards, key centers of decision making, had no women members.[43]

Thus, women swell the base of the educational pyramid, feminizing the elementary school, and men perch along the structure's top, issuing their directives and decisions. The pattern is familiar. It can be seen in the business office where a pool of secretaries, armed with memo pad and typewriter, put into operation the orders of their male commander; it happens on the hospital ward where female nurses, equipped with bedpan and thermometer, carry out the instructions

Girls use what boys invent.

SOURCE: Whitney Darrow, Jr., *I'm Glad I'm a Boy! I'm Glad I'm a Girl!*
New York, Simon and Schuster, 1970. Reprinted by permission of Windmill Books/Simon and Schuster.

of the male doctor. In education as in other fields, women have their
place—and it is not on top.

How does this imbalance in the school staffing pattern affect the
elementary school girl? She may be quite unaware of many of the
male bosses. School board members and superintendents may be little
more than shadowy, undefined figures who shuffle papers and talk
incessantly in some unimportant corner of her school world. However, the male boss in the form of the principal does emerge as an
important figure. Whenever an issue is too big or troublesome for the
teacher (usually female) to handle, the principal (usually male) is
called upon to offer the final decision, to administer the ultimate

punishment or reward. And children, so alert to body cues, so sensitive to messages transmitted through the silent language, must detect the teacher's change in demeanor, the slight shift in posture that transforms confidence into deference and respect. It would be hard to misinterpret the relationship. The teacher is the boss of the class; the principal is boss of the teacher. And the principal is a man. In the child's mind associations form. When a woman functions professionally, she takes orders from a man, and the image of female inferiority and subservience begins to come across.

Children seldom see a female superintendent, and the woman principal is becoming harder and harder to find. There is another staffing rarity, and this is the opportunity for children to work with a teacher who is noticeably pregnant, for many schools have written policies that require discontinuance of teaching at a specific time during pregnancy, sometimes as early as the third month. Women teachers who have been harmed by such regulations are taking their grievances to court, contending that such policies violate their equal protection rights under the fourteenth amendment.

A Virginia school teacher, Susan Cohen, is the first woman to successfully challenge the constitutionality of regulations concerning mandatory maternity leave. In her federal court suit, the judge noted, "Decision of when a pregnant teacher should discontinue working are matters best left up to the woman and her doctor."[44]

But even as Mrs. Cohen was winning her suit in Virginia, two women teachers in Cleveland lost their case against compulsory maternity leave. The following are comments taken from actual court records. They represent the puritanical views that some board members and educators hold about pregnant women.

Teachers suffered many indignities as a result of pregnancy, which consisted of children pointing, giggling, laughing, and making snide remarks.

Although no child was born in the classroom, a few times it was very close.

Where the possibility of violence and accident exists, pregnancy greatly magnifies the probability of serious injury.

The kids might think she has a watermelon in her belly.[45]

As increasing numbers of women challenge these attitudes and the regulations in which they are embodied, they are receiving assistance from the National Education Association through the Du Shane Emergency Fund. Lawsuits have now been instituted in situations involving forced maternity leave, loss of salary and retirement benefits, endangered tenure and seniority rights, and inequitable policies relative to reemployment after childbirth.

The dismissal of pregnant teachers also harms children, for pregnancy and birth can be presented and discussed in schools in a highly positive manner. A second-grade teacher brought his wife, who was eight months pregnant, into class to talk to the children. They were fascinated as she told them how the baby was growing inside her and a few, who felt the baby kick when they placed their hands on her stomach, were delighted and amazed. Almost daily after her visit they asked about the progress of mother and baby and with the teacher's help built a chart for the bulletin board on the development of a fetus. Later the teacher brought his wife to class again, this time with their four-month-old daughter, and a whole new learning area was opened—how to take care of a newborn infant.

Compulsory maternity leaves and related policies obviously do a disservice to women teachers. They deprive children as well, teaching them by omission that a pregnant woman is someone to giggle at or be embarrassed about and also denying them involvement in the fascinating process of birth.

Curricular materials as they now exist also harm elementary school children—particularly girls. What do girls learn about themselves from the image of women in school texts?

Sara's fourth-grade class has spent the past month studying the early history of America. The children's history text tells of the colonists' refusal to accept "taxation without representation," the war with England, and the struggle to conceptualize a new form of government. The text is replete with pictures and biographical sketches of George Washington, Ben Franklin, Paul Revere, Sam Adams. Although Sara has examined the text carefully, the only woman she can find mentioned is Betsey Ross. She wonders if there simply weren't any women in the colonies or if women never did anything worth writing about. It seems to her to have been a rather lopsided birth of the nation—having only founding fathers.

It is not only the history books that deny the young elementary school child heroic and positive female role models. If she wishes to read a biography about a famous American, she can turn for inspiration to Henry Hudson, Lewis and Clark, Robert Peary, Kit Carson,

Davy Crockett, Buffalo Bill, Abraham Lincoln, George Washington, Ben Franklin, Thomas Jefferson, Andrew Jackson, Woodrow Wilson, Mike Fink, and Albert Einstein, to name some of the more well-known figures. If for any reason she would like to read about a woman, she also has a choice: Annie Oakley, Amelia Earhart, and more recently, Shirley Chisholm. Of course other biographies about women do exist, but she will have to look a good deal harder to find them.[46]

Even in elementary math texts, sex stereotyping is blatant. Members of the Education Committee of the National Organization for Women in New York City conducted a study of math books that yielded the following results.

Mathematical problems in *Seeing Through Arithmetic Five* by Scott Foresman present math concepts in social contexts that strongly reinforce stereotyped sex roles. The following are some examples, with page numbers.

- Brownies are cooking and sewing to raise money. (p. 22).
- Boy is building with his father, thus stressing active work as related to males. (p. 26).
- Out of ten problems, five dealt with girls cooking and sewing. (p. 45)
- Problems dealing with club activities: girls are shown making sandwiches, and boys build dividers. (p. 65)
- Shows girls' 4-H club activities. Fourteen problems deal with sewing and cooking. (p. 84)
- Out of fourteen problems, three deal with mother cooking and girls helping. (p. 110)
- Girls and women are shown cooking and cutting cakes. (p. 133)
- Father takes boys on camping trip. Mother stays home and bakes. (p. 154).
- Boy goes out planting with father while mother stays home and bakes. (p. 183)
- Women and girls are shopping for food and sewing supplies. (p. 214)
- Problems deal with women cooking and sewing and men driving cars and hiking. (p. 220)
- Women and girls are shopping and cooking. Problems dealing with men have them building, repairing, and earning money. (p. 264)

Math Book 5 (Heath) contains fewer problems than the preceding book, but where there are problems, role teaching is just as evident. Some examples follow:

- Out of ten problems, five deal with boys working at physical activities, and two problems have girls babysitting and sewing. (p. 155)
- Out of five problems, one has girls sewing, and two problems have boys playing marbles while girls are jumping rope. (p. 166)
- There are twelve problems altogether; eleven dealing with boys earning money, building things and going places, while one deals with a girl buying a ribbon for a sewing project. (p. 173)
- Out of five problems, three deal with boys and men doing varied activities while one problem deals with one girl shopping and one girl sick. (p. 197)[47]

What about pleasure reading available to the elementary school girl? A committee of feminists examined lists of past Newbery Award Winners and books recommended by the American Library Association. They found that of all forty-nine Newbery Award Winners, books about boys outnumbered books about girls three to one, and in the ALA lists the ratio was two to one.[48] The committee also extracted sexist quotes that they felt would teach girls that it is discouraging and humiliating to have been born female. For example, a sympathetic male character in the 1967 Newbery Winner, *Up a Road Slowly*, gives the heroine the following advice: "Accept the fact that this is a man's world and learn how to play the game gracefully." And in the 1957 Newbery Award Winner, *Miracles on Maple Hill*, the author sets forth a less demanding code of behavior for girls than for boys, one that requires less in the way of courage and intelligence.

For the millionth time she was glad she wasn't a boy. It was all right for girls to be scared or silly or even ask dumb questions. Everybody just laughed and thought it was funny. But if anybody caught Joe asking a dumb question or even thought he was the littlest bit scared, he went red and purple and white. Daddy was even something like that, old as he was.[49]

School reading texts were also studied. It was found that the major reading series used in almost all public and private schools across the country teach that being a girl means being inferior. In these texts, boys are portrayed as being able to do so many things: they play with bats and balls, they work with chemistry sets, they do magic tricks that amaze their sisters, and they show initiative and independence as they go on trips by themselves and get part-time jobs. Girls do things too: They help with the housework, bake cookies and sit and watch their brothers—that is, assuming they are present. In 144 texts studied, there were 881 stories in which the main characters are boys and only 344 in which a girl is the central figure.[50] Furthermore, as Marjorie U'Ren, who examined the most recent textbooks adopted or recommended for second- through sixth-grade use in California, points out, females are depicted as having less mental perseverance and moral strength than males. "Not only are females more often described as lazy and incapable of independent thinking or direct action, but they are also shown as giving up more easily. They collapse into tears, they betray secrets, they are more likely to act on petty or selfish motives."[51]

Adults in these readers are also characterized by streotyped behavior. The men do a variety of exciting jobs; career possibilities include being an astronaut, explorer, inventor, scientist, writer, and so on. Occasionally, women in these texts work, but only in the sex-typed jobs of secretary, nurse, teacher, and librarian. Moreover, when women do fulfill the traditional role of housewife and mother, they are depicted as one-dimensional cardboard characters. The mother's activities are almost totally restricted to housekeeping and cooking. When she speaks, she often serves as a foil for father, asking him what can be done in a particular situation, and then taking his advice as he creatively and decisively solves the problem.[52]

The proverb "a single picture is worth a thousand words" suggests that pictures may have a powerful impact. We cannot leave children's texts without a look at how they are illustrated. U'Ren, in the California study, notes that only 15 percent of the text illustrations are of girls and women. The most important illustrations, those on book covers or by chapter headings are invariably of males; in group scenes, females are found making up the background. Although any photograph of a street scene shows an equal amount of males and females, in a textbook illustration there will usually be more men than women.[53] There is a further distortion in textbook pictures. Young girls, because they mature earlier, are often taller and heavier than are boys of a corresponding age. However, in textbook pictures girls are usually drawn smaller than boys, a bizarre contradiction of reality.[54]

One of the most overtly offensive books for young children is *I'm Glad I'm a Boy! I'm Glad I'm a Girl!*, illustrations from which are included in this chapter. In this book, captions under large cartoon figures announce the following role dispensations: boys are doctors, pilots, policemen, and Presidents; girls are nurses, stewardesses, metermaids, and First Ladies. This children's book was published in

1970.[55] One can only imagine the uproar if similarly subservient roles, complete with lower status and lower pay, were depicted as appropriate for black, Mexican, or native Americans.

Obviously authors and illustrators have not joined in a pernicious conspiracy to put down women. Discrimination is for the most part unintentional—although not completely. In a course called Writing for Children, one instructor warned, "The wise author writes about boys, thereby insuring himself a maximum audience, since only girls will read a book about a girl, but both boys and girls will read about a boy." And the Newbery Award winner *Island of the Blue Dolphins* was initially rejected by a publisher who wanted to change the sex of its courageous heroine.[56]

The result is that for a girl in search of an inspiring model, reading and history texts, biographies, and fiction offer a meager diet. Not only is there little that is inspiring, but there is far too much that is degrading and humiliating, that teaches a girl not to strive, not to achieve, and to be docile, dependent, submissive, and unobtrusive. Perhaps this robbery of proud and achieving models is part of what the *Old Mole* of Cambridge, Massachusetts refers to in its statement:

Our history has been stolen from us. Our heroes died in childbirth, from peronitis, overwork, oppression, from bottled up rage. Our geniuses were never taught to read or write. We must invent a past adequate to our ambitions. We must create a future adequate to our needs.[57]

Thus, because of the operation of the pervasive hidden curriculum —interaction patterns, a seductive reward system, unbalanced staffing and curricular materials—sex stereotypes introduced in the home are reinforced and refined in school. Young boys rebel against the hidden curriculum's demand for quiet and docile behavior and maintain the ability to deal with school life in an autonomous and independent manner. Although they do not generally win official school approval in the form of grades, there is no shortage of societal role models in the school itself and in books to assure the boy that success will eventually be his.

Young girls do not leave the elementary school with so little damage done. For them, a robbery has been perpetrated. This has not been accomplished by a swift, direct maneuver like the act of a pickpocket as he slips a wallet from his victim's pocket. Rather, it is a slow, subtle, and daily filching of self-respect as girls are seduced

Boys are Presidents.

SOURCE: Whitney Darrow, Jr., *I'm Glad I'm a Boy! I'm Glad I'm a Girl!*
New York, Simon and Schuster, 1970. Reprinted by permission of Windmill Books/Simon and Schuster.

by the reward system, as they shy away from challenging material,
as they are presented in life and in books with role models who are
subservient and apparently inferior to men.

THE LOSS OF
HUMAN POTENTIAL

Ironically, although artificial sex typing is encouraged in school—the
aggressive, superior male and the passive, inferior female—the real
purpose of biological differentiation between men and women is
totally ignored. Anything related to sexuality itself is the school's
Number 1 Taboo. In their homes, on television, and in movies, children see that men and women express love for one another. However,
it would be an incredibly rare experience to see a man and woman

Girls are First Ladies.

SOURCE: Whitney Darrow, Jr., *I'm Glad I'm a Boy! I'm Glad I'm a Girl!* New York, Simon and Schuster, 1970. Reprinted by permission of Windmill Books/Simon and Schuster.

stop, embrace, and kiss in the school corridor or to hear a pregnant woman talk to a class about what it is like to have a baby. This arid and ascetic denial of sexuality in the school often results in an atmosphere of underlying tension, particularly in the upper elementary grades. The repression of sexuality can be seen in graffiti scribbled on locker and bathroom walls; it is apparent in the nervous giggles that erupt when a student reads aloud from a literature text words like "body," "breast," and "bosom."

The school's persistent denial of sexuality generates an eerie kind of titilation. It becomes unnatural for a teacher to put her arm around a student, or even touch his arm to get his attention. In fact, many students back away instinctively, fearing active hostility. The mixed messages confuse them.

Pleasure is put down so often. The damper sits uneasily. Show me a school where children hoot and applaud when someone drops a tray in the cafeteria, or where straw wrappers hang from the ceiling, or where milk cartons fly through the air, and I'll show you a school that represses the normal exuberance of youth and substitutes titillation

Sexuality goes underground. Imagine a school where the young and pretty third-grade teacher falls in love with the male physical education teacher. The giggles and whispers and frenetic curiosity of the students seem way out of proportion to their response to a similar situation outside the school. The school encourages titillation by its very denial of the sexuality in us all.[58]

Thus, at the same time that it reinforces the artificial sex role trappings, the school makes a pariah of sexuality, barring it from the classroom. Each sex is shaped to fit a specified mold. But the cost is high. A whole range of behaviors and attitudes are denied to boys and girls. If boys cry, or like ballet, or write poetry, or play with dolls, they are subjected to taunts of "sissy" or "fairy." Girls who play football, climb trees, or experiment with chemistry sets are labeled "tomboys."

A man ought no more to value himself for being wiser than a woman, if he owes his advantage to a better education, than he ought to boast of his courage for beating a man when his hands were bound.

Mary Astell, *An Essay in Defense of the Female Sex*, 1721

But sex stereotyping does more than deny access to boys and girls of a wide variety of behaviors and activities that would make their lives richer and fuller. For girls, as they are molded into roles of women, there is a concomitant ebbing away of pride and self-esteem. The loss of dignity, the growing feelings of inferiority that comes of being made female have been documented in numerous studies. It has been shown that as boys and girls progress through school, their opinions of boys become higher, and, correspondingly, their opinions of girls become lower.[59] Thus children learn that boys are worth more. In another study it was found that grade school boys were more certain that it's great to be male; they were more confident and assertive. In contrast, girls were not particularly enthusiastic about having been born female. They were less confident about their accomplishments, their popularity, and their general adequacy. Rather than concentrating intensely, as did boys, on their present lives, they looked forward with hope and interest to their adolescent and adult futures.[60]

This hope placed in the future is particularly ironic since girls' options become more confined as they grow older. Even as young girls look for better times at a later date, they are aware of the restricted nature of their future role options.

Over 700 fourth-, fifth-, and sixth-grade girls were asked what they would like to become when they were grown up. Almost all selections made by these young girls fell into one of four categories. Each girl chose to become a teacher, a nurse, a secretary, or a mother. Fantasy played no part at all in their decisions. On the other hand, when boys were asked the same question, their choices were not restricted; for them, the world was wider. At each of the three grade levels, about 15 percent of their choices were based on pure fantasy. For example, one boy said, "I would like to be a businessman and sit and work a big deal." Another fantasized, "I would like to be a cop and have adventures."[61]

Restriction of options, feelings of inadequacy, a growing sense of inferiority—these are the legacy bequeathed to the female, and she knows it at a very young age. Although the pattern of underachievement in males begins at grade one, girls often aspire and achieve only until the fifth and sixth grades. This is the point at which they develop a conception of how limited their role in life will be. In this role, there is little room for their high aspiration and achievement. The "why bother" attitude takes over.[62]

Let us for a brief moment leave the facts and figures, the studies that show limited career options and decreasing self-esteem. Let us turn to one elementary school girl who wrote the following letter that appears in a book called *Children's Letters to God*.[63] She asks,

Dear God,
Are boys better than girls? I know you are one, but please try to be fair.

Love,
Sylvia.

The authors recently showed this letter to some friends, and their reactions were: "How cute!" and "How sweet!" It is our opinion that this letter is not cute, and if it is sweet, it is only in the most pathetic sense. It is the expression of a devastating loss at a very young age.

NOTES

[1]Thomas Lyles, "Grouping by Sex," *National Elementary Principal*, 46, no. 2 (November 1966), 38–41. Copyright 1966, National Association of Elementary School Principals, NEA. All rights reserved.

[2]"No Girls (Or Lady Teachers) Please," *Nation's Schools*, 83, no. 4 (April 1969), 68–69.

[3]Phil Jackson, *Life in Classrooms*, New York, Holt, Rinehart and Winston, 1968, p. 5

[4]*Ibid.*, pp. 33–37.

[5]Melvin Silberman, ed., *The Experience of Schooling*, New York, Holt, Rinehart and Winston, 1971, pp. 9–58.

[6]Robert Goldhammer, *Clinical Supervision*, New York, Holt, Rinehart and Winston, 1969, pp. 11–21.

[7]George Spindler, ed., *Education and Culture*, New York, Holt, Rinehart and Winston, 1963, pp. 148–149.

[8]Sandra Bem and Daryl Bem, "We're All Nonconscious Sexists," in Daryl J. Bem, *Beliefs, Attitudes, and Human Affairs*, Monterey, Calif., Brooks/Cole, Copyright 1970 by Wadsworth Publishing Co.

[9]Robert Sears, Eleanor Maccoby, and Harry Leven, *Patterns of Child Rearing*, Evanston, Ill., Row, Peterson, 1957.

[10]Susan Goldberg and Michael Lewis, cited in Bem and Bem, *op. cit.*

[11]Jerome Kagan, "Acquisition and Significance of Sex Typing," in Martin and Lois Hoffman, eds., *Review of Child Development*, New York, Russel Sage Foundation, 1964, pp. 137–167.

[12]Sears, Maccoby, and Levin, *op. cit.*

[13]Kagan, *op. cit.*

[14]Uri Brofenbrenner, "Some Familial Antecedents of Responsibility and Leadership in Adolescents," in Luigi Petrullo and Bernard Bass, eds., *Leadership and Interpersonal Behavior*, New York, Holt, Rinehart and Winston, 1961, p. 260, as quoted in Jo Freeman, *The Social Construction of the Second Sex*, Pittsburgh, Know, Inc., 1970, p. 9.

[15]Frances Bentzen, "Sex Ratios in Learning and Behavior Disorders, *National Elementary Principal*, 46, no. 2 (November 1966), 13–17.

[16]Patricia Sexton, "Are Schools Emasculating Our Boys?," *Saturday Review*, 48 (19 June 1965), p. 57.

[17]William J. Goldman and Anne May, "Males: A Minority Group in the Classroom," *Journal of Learning Disabilities*, 3, no. 3 (May 1970), 276–278.

[18]William McFarland, "Are Girls Really Smarter?," *Elementary School Journal*, 70, no. 10 (1968), 14–19.

[19]Michael Palardy, "For Johnny's Reading Sake," *Reading Teacher*, 22, no. 8 (May 1969), 720–724.

[20]Le Trippot, "Elementary Education—A Man's World," *Instructor*, 78, no. 3 (November 1968), 50–52.

[21]Timothy Weaver, "Humor and Education," *Phi Delta Kappan*, 52, no. 3 (November 1970), 1966–1968.

[22]Jerome Kagan, "The Child's Sex Role Classification of School Objects," *Child Development*, 35, no. 4 (December 1964), 1051–1056.

[23]William Meyer and George Thompson, "Teacher Interactions with Boys, as Contrasted with Girls," in Raymond Kuhlens and George Thompson, eds., *Psychological Studies of Human Development*, New York, Appleton-Century-Crofts, 1963, pp. 510–518.

[24]Phil Jackson and Henriette Lahaderne, "Inequalities of Teacher-Pupil Contacts," in Melvin Silberman, ed., *The Experience of Schooling*, New York, Holt, Rinehart and Winston, 1971, pp. 123–134.

[25]Robert Spaulding, "Achievement, Creativity, and Self-Concept Correlates of Teacher-Pupil Transactions in Elementary School," Cooperative Research Project No. 1352, 1963, U.S. Dept of Health, Education and Welfare, Office of Education, Washington, D.C.

[26]Pauline Sears and David Feldman, "Teacher Interactions with Boys and Girls," *National Elementary Principal*, 46, no. 2 (November 1966), 30–35.

[27]Gary Peltier, "Sex Differences in the School: Problem and Proposed Solution," *Phi Delta Kappan*, 50, no. 3 (November 1968), 182–185.

[28]Bentzen, "Sex Ratios in Learning and Behavior Disorders," *op. cit.*

[29]Richard Waite *et al.*, "First-Grade Reading Textbooks," *Elementary School Journal*, 67, no. 7 (April 1967), 366–374.

[30]John McNeil, "Programmed Instruction Versus Visual Classroom Procedures in Teaching Boys to Read," *American Educational Research Journal*, 1, no. 2 (March 1964), 113–120.

[31]Ralph Preston, "Reading Achievement of German and American Children," *School and Society*, 90, no. 2214 (October 1962), 350–354.

[32]Steven Asher and John Gottman, "Sex of Teacher and Student Reading Achievement," paper presented at the American Educational Research Association, April 1972.

[33]Jerome Bruner, *Toward a Theory of Instruction*, Cambridge, Mass., Belknap Press of Harvard University, 1966, pp. 123–124.

[34]Melvin Silberman, "Classroom Rewards and Intellectual Courage," in Silberman, ed., *The Experience of Schooling, op. cit.*

[35]Vaughn Crandall and Alice Rabson, "Children's Repetition Choices in an Intellectual Achievement Situation Following Success and Failure," *Journal of Genetic Psychology*, 97, (September 1960), 161–168.

[36]Eleanor Maccoby, "Woman's Intellect," in Seymour Farber and Roger Wilson, eds., *The Potential of Woman*, New York, McGraw-Hill, 1963, p. 33.

[37]Norma Hare, "The Vanishing Woman Principal," *National Elementary Principal*, 45, no. 5 (April 1966), 12–13.

[38]Patricia Sexton, *The Feminized Male*, New York, Random House (Vintage), 1969, pp. 141–143.

[39]Material presented by Bernice Sandler for the record to the Committee on the Judiciary, House of Representatives, 92nd cong., Hearings on Equal Rights of Men and Women, 1971.

[40]Hare, *op. cit.*

[41]Sexton, *The Feminized Male, op. cit.*

[42]Sandler, *op. cit.*

[43]Sexton, *The Feminized Male, op. cit.*

[44]NEA Du Shane Emergency Fund Division, "Discriminating Against the Pregnant Teacher," *Today's Education*, 60, no. 9 (1971), 33–35.

[45]*Ibid.*, p. 33.

[46]Seymour Metzner, "Literary Voyages in American History," *Elementary School Journal*, 66, no. 5 (February 1966), 235–238.

[47]Anne Grant West, ed., *Report on Sex Bias in the Public Schools*. Copyright 1971 by Education Committee, NOW, NYC.

[48]The Feminists on Children's Literature, "A Feminist Look at Children's Books," *School Library Journal*, 17, no. 5 (January 1971), 19–24.

[49]*Ibid.*

[50]Betty Miles, "Harmful Lessons Little Girls Learn in School," *Redbook*, 86 (March 1971), 168–169.

[51]Marjorie U'Ren, "The Image of Women in Textbooks," in Vivian Gornick and Barbara Moran, eds., *Woman in Sexist Society*, New York, Basic Books, 1971, pp. 218–225.

[52]*Ibid.*

[53]*Ibid.*

[54]The Feminists on Children's Literature, *op. cit.*

[55]Whitney Darrow, *I'm Glad I'm a Boy! I'm Glad I'm a Girl!*, New York, Simon and Schuster (Windmill), 1970.

[56]Alleen Pace Nelson, "Women in Children's Literature," *College English*, 32, no. 8 (May 1971), 918–926.

[57]The *Old Mole* as quoted in The Feminists on Children's Literature, *op. cit.*, p. 19.

[58]Sidney Simon, "Nourishing Sexuality in the Elementary School," *National Elementary Principal*, 50, no. 4 (December 1971), 57–60. Copyright 1971 by National Association of Elementary School Principals, NEA. All rights reserved.

[59]Stevenson Smith, "Age and Sex Differences in Children's Opinions Concerning Sex Differences," *Journal of Genetic Psychology*, 54, (March 1939), pp. 17–25.

[60]Patricia Minuchin, "Sex Differences in Children: Research Findings in an Educational Context," *National Elementary Principal*, 46, no. 2 (November 1966), 45–48.

[61]Robert O'Hara, "The Roots of Careers," *Elementary School Journal*, 62, no. 5 (February 1962), 277–280.

[62]Eleanor Maccoby, "Sex Differences in Intellectual Functioning," in Eleanor Maccoby, ed., *The Development of Sex Differences*, Stanford, Stanford University Press, 1966.

[63]Eric Marshall and Stuart Hample, compilers, *Children's Letters to God*, New York, Simon and Schuster (Pocket Books), 1966.

6

Living down to expectations: the high school years

When we look at what men are like after years spent in schools, we find they suffer from the loss of avenues that have been blocked. They may have learned not to cry, that the only place for poetry is in required English courses, that the kitchen is a place to stay out of, that babies are strange creatures to be held at arm's length, awkwardly. As we shall soon see, however, in terms of intellectual achievement, general sense of self-esteem, and financial potential, men are in a far more favorable position than are women who have completed high school or college. Consequently, in this chapter our concern will be focused where the most harm has been done—on the young woman who is likely to emerge from the classroom with promise and potential schooled out.

BIASED STORYTELLERS

During the high school years, all students make some crucial decisions. It is at this time that schools of higher education and careers are chosen, as are marriage partners and life styles. As a young woman attempts to make these choices, she looks to the school environment for help. A good or bad report card, a friend's advice, a session with the guidance counselor, a teacher's casual comment, a compelling biography—these are the stuff decisions are made of, and too often there is little in the school environment that nourishes and inspires women and a great deal that discourages, inhibits, and sets a hard, low ceiling on their aspirations. Even more than in the elementary school, there is a sexist bias in the high school curriculum. This bias is so insidiously pervasive that only when consciousness is intensely heightened can one begin to comprehend the discriminatory nature of much of the material and to realize its harmful impact.

If a student were to tell what American life was (and is) like, based on the reading of academic books, (s)he would have to conclude that it had very few women. History, for example, is exactly that—"his story." In the decisions and deliberations of who should be celebrated in the history text, *women are selected out.* Janice Trecker, in a thorough analysis of twelve of the most popular U.S. history texts used in public schools, comments on this calculated neglect.

Ask most high school students who Jane Addams, Ida Tarbell or Susan B. Anthony were and you may get an answer. Ask about Margaret Sanger, Abigail Duniway or Margaret Brent and you will probably get puzzled looks. Soujourner Truth, Frances Wright, Anna Howard Shaw, Emma Willard, Mary Bickerdyke, Maria Mitchell, Providence Crandall and scores of others sound like answers from some historian's version of trivia. Interest in the fate of obscure Americans may seem an esoteric pursuit, but this is not the case. History, despite its enviable reputation for presenting the important facts about our past, is influenced by considerations other than the simple love of truth. It is an instrument of the greatest social utility, and the story of our past is a potent means of transmitting cultural images and stereotypes.[1]

Not only are individual women omitted, but the areas in which women have made their greatest contributions—theatre, dance, music, day to day life in homes—are ignored as well. Often, pages will be devoted to discussing the details of various battles in various wars, but intellectual, cultural, and social achievements in which women have traditionally been involved will be totally excluded, or glossed over or tagged onto a chapter's end almost as an afterthought. For example, in its discussion of the frontier period, one high school text spends five pages discussing the six-shooter and scarcely five lines on frontier women. In another two-volume high school text, there are only two sentences in which the women's suffrage movement is described (one sentence in each volume). The most glaring omission of all is the lack of a single word about birth control, the fight for its acceptance by Margaret Sanger and other physicians, or the impact it had on the lives of women. Moreover, there is incredibly little information on prejudice that is still going on—for example the legal challenges to discrimination in hiring, promotion, and unequal pay.

When women are presented in these texts, they are often drawn as creatures concerned with trivia, helpless and ineffectual when it comes to serious matters. One text spends more time talking about the length of women's skirts than about their struggles to achieve civil and political rights. Another text barely alludes to the feminists, yet spends a whole column on the Gibson girl, describing her as "completely feminine, and it was clear that she could not or would not defeat her male companion at golf or tennis. In the event of a motoring emergency, she would quickly call upon his superior knowledge."[2] Trecker concludes that a student reading these texts might be limited to the following description of the history and contributions of the American woman:

> *Women arrived in 1619 (a curious choice if meant to be their first acquaintance with the new world). They held the Seneca Falls Convention on Women's Rights in 1848. During the rest of the 19th century, they participated in reform movements, chiefly temperance, and were exploited in factories. In 1923 they were given the vote. They joined the armed forces for the first time during the second world war and thereafter have enjoyed the good life in America.[3]*

The result is that ignorance about women in history is almost total. Gerda Lerner asked her history seminar at Sarah Lawrence College to list ten American women who had played important roles before 1950. Most of her students could not.[4] I asked the same question to students and the demonstration of ignorance was similar.

In history texts women are relegated to secondary roles mainly by sins of omission. In literature and language texts they are also relegated to secondary status not so much because they are left out but because of the distasteful way they are put in. They are portrayed as insipid, passive, and ineffectual. When they do act, it is often for malicious or destructive reasons. The following list describes what females do in *Roberts English Series* texts used at the junior high school level:

- Count votes for males who were nominated
- Accompany men to the hunt
- Find their beauty is shortlived
- Sit with their fans in their hands and gold combs in their hair
- Put cream on their faces and "lie in bed staring at the ceiling and wishing (they) had some decent jewelry to wear at the . . . Ball"
- Poison their husbands
- Die because they never knew those simple little rules . . .
- Get eaten up by alligators
- Cut and gather grain and sing to no one
- Listen to men give speeches
- Rear children
- Do silly, ridiculous things (James Thurber)
- Ride with the devil.[5]

It is hardly a proud catalogue of activities that would inspire courage, dignity, and leadership in female students.

Diane Staven has analyzed the way women are treated in fiction popular with junior high school and high school males. She notes that "girl friends and mothers are almost always unrealized or unpleasant characters—one-dimensional, idealized, insipid, bitchy, or castrating—while sexually neutral characters such as sisters and little old ladies are most often well conceived and likeable."[6] A list of quotes from these books indicates the demeaning and even hostile way in which females are depicted:

Women in the States . . . have forgotten how to be women; but they haven't yet learned how to be men. They've turned into harpies, and their men into zombies. God, it's pitiful!

Remember—she's a female, and full of tricks.

Men . . . like to talk about women as though they had some sort of special malignant power, a witchlike ability to control men.

Polly . . . says I'm a witch . . . I was being nasty . . . Girls just do those things, I guess . . .

Even old girls like my mother. If she hadn't torpedoed my father's idea to buy a garage, he might not have taken off.

[Polly] . . . began to think she should run the show. That's where I had to straighten her out. And after I got her straightened out she seemed happier.[7]

Fiction written for young women is also insulting, for it frequently suggests that the only interest a female has is in being popular with males. Unlike stories about men in which the protagonist must solve the central question of "What shall I be?" for heroines the question of greatest, and often only import, is "Who shall he be?" Women do not stand alone in these stories. The plot interest results from the way they relate to male characters.

There is the prevalence of what has been termed the "cop-out" book. These are stories in which a girl, in order to grow into womanhood, must forego her tomboy ways—and in the process relinquish a good deal of spirit, independence, and autonomy. In a widely used bibliography, there is an entire section called "From Tomboy to Young Woman." Here are a few descriptions from the bibliography that depict this metamorphosis:

A Girl Can Dream *by Betty Cavanna (Westminster, 1948): Loretta Larkin, tops in athletics but poor in social graces and jealous of a classmate who shines socially, finds out that being "just a girl" can be fun.*

Billie *by Esphyr Solbodkina (Lothrop, 1959): Billie, who wore faded jeans and played boys' games because she didn't like being a girl came to think differently after she took ballet lessons to limber up a sprained ankle.*[8]

So young girls learn from the fiction they read that ugly ducklings will become swans and the sparks of spunky tomboyishness and individuality must be put out by the damper of passive womanhood, the role to which they must conform.

In standard literature anthologies, there is a sex bias similar to that in history books. Too often women are missing. *The Norton Anthology,* used both at high school and college levels, includes the works of 169 men and 6 women; *American Prose and Poetry* offers works by 86 men and 10 women.[9] Evidently the critical sensibility that labels certain writers "great" has decided that most women authors are minor, recommended for reading if the student has a little spare time. Thus, literature as taught in schools is a biased mirror reflecting the male life style. There are few "portraits of the artist as a young woman" and so little chance to contemplate the feminine experience, given sharper definition and richer meaning through literature.

> Representation of the world, like the world itself, is the work of men; they describe it from their own point of view, which they confuse with absolute truth.
>
> Simone de Beauvoir

The sexual bias against women so obvious in history and language texts and in fiction also pervades the social sciences. Although 51 percent of the population is female, only 15 percent of the sociologists are.[10] Thus, research both in laboratories with white mice and in colleges with sophomores, has been carried out, for the most part, from a masculine point of view. Topics that are selected for investigation have been those that pique masculine curiosity, and conclusions reached are often distorted by biases peculiar to men—particularly conclusions about the female sex.

One has only to look through the table of contents in frequently used sociology and psychology texts to find that there is little listed under the category "woman"—if there is such a category at all. Jo Freeman notes that:

One soon realizes that when the author talks about "man" he means male. Major research has been done—such as that on achievement motivation—from which women were systematically excluded because their inclusion "messed up the model," and there was no curiosity as to why this was so. Major books have been written, on such relevant topics as the occupational structure, in which whole sections are devoted to "minority groups," but only a footnote to women (one third of the labor force.)[11]

Feminists are now beginning to analyze the pronouncements of many of the noted authorities whose texts form a basic staple of social science courses. They are finding that their remarks about women are often contemptuous and insulting. Sigmund Freud, for example, who initiated the wild goose chase for that elusive chimera, the vaginal orgasm, has asked, "The great question that has never been answered, and which I have not been able to answer despite my thirty years of research into the feminine soul is: What does a woman want?"[12]

Bruno Bettelheim, a prominent contemporary male psychologist, has, with disquieting certitude, supplied the answer for misogynists who might still be wondering: "We must start with the realization that, as much as women want to be good scientists and engineers, they want first and foremost to be womanly companions of men and to be mothers."[13]

The total potential of women has also been disregarded in remarks by Benjamin Spock whose texts are not only found in the nurseries of countless, uncertain mothers, but also on required reading lists in various psychology and sociology courses. He has written:

Women are usually more patient in working at unexciting repetitive tasks. . . . Women on the average have more passivity in the inborn core of their personality. . . . I believe women are designed in their deeper instincts to get more pleasure out of life—not only sexually but socially, occupationally, maternally—when they are not aggressive. To put it another way I think that when women are encouraged to be competitive too many of them become disagreeable.[14]

Naomi Weisstein, in a perceptive article "Kinder, Kuche, Kirche as Scientific Law: Psychology Constructs the Female," notes that "there isn't the tiniest shred of evidence to indicate that those conclusions have anything to do with women's real potential." She indicates that the literature of personality from which the psychological picture of women has been drawn rests for the most part on the shaky base of "years of intensive clinical experience." Freud, for example, demonstrated the existence of the castration complex from experimental reports of a man committed to Freudian theory—a source that hardly seems irrefutable. Another flaw is that much of the psychological literature is based on the concept of innate traits, and there is not sufficient emphasis given to the effects of social context. Weisstein draws upon an event from personal experience to point out erroneous concepts about men and women that are taught in school. While a graduate student at Harvard University, she and other members of a seminar were asked to identify which of two piles of a clinical test had been written by females and which by males. After several weeks of intensively studying the differences between men and women, only four of the twenty members of the seminar were able to identify the piles correctly. Such a result is well below chance, and Weisstein concludes, "Students are judging knowledgeably within the context of psychological teaching about the differences between men and women; the teachings themselves are simply erroneous."[15]

Home economics is another curricular area that draws a tight box around female potential—and not simply because it is a segregated subject that places a female label on various types of work. Dorothy Lee has analyzed various teachers' manuals and guides used across the country in home economics programs; she has found that objectives listed in these manuals teach a woman to assume characteristics and traits that will be pleasing to others rather than suggest she develop a code of behavior that satisfies an internal standard:

Personality Development. Objectives: Desire and ability to know and use approved social customs and good manners. Make and keep good friends. Possess good personality traits. Problems:

a. *Get along with people by having good manners.*
b. *How to develop good manners at home.*
c. *Careful grooming to make you pleasing at first sight.*
d, e, f, g, h. *deal with being a good guest and a good hostess and having a good voice.*
i. *How to be popular, and make and keep friends. Five points listed under this deal with good manners, two with dating procedures, five with how to behave in public.*[16]

There is little in such objectives that has to do with moral courage, the ability to take a well-considered position on an issue and affirm it, even if this means not being popular and pleasing to everyone. Small wonder the empirical research indicated that individuals whose sex role identification is feminine have a greater need for social approval and those whose sex role identification is masculine exhibit greater need for self-approval.[17] And small wonder that a class of women students will tend to avoid heated argument and debate, retreating from positions and hastily deferring to one another when lines of polarization threaten to divide the classroom.

There are other elements in the curriculum that ignore the needs of women. High school and college athletics programs are well known for heavy emphasis on sports, such as football, that heap school and community laurels on male athletes. No such acclaim is given to female team sports (more on this later). Furthermore, training in self-defense, by which women could learn to protect themselves and move about with increased self-confidence, is seldom provided. There is also little stress placed on sports that emphasize individual talents and abilities—such as skating, tennis, swimming, golf, or skiing—and that could provide continued physical exercise for women, as well as men, after they leave school.

As of 1969, nearly half of the schools in America offered sex education courses. It seems that these courses should provide a forum for frank discussion among students about what *is* "appropriate" sex role behavior and perhaps lead to ways for increasing the options of both males and females. Often, feminists supported the implementation of sex education courses. However, these courses, caught in a controversy of their own, too often ignore feminists' concerns. They do not provide information on contraception, nor do they emphasize the devastating effects that may result from overpopulation. Instead they endorse the traditional sex roles in which women are weak and submissive and men, dominant and strong.[18]

Sonia Sanchez, a black poet who teaches English at Manhattan Community College, has noted that white middle-class and upper-class America "knows its history and understands it fully. And they learn it in schools. We don't learn anything about ourselves so therefore we were like Topsy, we just grew. So now we study our history to know the kinds of people we've been, the kinds of people we can be. . . . A people who don't know their history can never be anything."[19]

All women, but especially Third World, Asian-American, Puerto Rican, chicana, and black women—have the need and the right to confront past and present and to see that they have played a proud and essential part in the course of events. When these women do achieve that realization, their response is often moving and powerful.

Kathleen Chamberlain, who joined other teachers at Manhattan Community College to initiate a woman's studies program, tells of the response of minority women. A Dominican student in the women's studies course wrote in her first paper:

I've been left out and unvoiced in the past, not only as a woman but as an individual from a Latin culture in America. But those days of being left out are gone, never to return. I know what I want in the future: To be treated as an equal economically, socially, and politically and to help those still oppressed to "see the truth."[20]

And another student, after realizing the dearth of writing by or about Puerto Rican women, spoke to the women's studies class with urgency and emotion, "I have a message for my Puerto Rican sisters: Write! Write all you can."[21]

"One study of folklore in a primitive society found that the stories passed down through the generations portrayed the elders as wise, courageous, and powerful, and then it was found that the storytellers were the elders of the tribe."[22] A study of material offered in the schools suggests that we have our own biased storytellers, and they are white and male. It must at last be time to put sexual and racial perspective and balance into what women and men learn in school.

THE QUEST FOR MEDIOCRITY

When a visitor to a high school walks through the classrooms, (s)he may first be struck by all the academic apparatus—shelves of books, worksheets, piles of graded tests, and compositions. However, if (s)he should glance at the classroom bulletin board, (s)he may notice signs and announcements that tell of a very different side of school life. For example, here is an October 1971 list of announcements that was posted in a Wisconsin high school classroom.

> *WEEKLY ANNOUNCEMENTS*
> Monday, September 27
> The Drill Team will practice at 6:30 tonight in the new gym.
> Tuesday, September 28
> Sophomore football at East Troy at 7:00 tonight.
> Cross country meet at Mukwonago today.
> Wednesday, September 29
> Regular schedule of classes
> Thursday, September 30
> Frosh football at Wilmot at 4:30
> Friday, October 1 HOMECOMING! ! ! !
> There will be a pep assembly this afternoon. We will follow the "B" schedule.
> Homecoming Football game with Wilmot tonight! ! ! !

If the visitor should take a few moments to flip the pages of the high school yearbook, (s)he would become even more aware of the myriad of social activities that are an integral part of high school life. (S)He would find a variety of clubs that convene to satisfy interests that range from stamp collecting to scuba diving. (S)He might close the yearbook slightly dazed, for when one considers the primarily academic function of school, the extent of social and extracurricular activities available is enormous.

Although these clubs and organizations vary, they all have a single common denominator. Except for an advisor, they include no young children, no full-grown adults, none of the elderly. For the high school student, most social interaction is with peers, and as a result of this exclusiveness, an adolescent society is formed, a subculture unique unto itself with its own peculiar set of norms and behavior patterns.

> ... A high school woman has special problems. ... Every so often there are "pep rallies" where muscular football players are paraded before us for adulation, while cheerleaders (all women, of course) scream praise for the young studs.
>
> Brooke, Spleen-Williams "Gettin' It Together in The High Schools" *Women*, Winter 1971

Within the confines of this adolescent society, pressure exerted by the peer group becomes extremely powerful, and this peer pressure operates to impose artificial, stereotyped definitions of male and female roles. In fact, this subculture becomes a microcosm reflecting in heightened and exaggerated images the sex typing that goes on in society at large. For example, in the high school social pecking order, the most envied male is usually the football star, and as his counterpart, it is likely that the most admired female will be a member of the cheerleading squad. The sex typing is blatant. Being successfully male means winning in physical combat, whereas being successfully female means attractively and enthusiastically supporting men in their achievements.

The nature of the male-female relationship in high school results in very different avenues along which each sex must travel to be considered successful. James Coleman analyzed the "adolescent society," (the title of his book) in the late 1950s. His comments present an overview and offer a perspective that is still highly pertinent today: "There is the suggestion that the girls' culture derives in some fashion from the boys: the girl's role is to sit there and look pretty, waiting for the athletic star to come pick her. She must cultivate her looks, be vivacious and attractive, wear the right clothes, but then wait—until the football player whose status is determined by his specific achievements comes along to choose her."[23]

The high school woman must try to make herself as attractive as she possibly can, for her success will be determined not as much by any of her own accomplishments as by the quantity and quality of males she manages to gather around her. Popularity with boys becomes of overriding importance. As one student commented, "Failure

is not being accepted by men. It is the shame of being a wallflower."
Spending a dateless Saturday night is anathema, and the young
woman will do almost anything to avoid such ostracism. She may buy
books such as *On Becoming A Woman—What Every Teenage Girl
Should Know* and follow advice like:

*And while we're on the subject of smells, let's be blunt. You can
look like an angel, but if you don't use a deodorant, you're in trouble.
Maybe your best friends won't tell you, but your phone won't ring.
. . . A truly feminine woman who is happy to be a woman really
likes men. . . . Now let's get one thing clear though—this doesn't
mean you should dash out on the ball field and play ball with the
guys. We said friend, not competitor. Stick to your own sex or else
when the time comes for dating you'll be classified as a good Joe, not
a good prospect for dating.*[24]

The high school woman spends an inordinate amount of time
worrying about physical attractiveness and popularity. This concern
with social success can be seen in a national interview sample of
adolescents taken in 1966: 65 percent of the boys and only 21 percent of the girls worried most about achievement; 16 percent of the
boys and 44 percent of the girls worried most about acceptance by
others; 19 percent of the boys and 62 percent of the girls worried
most about personal characteristics.[25]

As the young woman learns to consider herself as a commodity,
she accents her physical attractiveness and plays down her intellectu-
ality, muting high academic abilities so as not to frighten away any
potential buyers. In a study of ten high schools, Coleman asked both
boys and girls how they would most like to be remembered. Neither
boys nor girls wanted to be remembered as the class's most brilliant
student—but girls were far more definite about their rejection of this
brilliant student role. In the schools Coleman studied, the average IQ
of boys was lower than that of girls. Interestingly, however, in each
school the IQ of the male named best scholar was consistently higher
than that of the female named best scholar. The brightest girls were
smart enough to skirt the brilliant student role and avoid being considered "too brainy."[26]

This courting of mediocrity rather than excellence can also be
seen in differing male and female patterns of underachievement.
Eleanor Maccoby notes these separate patterns as she summarizes the
findings of M. C. Shaw and J. T. McCuen in their study, "The Onset
of Academic Underachievement in Bright Children."

There is evidence that girls who are underachievers in high school usually begin to be so at about the onset of puberty, while for boys underachievement in high school usually has an earlier onset. This contrast is a further indication that the achievement drop off among girls as they reach maturity is linked to the adult female sex role.[27]

It is during adolescence that interest in boys begins, as does the growing realization that being too smart doesn't get a woman anywhere but home on Saturday night.

It must be made clear that the high school woman does not learn that she should be an idiot. Rather, the message is, "Don't be *too* smart or *too* successful." As Margaret Mead comments, ". . . throughout her education and her development of vocational expectance, the girl is faced with the dilemma that she must display enough of her abilities to be considered successful, but not too successful . . ."[28] The goal is to avoid either extreme and find that perfectly uncontroversial level of mediocrity.

To better understand the high school woman's quest for mediocrity, we must look ahead briefly and observe this phenomenon among college women. In the past, college women avoided the scholarly image and even wove intricate webs of subterfuge to disguise academic competence. In interviews conducted in 1947 at Barnard, college women expressed the confusion they were experiencing in trying to fulfill two conflicting roles—that of aggressive, intellectual student in the classroom and that of passive not-too-bright date on the weekends:

My mother thinks that it is very nice to be smart in college but only if it doesn't take too much effort. She always tells me not to be too intellectual on dates, to be clever in a light sort of way.

I was glad to transfer to a women's college. The two years at the co-ed university produced a constant strain. I am a good student; my family expects me to get good marks. At the same time, I am normal enough to want to be invited to the Saturday night dance. Well, everyone knows that on campus the reputation of a brain killed a girl socially. I was always fearful lest I say too much in class or answer a question which the boys I dated couldn't answer.

Their comments also reveal the incredible variety of ploys they had developed to hide intellectual talent.

> When a girl asks me what mark I got last semester, I answer, "Not so good—only one A." When a boy asks the same question I say very brightly with a note of surprise, "Imagine, I got an A!"

> One of the nicest techniques is to spell long words incorrectly once in a while. My boyfriend seems to get a great kick out of it and writes back, "Honey, you certainly don't know how to spell."

> It embarrassed me that my high school steady got worse marks than I. A boy should naturally do better in school. I would never tell him my marks and would often ask him to help me with my homework.[29]

As high a figure as 40 percent of the Barnard women admitted that they faked being dumb. In 1949, the study was replicated at Stanford University; there, 46 percent of the women interviewed acknowledged that they pretended intellectual inferiority when talking with men.[30]

The pattern is being repeated today. A similar study was conducted at Stanford in 1969, and 40 percent of the women there admitted to playing dumb when in male company.[31] And when I talk in my college classes about the comments made by the Barnard women in the 1940s and Coleman's analysis of high school in the late 1950s, I get looks of immediate recognition, and student response tells me that many of these norms are still very much in effect. The ploys women use to hide talent may not be quite as blatant, but they are still there. Female students tell me that, when on a date, they maneuver the conversation to a topic with which their male companion is familiar and then sit back and listen to his opinions, asking the appropriate questions when he seems to be running out of things to say. In short, an extremely high number of high school and college women are still practicing the extraordinary behavior of pretending to be less than they are.

> Women have served all these centuries as looking-glasses possessing the magic and delicious power of reflecting the figure of man at twice its natural size.
>
> Virginia Woolf

So for the high school and for the college woman, social pressure makes education not a process of growth toward full potential, but rather a distasteful matter of hiding ability, playing down competence, nipping success in the bud before it loses the only achievement that seems to be of any real meaning—that of male attention and approval.

A woman who is guided by the head and not the heart is a social pestilence; she has all the defects of a passionate and affectionate woman, with none of her compensations: she is without pity, without love, without virtue, without sex.

Honore de Balzac

Interestingly, the need to achieve that the young girl takes with her, preserved partially intact from elementary school, is not obliterated, but rather rerouted into what society considers a more "appropriate" channel. The young woman learns to direct her achievement motive into social rather than academic areas. She uses her ability in a drive for social success, and for her, the ultimate achievement is marriage.

This destruction of women's need for academic success can be seen on tests designed to measure achievement motivation. These projective tests usually consist of stimulus pictures about which students write brief stories. These stories are analyzed to ascertain the extent to which they reflect the author's need to achieve. It has been found that there is a strong correlation between males who score high on tests for achievement motivation and males who have high academic averages. No such correlation has been found for females. In fact, women who discontinue their education after high school score higher on achievement motivation tests than do women who go to college. Also, women who prefer marriage to a career, or who actually marry, receive higher scores on achievement motivation tests than do women who pursue careers.[32] Furthermore, it has been demonstrated that female graduate students who have experienced a substantial time interruption in their training display significantly greater achievement motivation when competing against a male than do younger graduate females or undergraduate females. It seems that when a woman is older and the possibility of romantic involvement is somewhat less prominent, she feels free to express her need for achievement and success in academic areas.[33]

Simone de Beauvoir has noted that advancement through education has not been part of the socialization of white women: ". . . the girl, since childhood . . . has looked to the male for fulfillment and escape; he wears the shining face of Perseus or Saint George; he is the liberator; he is rich and powerful, he holds the key to happiness."[34] Beauvoir believes that the white adolescent female turns away from independence and assertiveness, embraces a perceived femininity, and hopes that through involvement with a successful man, her own social status will be elevated.

It appears that norms that affect the adolescent black woman are quite different. In a study by Joyce Ladner, it was shown that young black women in families with middle-class aspirations resisted emotional involvement with men. For them, acquisition of an education was perceived as the key to upward mobility. "If you want a good job you have to get some sort of education. . . . All of my sisters and brothers graduated from school so I just wanted to stay in school and make the record right. . . . I can marry right now but I'm not ready yet." In short, "the Black girl shoulders responsibility along with her initial independence. This is what she perceives femininity and womanhood to be."[35] She will need every ounce of independence and responsibility she can muster; for she is caught in the jaws of a double bind in which the discrimination that she must confront will be increased immeasurably.

High schools must recognize the damage done by insidious social pressures operating on female students, pressures that are highlighted and emphasized in the school environment. They must become aware of the by-products of self-abasement and degradation that accumulate over years of pretended inferiority and of how female students sacrifice ability and talent in order to fulfill the traditional feminine role. Until steps are taken to alter an environment that encourages one sex to prostitute itself academically, any notion of educating all students to their fullest potential is little more than hypocrisy.

DOWN AND OUT:
THE SEXUAL DOUBLE STANDARD

The same environment that persuades the high school woman to forego academic achievement also propels her onto the precarious tightrope of sexual involvement. Although sexual mores are becoming more liberal, the high school woman is still left to thread her way through conflicting norms: On the one hand the "new freedom" tells her she has as much right as her male counterpart to engage in sexual relations; on the other hand there are very clear and obvious vestiges of a value system that places high store on virginity and "purity."

The conflict implicit in attracting men—but not too far—is a very real and painful dilemma. It is still the young woman's bewildering role to flash a potpourri of messages that would dizzy the most skillful traffic policeman—green lights and come ahead signals, and when things begin to move too fast and far, warnings and stop signs at the appropriate moments. It is a frustrating and potentially harmful juggling act for the young woman. Later in married life, when stop signs are no longer needed, she may find that she is imprisoned in her stop and go role.

The sexual double standard is a powerful norm that shapes behavior in adolescent society: On the hunting ground for dates and marriage partners, sexual involvement is fair game for men, but to maintain a position in a respected clique or group, the young woman is forced to keep her virginity and/or her reputation intact.

Official policy in many high schools reinforces this sexual double standard and is nowhere more draconian than in the punitive treatment of pregnant high school women. Of 17,000 school systems surveyed across the country in 1970, only 5,450 provided for the continuing education of school-age pregnant women, despite the fact that state funds are often made available for that purpose.[36] Besides the basic theft of her education, this abrupt dismissal may have other deleterious effects—depriving her of associations with peers and teachers at the very time when their support may be most needed. Each year approximately two hundred thousand school-age women in the United States drop out of school, give birth, and do not have the funds for their adequate support. The problem is being attacked nationally by a task force from the Department of Health, Education, and Welfare, and The National Alliance Concerned with School-Age Parents has begun to express concern as has the American Civil Liberties Union.

In its pamphlet *Academic Freedom in the Secondary Schools*, ACLU states ". . . the right of an education should not be abrogated because of marriage or pregnancy unless evidence proves that the student's presence in the schools or classroom does, in fact, disrupt or impair the educational process."[37] The report of the Atlanta Adolescent Pregnancy Program, a program designed to meet the needs of pregnant school age women, makes the following comment about the existing situation: "In general, the underlying belief which dictates expulsion from school is that the pregnant school girl is a 'bad girl,' pregnancy being a clear indication that she has had coitus at least once. The AAPP findings, however, indicate that the pregnant school girls are not promiscuous, have usually just begun sexual intercourse, and cannot be differentiated by psychological testing or by any other means from students who are not pregnant." The report also notes that if it is just to dismiss a pregnant woman because she has experienced coitus, "then authorities should expel her coital partner."[38]

Help and education for the young woman after she becomes pregnant are only part of the responsibility. Counseling and birth control information should be provided by competent school personnel so that pregnancy may not be the result of naiveté and ignorance. Only when high school women have access to information about how and when to get or not to get pregnant and only when they are no longer condemned or shamed (any more than are men) for sexual participation, will they be able to carve out future social, academic, and professional goals in dignity and confidence.

SEGREGATED EDUCATION

Whenever educational opportunities are segregated because of a distinction such as race or sex, superior facilities are awarded to the group to which society accords superior status. This has long been apparent to both casual observers and diligent researchers looking at racially segregated schools. One has only to remember the experiments in Greely, Colorado, or Fairfax County, Virginia, to see that it applies to sexually segregated education also: "In working with boys, we employ more science materials and equipment. . . . From studying the atom, for example, a boy's class moved into a study of nuclear fission. It is unlikely that girls would respond that way. Or another example, mold can be studied from a medical standpoint by boys and in terms of cooking by girls."

At all levels of schooling, there is occasional segregation on the basis of sex. In elementary school, there is the separated lining up— girls on one side of the room, boys on the other. In many schools eating lunch is a segregated activity, and in some schools a child's sex determines the play area; girls are shuttled off to one section of the schoolyard, and boys are restricted to another. All these separations subtly reinforce the stereotype that the other sex is alien, different, foreign, indeed as the cliché puts it—"opposite."

> We deny the right of any portion of the species to decide for another portion, or any individual for another individual, what is and what is not their "proper sphere." The proper sphere for all human beings is the largest and highest which they are able to attain to.
>
> Harriet Mill

At the secondary level, this occasional segregation often becomes overt school policy in the form of Boys Only and Girls Only courses. Girls are herded into courses in home economics; they are taught to cook and sew; they are often barred from industrial arts courses where boys learn woodwork, metal work, electric shop, and sometimes printing and mechanical drawing. Because of this separation girls are taught in school that their right and proper lot in life is that of homemaker and also that it is quite appropriate to be helpless when it comes to any task requiring technical or mechanical skill. Correspondingly, boys learn that housework is something of which they need have no knowledge.

Suppose that a white male college student decided to room with a black male friend. The typical white student would not blithely assume that his roommate was better suited to handle all domestic chores. Nor should his conscience allow him to do so even in the unlikely event that his roommate would say, "No, that's OK. I like doing housework. I'd be happy to do it." We suggest that the white would still feel uncomfortable about taking advantage of the fact that his roommate had simply been socialized to be "happy" with such an arrangement. But change this hypothetical black roommate to a female marriage partner and his conscience goes to sleep.[39]

It is no wonder that the married man's conscience goes to sleep, and that his wife allows it to! School has taught them that this is the appropriate division of labor.

This rigid sex stereotyping of home economics for girls only and shop for boys only is being challenged. The following excerpt is public testimony given in the U.S. courthouse, Brooklyn, New York.

The witness: *I asked Miss Jonas if my daughter could take metal working or mechanics, and she said there is no freedom of choice. . . .*

I didn't ask her anything else because she clearly showed me that it was against the school policy for girls to be in the class. She said it was a Board of Education decision. . . .

> Q. *Now, after this lawsuit was filed, they then permitted you to take the course, is that correct?*
> A. *No, we had to fight about it for quite a while.*
> Q. *But eventually they did let you in the second semester?*
> A. *They only let me in there.*
> Q. *You are the only girl?*
> A. *Yes.*
> Q. *How did you do in the course?*
> A. *I got the medal for it from all the boys there.*
> Q. *Will you show the court?*
> A. *Yes (indicating).*
> Q. *And what does the medal say?*
> A. *Medal 1970 Van Wyck.*
> Q. *And why did they give you that medal?*
> A. *Because I was the best out of all the boys.*

The Court: *I do not want any giggling or noises in the courtroom. Just do the best you can to control yourself or else I will have to ask you to leave the courtroom. This is no picnic, you know. These are serious lawsuits.*[40]

Nowhere are the detrimental effects of segregation more obvious than in high school athletics programs, where more monies and facilities are awarded to boys' sports, as are more school and community acclaim, than to girls' sports. It is a familiar experience to open the town or city newspaper and see headlines lauding the most recent exploits of the boys' football or basketball team. Victories of girls' teams, if they are reported at all, get smaller headlines and are tucked away into unobtrusive spots reserved for news of far less importance. High school women have also gone to the courts with testimony against separate and unequal physical education programs.

> Q. *You are taking gym now, is that correct?*
> A. *Yes, I am.*
> Q. *Do you have the same activities in your gym classes that the boys do?*
> A. *No, we don't. Right now we're doing folk dancing and we asked—there were about twenty girls in the class that I knew who*

would like—who would have liked to go out and run track as the boys do. They play ball out in the recreational fields, and I asked one of the gym teachers if we could get a group of girls who would like to go out and run track or play ball in the fields. Since there are about six or seven gym teachers and since they divide the boys' classes up with teachers taking certain groups out, if we could do this in our class. First she said I should get the names of fifty girls who would want to do it. I proceeded to ask around and I had about thirty girls in the first day who wanted to do it, and then the next day in gym she said to forget about it because she had spoken to Mrs. Klein, the head of the girls' Health Education Department. She said that just couldn't be done.

Q. *Are the girls able to go out at all or is it just a question of running track?*

A. *The girls are only allowed to go out in the very, very early part of the term, at the beginning of September, and then again in June, which comes to a total of about three weeks. When the boys go out—they go out all the time, except, you know, when the weather just doesn't permit.*

Q. *Do the boys and girls have the same equipment in their gym classes?*

A. *The only equipment in my years of gym in Jamaica High School, the only equipment I've ever seen is a basketball and a volley ball. And the boys have ropes. They have pegboards that they use for climbing. I don't know. I've never been in the boys' gym. I've only heard from friends but I know the equipment that we use and it's not the same. . . . All I've ever seen is a basketball and a volley ball and a record player.*

Q. *What other programs in gym do you have? You play baseball?*

A. *We don't. We spend a lot of time—I think there are a few weeks that we are supposed to be playing baseball, but everytime we keep learning over and over again, which leaves about two or three days left to actual game playing.*

Q. *You play volley ball?*

A. *Yes, we play volley ball also.*

Q. *And when you go outside, what sort of classes do you have?*

A. *We play this game. I don't know. It's called Ogre Take, where you just throw the ball and you run around.*

Q. *And you're running around a lot?*

A. *There is no equipment, though, and when I asked if we could play soccer, since I saw other—the boys' gym classes playing it and* *since I've played soccer on my own time, I was told that the boys use the fields and, you know, because of that we're not allowed to use them. Because they get priority. The teacher told me that.*[41]

There is also exclusion of women students throughout high school extracurricular activities. There are segregated clubs and activities; there are honors, awards, and prestigious positions that are available only to male students. Again, we can turn to court testimony to observe the harm done by this pervasive form of segregation.

Q. *Are there any classes or programs within the classes that are open to male students and not to female students?*

A. *Well, within my physics class last year, our teacher asked if there was anybody interested in being a lab assistant, in the physics lab, and when I raised my hand, he told all the girls to put their hands down because he was only interested in working with boys.*

Q. *Did you make any further attempts to become a lab assistant?*

A. *Yes. I spoke to Mr. Chailiff. He is the head of the student organization, and I told him what my physics teacher had said and he said he would see, you know, what might be done; but I never heard about it again.*

Q. *Are there any other activities in the school that women are not members of and have you attempted to be in any other activities?*

A. *Yes. There is an Honor Guard, which are students who, instead of participating in gym for the term, are monitors in the hall, and I asked my gym teacher if I could be on the Honor Guard Squad. She said it was only open to boys. I then went to the head of the Honor Guard, a Mr. Baron, who said that he thought girls were much too nasty to be Honor Guards. He thought they would be too mean in working on the job, and I left it at that.*[42]

At times entire schools are segregated on the basis of sex, and then the effects are more comprehensive and far-reaching in their consequences. In New York City, for example, there are four specialized academic high schools of very fine quality. Until recently women were not allowed to attend two of these—Stuyvesant and Brooklyn Technical—both of which prepare for higher education leading to careers in science, math, and technology. In 1969, Alice de Rivera, a fourteen-year-old student, challenged the legality of the segregated academic high school, and in a celebrated case settled through conciliation settlement, desegregated Stuyvesant High.[43]

There is much challenging still to be done. Vocational-technical

high schools also segregate in a variety of ways and thereby discriminate against women. During the 1970–1971 academic year, a
Board of Education catalog, *The Public High Schools, New York City,*
listed seventeen segregated high schools for either boys only or girls
only.[44] Of these seventeen, twelve were for male students and only
five for females. Even when these vocational schools are co-ed, there
is separated course work within the integrated structure. There are
more boys-only courses offered; moreover, the skills taught women
for the most part hold potential for modest economic returns whereas
the skills men learn open avenues toward well-paid employment.
An encouraging change must be mentioned in that the vocational-
technical courses in the 1971–1972 catalog are no longer segregated
by sex.

Thus in schools, seeds are sewn that later grow into the hard
reality of economic discrimination against women—a particularly
repugnant flowering when one considers that two-thirds of all adults
on welfare are women, more than half of the poor blacks in America
are in families headed by women, and the unemployment of teenage
girls, both black and white, is higher than for any other group in the
country.[45]

This kind of segregation is tangible. It has been put down on
paper as official admissions policy. Throughout education, however,
there is subtle separation of the sexes that is not achieved by stated
rules or closed classroom doors. As one looks at class enrollments,
(s)he cannot help but notice that certain subjects seem to sport in-
visible but extremely effective Women Only and Men Only tags. In
effect there is a sexually divided curriculum, a tacit and ubiquitous
agreement that women belong in various fields in the humanities and
in courses stressing social service, and boys belong in math and
science. As girls become indoctrinated in the concept of the great
curricular divide, they grow progressively clumsier and more awk-
ward in male fields. It has been empirically proven that children
avoid involvement with materials that are stereotyped as characteristic of the opposite sex.[46] Female avoidance and expressed incompe-
tence in math and science, for example, begins in the elementary
school. Dr. Paul Torrance instructed fourth,- fifth,- and sixth-graders
to figure out principles underlying science toys. Boys demonstrated
about twice as many ideas as girls did. Then Torrance participated in
conferences with the children stressing the importance of girls' involvement with science. The next year, when he repeated the experiment, the performances of boys and girls were almost identical. However, both boys and girls stated that they thought the boys' ideas

were better.[47] By the ninth grade, 25 percent of boys and only 3 percent of girls are considering careers in science or engineering.[48] By the time they are ready for college, boys score fifty points higher on the math college board exam. However if the math problems are reworded to include homemaking terms, girls' scores increase, even though the abstract reasoning required to figure out solutions remains the same.[49]

In 1954, the Brown case decided that separate was not equal. It is not equal in 1971. It is not equal when boys' gym classes have elaborate equipment that enables them to participate in a variety of sports while girls practice waist slimming exercises to the music of a record player. It is not equal when a "boys only" vocational school offers courses like electrical engineering and a "girls only" vocational high school has a preponderance of offerings in the clerical skills.

If a female student is less well-to-do, she may be segregated and channeled early during her high school career into courses in clerical skills and cosmetology. If she is wealthier, she may be tracked later— out of math and science courses, out of medical and law schools, and into English courses, education, home economics, library science, and social work.

In 1967 the medium income for a white man was $7,396; for a nonwhite man $4,777; for a white woman $4,279, and for a nonwhite woman $3,194.[50] The roots of this disparity lie, at least partially in high schools and colleges where women are relegated, either forcibly or by tradition, into courses that have potential for meager economic returns. Thus segregated education not only reinforces the artificial notion that the interests and abilities of each sex are so different as to require separated learning opportunities, but it actually institutionalizes and perpetuates economic discrimination against women.

TEACHERS AS CARRIERS: THE SOCIALIZATION CIRCLE

We have surveyed a number of ways that schools discriminate against women. Above and beyond these, another harmful force is at work: ironically, teachers, former victims of sex typing in the socialization process, become its new transmitters. This transmission becomes obvious in the following study in which junior high school teachers were asked to select adjectives that they felt would describe good male and good female students. Here are the teachers' responses, stereotypes in miniature of the male and female roles.[51]

Adjectives Describing Good Female Students		Adjectives Describing Good Male Students	
appreciative	sensitive	active	energetic
calm	dependable	adventurous	enterprising
conscientious	efficient	aggressive	frank
considerate	mature	assertive	independent
cooperative	obliging	curious	inventive
mannerly	thorough		
poised			

Sometimes these stereotypes get transmitted directly, and one way the high school woman learns to stop achieving is simply by listening to what her teachers and counselors tell her. When a female high school student enters a counseling session, it is all too likely that within that microcosm she may come face to face with the prejudices and stereotypes that pervade society at large. Too often counselors dichotomize professions into those "appropriate" for men and those "appropriate" for women. In fact, it has been empirically demonstrated that counselors respond more positively to female clients who hold traditionally feminine career goals than to those who wish to make their way in professions usually reserved for men.[52] Kathleen Chamberlain reports:

> Women have frequently told me that their high school guidance counselors had advised them to become legal secretaries when they wanted to become lawyers, nurses when they wanted to become doctors. (And this socialization process starts early. A friend who teaches fourth graders at a New York City public school—children who will go to a community college someday if they get to college at all— told me that when she asks the girls in her class what they wanted to be when they grew up, they answered not nurses, but nurses' aides, not secretaries, but typists).[53]

Ironically, instead of cementing stereotypes, guidance counselors could be playing a very crucial role in tearing them down, as is demonstrated by the following study. The Strong Vocational Interest Blank was administered to a group of high school women, first with standard instructions and then with "role-playing" instructions. The role playing instructions were: "Pretend men like intelligent women," and "pretend a woman can combine a demanding career with raising a family and perform both well." The role-playing set of instructions raised the measured career interest of these women in six occupations (author, artist, psychologist, lawyer, physician, and life insurance saleswoman).[54]

The lowered expectations that teachers and counselors hold for female students do not even have to be stated to have their effect. In countless nonverbal ways they are transmitted, almost intangibly, and the impact they have on the student is devastating. This phenomenon—that one person's expectations for another's behavior should come to serve as a self-fulfilling prophecy—has far-reaching implications as can be seen in the following experiment.

At the very beginning of the school year, each of eighteen teachers in an elementary school was given names of those children in the classroom who in the academic year ahead would show dramatic intellectual growth. These predictions were allegedly based on children's scores on a test of academic blooming. In reality, the criterion for selection had nothing to do with ability; rather, the children were chosen by a table of random numbers. At the end of the year, it was found that, for children whom the teacher expected to make dramatic gains, IQs increased significantly above those of a control group. The experimenters, Robert Rosenthal and Lenore Jacobson comment on the subtle ways in which expectations are transmitted: "By what she said, by how and when she said it, by her facial expression, postures, and perhaps by her touch, the teacher may have communicated to the children of the experimental group that she expected improved intellectual performance." Although the research methodology in the Rosenthal and Jacobson experiments has been criticized, few would discount the power of the self-fulfilling prophecy, the phenomenon these researchers define.[55]

This experiment has profound importance for all levels of education. Female students at the high school level, are enmeshed in an environmental web where not as much is expected of them, and almost osmotically they imbibe the message. Naomi Weisstein comments on the effect of the self-fulfilling prophecy: "In light of the social expectations about women, it is not surprising that women end up where society expects them to; the surprise is that little girls don't get the message that they are supposed to be stupid until they get into high school . . ."[56]

This is the discriminatory network in which the young woman is enmeshed: curricular materials without intelligent and courageous women; segregated and unequal facilities; a social context in which women are shaped into the demeaning posture of pretended inferiority, and where, in a pathetic enactment of the self-fulfilling prophecy, they live down to the expectations of those who are teaching them.

The product that results from years of sexist schooling gives cause for concern. Although women make better high school grades than do men, they are less likely to believe that they have the ability to do college work.[57] In 1968, the President's Commission on the Status of Women reported that more than twice as many girls as boys from the top 10 percent of high school seniors have no college plans.[58] A variety of other studies demonstrate that, of the brightest high school graduates who do not go to college, 75–90 percent are women.[59]

Moreover, high school women have no conception of how and where to put their talents and abilities to work. Although adolescent girls view homemaking as inferior to careers that are open to men, they also feel that men view intelligent women with distate and marriage and a career are not really compatible.[60] In another study, a devastating sense of pessimism was revealed as only 25 percent of women from blue collar families said that they actually expected to reach their chosen profession.[61] In short, young women graduate from high schools all over the country with little confidence, optimism, and hope—for these have been quite thoroughly schooled away.

Some schools, at least in small ways, are beginning to soften sex stereotypes and sexist practices that deny females, and also males, a wide range of options. In the spring of 1972 a Brotherhood Program was presented in a small Wisconsin high school. It was written by Nancy Lindberg, the school's guidance counselor, a woman concerned about the way sexism is limiting the potential of her students. During the program a young man and a young woman, as part of a tableau, read the following passages for their classmates.

I am a young man. Let me show my manliness, not by fighting or being tough but by being a real person, with the spectrum of emotions. If I'm happy, let me laugh. If I'm sad, don't shame me for my tears. I, too, can cry.

I am a young woman. Don't limit my horizons. I want to try many things. Let my own abilities and interests decide what's right for me, not tradition and law. Don't pity me if I'm not beautiful. I must do more with my life than stand and be beautiful.

As we shall see later, this small midwestern school is not alone as it tries to discard restricting stereotypes. And as the network of sexist practices begins to be eradicated in more and more high schools across the country, equality of opportunity will become a daily happening and not merely an empty phrase.

NOTES

[1]Janice Trecker, "Women in U. S. History Textbooks," *Social Education*, *35*, no. 3 (March 1971), p. 249. Reprinted by permission of the National Council for the Social Studies and the author.

[2]*Ibid.*, p. 255.

[3]*Ibid.*, p. 252.

[4]Anne Grant West, "Women's Liberation or, Exploding the Fairy Princess Myth," *Scholastic Teacher*, Junior High Edition, November 1971, p. 10.

[5]Mary Ritchie Key, "Male and Female in Children's Books—Dispelling All Doubts," *American Teacher*, February 1972, p. 17. Reprinted by permission of *American Teacher*.

[6]Diane Staven, "The Skirts in Fiction About Boys: A Maxi Mess," *School Library Journal Book Review*, *95*, no. 1 (January 1971), 66–70.

[7]*Ibid.*

[8]The Feminists on Children's Literature, "A Feminist Look at Children's Books," *School Library Journal*, *17*, no. 5 (January 1971), 19–24.

[9]Elaine Showalter, "Women and the Literary Curriculum," *College English*, *32*, no. 8 (May 1971), 855–862.

[10]Arlie Hochschild, "The American Woman: Another Idol of Social Science," *Transaction*, *8*, no. 63 (November–December 1970), 13.

[11]Jo Freeman, "Women's Liberation and Its Impact on the Campus," *Liberal Education*, *57*, no. 4 (December 1971), 474.

[12]Sigmund Freud, quoted in "Know Your Enemy: A Sampling of Sexist Quotes" in Robin Morgan, ed., *Sisterhood is Powerful*, New York, Random House (Vintage), 1970, p. 34.

[13]Bruno Bettelheim, quoted in Naomi Weisstein, "Woman as Nigger," *Psychology Today*, *3*, no. 10 (1969).

[14]Benjamin Spock, quoted in Morgan, *op. cit.*, p. 34.

[15]Naomi Weisstein, "Kinder, Kuche, Kirche as Scientific Law: Psychology Constructs the Female," in Morgan, *op. cit.*

[16]Dorothy Lee, "Discrepancies in the Teaching of American Culture," in George Spindler, ed., *Education and Culture*, New York, Holt, Rinehart and Winston, 1963, p. 187.

[17]Gilbert Becker, "Sex Role Identification and the Needs for Self and Social Approval," *Journal of Psychology*, *69*, no. 1 (May 1968), 11–15.

[18]Claire Doubrousky, compiler, "What We Have Found," in Anne Grant West, ed., *Report on Sex Bias in the Public Schools*, New York, Education Committee, NOW, 1971.

[19]Kathleen Chamberlain, "Women Students at Manhattan Community College," to be published by KNOW, Inc. Reprinted by permission of the author.

20*Ibid.*

21*Ibid.*

22Hochschild, *op. cit.*, p. 13

23James Coleman, *The Adolescent Society*, New York, The Free Press of Glencoe, 1961, p. 42.

24Quoted in Joan Robins, *Handbook of Women's Liberation*, North Hollywood, NOW, 1970, p. 33.

25Patricia Sexton, *The Feminized Male*, New York, Random House (Vintage), 1969, p. 112.

26Coleman, *op. cit.*

27Eleanor Maccobey, editor, *The Development of Sex Differences*, Stanford, Calif., Stanford University Press, 1966, p. 31, in reference to Merville C. Shaw and John J. McCuen, "The Onset of Underachievement in Bright Children," *Journal of Educational Psychology, 51*, no. 3 (June 1960), 103–109.

28Margaret Mead, *Male and Female*, New York, William Morrow, 1949, p. 320.

29Maria Kamarovsky, "Cultural Contradictions and Sex Roles," *American Journal of Sociology, 52*, no. 3 (November 1946), 184–189.

30Paul Wallen, "Cultural Contradictions and Sex Roles: A Repeat Study," *American Sociological Review, 15*, no. 2 (March 1950), 288–293.

31Carole Leland, "Women-Men-Work: Women's Career Aspirations as Affected by the Male Environment," Ph.D. diss., Stanford University, 1966.

32James Pierce, "Sex Differences in Achievement Motivation of Able High School Students," *Cooperative Research Project*, no. 1097, December 1961.

33Barry Lubetkin and Arvin Lubetkin, "Achievement Motivation in a Competitive Situation: A Comparison of Undergraduates, Younger Graduate Students, and Older Female Graduate Students," U.S. Department of Health, Education and Welfare, April, 1968.

34Simone de Beauvoir, as quoted in Diana T. Slaughter, "Becoming an Afro-American Woman, *School Review, 80*, no. 2 (February 1972), 299–318.

35Slaughter, *ibid.*

36"Pregnant Teen-agers," *Today's Education, 59*, no. 7 (October 1970).

37*Ibid.*, p. 89.

38*Ibid.*

39Daryl Bem and Sandra Bem, "We're All Nonconscious Sexists," *Psychology Today, 4*, no. 6 (November 1970), p. 116.

40Excerpts of testimony quoted in West, *Report on Sex Bias in the Public Schools, op. cit.*

41*Ibid.*

42*Ibid.*

43*Ibid.*

44*Ibid.*

45Material presented by Bernice Sandler for the record to the Committee on the Judiciary, House of Representatives, 92nd cong., Hearings on Equal Rights for Men and Women, 1971.

[46]Charles Elton and Harriett Rose, "Traditional Sex Attitudes and Discrepant Ability Measures in College Women," *Journal of Counseling Psychology*, 14, no. 6 (November 1967), 538–543.

[47]Paul Torrance, *Guiding Creative Talent*, Englewood Cliffs, N.J., Prentice-Hall, 1962.

[48]Bem and Bem, *op. cit.*

[49]*Ibid.*

[50]Facts About Women in Education, prepared by the Women's Equity Action League, Cleveland, Ohio, 1971. Can be obtained from WEAL, 1253 4th St., Washington, D.C. 20024.

[51]B. J. Kemer, "A Study of the Relationship Between the Sex of the Student and the Assignment of Marks by Secondary School Teachers," Ph.D. diss., Michigan State University, 1965.

[52]Arthur Thomas and Norman Stewart, "Counselor's Response to Female Clients with Deviate and Conforming Career Goals," *Journal of Counseling Psychology*, 18, no. 4 (July 1971), 352–357.

[53]Chamberlain, *op. cit.*

[54]H. S. Farmer and M. J. Bohn, "Home Career Conflict Reduction and the Level of Career Interest in Women," *Journal of Counseling Psychology*, 17, no. 3 (May 1970), 228–232.

[55]Robert Rosenthal and Lenore Jacobson, "Pygmalion in the Classroom: An Excerpt," in Melvin Silberman, ed., *The Experience of Schooling*, New York, Holt, Rinehart and Winston, 1971, p. 115.

[56]Weisstein, *op. cit.*

[57]Patricia Cross, "College Women: A Research Description," *Journal of the National Association of Women Deans and Counselors*, 32, no. 1 (Fall 1968), 12–21.

[58]Quoted in West, "Women's Liberation or, Exploding the Fairy Princess Myth," *op. cit.*

[59]Facts About Women in Education, *op. cit.*

[60]E. Mathews, "The Marriage-Career Conflict in the Career Development of Girls and Young Women," Ph.D. diss., Harvard University, 1960.

[61]West, Women's Liberation or Exploding The Fairy Princess Myth, in reference to Ethelyn Davis, "Careers as Concerns of Blue-Collar Girls," in Arthur B. Shostak and William Gomberg eds., *Blue-Collar World/Studies of the American Worker*, Englewood Cliffs, N.J., Prentice-Hall, 1964, pp. 154–164.

7
The male university

Finding . . . that the young women did no manner of harm, we very cautiously admitted them to some of the recitations of lectures in the university building itself, providing always that they were to be marched in good order, with at least two teachers, one in front and the other in the rear of the column as guards.

> President of the University
> of Missouri, 1870[1]

A century ago, in Missouri at any rate, women were alien to higher education, considered almost like animals, needing the restraining influence of guards to keep them from creating havoc in the orderly male university. And a few years earlier, when the University of Michigan was debating whether to admit women, its president had noted that "Men will lose as women advance, we shall have a community of defeminated women and demasculated men. When we attempt to disturb God's order, we produce monstrosities."[2]

Such biased statements about the nature of woman and her capabilities become less shocking when one considers the social context in which they were spoken. For two hundred years after the establishment of Harvard in 1636, it was not possible for a woman to attend college in this country. Not until the mid 1800s did Oberlin become the first college to admit women, followed by Elmira Female College in 1855.

The major force that opened the doors of higher education to women was the Civil War, and the major thrust behind this new privilege was not ideological commitment, but rather economic need. As the young men of the country were drawn away from campuses and onto battlefields, colleges were confronted with shrinking enrollments and potential financial collapse. In some cases, their very existence was threatened, and they were forced to fill enrollment lists with women and general funds with their admissions fees.

Immediately following the Civil War, the number of colleges admitting women almost doubled. It is significant that the all-male institutions most ready to accept female students were those in need of economic help. It was not until approximately 1900 that most graduate and professional schools would allow women to attend.[3]

When we look, even briefly, at this past history, there is no doubt that we've come a long way, baby, since the bizarre quotes of past university presidents or the closed door policies. However, when we look at higher education today, there is also no doubt that equal education for women is a goal that is far from achieved and that the main purpose of colleges and universities is still to educate men. This chapter will highlight sexist practices that pervade higher education and that serve as a special deterrent to the university woman.

DEAD ENDS AND
DO NOT TRESPASS SIGNS

An integral part of university student life, particularly for the graduate student, is the gripe session over midnight cups of black coffee. There is often cause for staying up late and much to complain about, for the path to academia's ultimate rite of passage, the doctorate, is one punctuated by innumerable obstacles: the completion of a long list of required courses, first at the undergraduate and then at the graduate level; a comprehensive exam, sometimes lasting several days, tapping the knowledge gained over years of study; the painstaking research and writing that will hopefully become a completed dissertation; and finally, the oral defense where a professor's comment, sometimes based on insight or logic, sometimes on whim or the momentary need for an ego trip, can cause months of rewriting.

> A woman needs what will make her a queen of the household and of society, while man needs what will fit him for the harder, sterner duties of life, to which ladies should never be driven except in cases of exigency.
>
> She cannot afford to risk her health in acquiring a knowledge of the advanced sciences, mathematics, or philosophy for which she has no use. . . . Too many women have already made themselves permanent invalids by an overstrain of study at schools and colleges.
>
> Editors of a student newspaper, Agricultural College of Pennsylvania, 1889.

When a woman decides to attend a college or university, whether enroute to a bachelor's degree or a doctorate, she has a good deal to complain about, for many additional obstacles make the traveling tough. She first runs into this obstacle course when as a high school senior she submits an application to college. These obstacles, reserved for women only, will continue to frustrate throughout her undergraduate and graduate work; and they will persist during her professional life in academia. To begin where the obstacle course begins, we will join two high school seniors as they encounter the first barrier that women must hurdle along the higher education route:

Sue and Jim had been dating since their sophomore year and were almost inseparable. They walked to classes together, studied together, and joined the same clubs and activities. It was almost a joke around Cony High School, and the senior year book was filled with references to "the dynamic duo."

Planning to continue their close friendship, they each applied to the same co-educational colleges. Their records were similar—and good, each having a B+ average, college board scores in the 600's, and strong recommendations from teachers. They waited for acceptances in confident expectation.

During the spring, Sue and Jim would rush home from school, check their mail boxes, and then phone each other to compare notes. As the replies came in, Sue's excitement and anticipation became a hurt bewilderment. While Jim had been accepted at every school but one and had received a number of scholarship offers, her records showed four rejections and no money offered.

This particular episode is fictional, but recent investigations suggest that it could easily happen. From 75 to 90 percent (depending on the particular study) of the well-qualified students who do not go on to college are women, and although more women than ever received bachelor's degrees in 1970 (344,465) the percentage of recipients who were female (43 percent) was actually lower than in 1899 (53 percent).[4] This disparity is caused partly by the pressures applied to females that create lowered aspirations and partly by the simple fact that it is harder for women to get admitted. This discrimination in college admissions policies was demonstrated empirically in a 1971 study: Using a sample of 240 colleges across the country, researchers found that except in cases of clearly outstanding women, males were accepted more frequently than females with qualifications identical in every respect except gender.[5] In March 1971, Dr. Bernice Sandler cited the following examples of discriminatory admissions policies in testimony before the House Judiciary committee:

For the last decade at the University of Michigan, according to G. C. Wilson, Executive Associate Director of Admissions, the Office of Admissions has "adjusted" requirements to insure that an "overbalance"—that is, a majority—of women would not occur in the freshman class for a number of years, despite the fact that in terms of grades and test scores, there are more qualified female applicants than males. At Pennsylvania State University, an artificial ratio of 2.5 men to every female is deliberately maintained. . . . In graduate school, the quota system is even more vicious. At Stanford, for example, the proportion of women students has declined over the last ten years, even though more and equally or better qualified women have applied for admission to graduate school. (One out of every 2.8 men who applied was accepted; only 1 woman out of 4.7 applicants was accepted.)[6]

Recent investigation has also shown that women receive fewer scholarships and less financial aid than men—$518 as an annual average for females, $760 for males.[7] Many scholarships, both at the graduate and undergraduate levels, are limited to men only. A study by the Women's Equity Action League has disclosed that less than 10 percent of the White House Fellows or Fulbright Fellowship Award winners have been women.[8] Moreover, practically all federal aid, both scholarships and loans, is available only for students enrolled in full-time study, a requirement that many married women find impossible to meet.[9]

What happens when a young woman surmounts the admissions hurdle and arrives on the college campus?

Although it was past midnight, Diane could not stop thinking of all the events that had been crowded into her first week at college. Already she had been to a round of parties and mixers where she met the "Big Men on Campus," the captain of the football team, the president of the student body and of the school council. She had also gone to all of her classes, and it seemed that her professors were knowledgeable and excited about their subject matter. In her initial enthusiasm she had even attended the Convocation, although warned it would be dull, and had patiently listened to the president of the college drone a series of generalizations welcoming the new students.

Suddenly, Diane's pleasant thoughts were interrupted by a jarring realization. Of all the important people she had met at college— student leaders, professors, deans, the president—not a single one had been female.

In casual social interaction at parties and in classrooms, the woman on campus learns that she is on borrowed territory. In contrast to the young boy in the "feminine elementary school," she is now the fish out of water, the out-of-place female who can exert little, if any, influence on surroundings that seem to be totally controlled by men. The results of a 1970 survey of 454 colleges and universities that hold corporate membership in the American Association of University Women demonstrate that it is indeed a male population of students, faculty, and administration that controls and operates higher education. The survey shows that students elected to leadership positions—the president of the student body or the college class, the Chairman of the Union Board of Governors or Campus Judicial Board—are invariably males. When women hold student positions, they are generally appointive rather than elective positions, such as editor of the yearbook or literary magazine, student chairman of the activities committee or freshman orientation.[10] At the graduate level, women, particularly if they are married, are not only absent from positions of leadership, but from general social interaction as well. In a national sample, it was found that married women knew fewer persons in their departments than did either married men, single men, or single women.[11] In another study, when full-time graduate students were asked: How many of the people you see socially are fellow graduate students, 22.8 percent of the married

TABLE 2. Students in Campus Leadership Positions (1967–1970)

| Position | Coed schools (376) | | | |
	% Men 3 years	% Women 2–3 years	% Co*	Total responses
President, student body	84.3	4.8	.5	370
Class President	75.5	6.1	7.8	294
Chairman, Union Board of Governors	64.6	12.3	2.4	209
Captain, Debate	65.3	8.3	2.4	170
Chairman, Campus Judicial Board	68.0	8.8	8.3	252
Editor, yearbook	16.6	49.2	8.5	362
Chairman, activities committee	47.0	27.0	5.0	259
Chairman, freshman orientation	39.8	24.3	18.5	259
Editor, literary magazine	38.8	29.6	6.0	263
Editor, campus paper	38.6	24.9	8.8	37.3

*Respsonibility shared by both men and women.
SOURCE: *AAUW Journal*, November 1970.

men replied, "Almost none." For women, the figure was almost twice as high.[12]

Table 2 summarizes the AAUW findings on student positions in 454 colleges and universities and emphasizes the need to encourage women to assume more leadership on college campuses.

Not only are student leaders male, but for the most part, so are teachers and administrators. In institutions of higher education across the country, less than one-quarter of the faculties are female, and when women are present, it is generally at the lower rungs, as instructors and assistant professors.[13] Moreover, 92 percent of the institutions responding to the AAUW survey reported that they do not include women in top-level administrative positions.[14] So the young undergraduate woman may peruse the list of faculty and administration in the college catalogue and wonder—where are the competent female leaders, the role models whom she can observe, talk with, emulate and who will help her develop her own goals and define and test her own unique life style? (An expanded discussion of female faculty and administration in higher education can be found on pages 160–166.

Although it is highly desirable to have more women in influential positions, it is very possible for men to provide college women with the encouragement they need, and researchers have found that "non-romantic relationships with men, including those with teaching fellows and graduate assistants, are important in shaping women's career and educational aspirations."[15] Unfortunately, those relationships too often discourage rather than inspire. The following is a list of comments that professors have made to their female students— particularly to graduate students. They are brief and clear examples of the way prejudice and discrimination surface in everyday conversation.

I know you're competent and your thesis advisor knows you're competent. The question in our minds is are you really serious about what you're doing.

The admissions committee didn't do their job. There is not one good-looking girl in the entering class.

Have you ever thought about journalism? [to a student planning to get a Ph.D. in political science]. I know a lot of women journalists who do very well.

No pretty girls ever come to talk to me.

A pretty girl like you will certainly get married; why don't you stop with an M.A.?

You're so cute. I can't see you as a professor of anything.

The girls at [X university] get good grades because they study hard, but they don't have any originality.

[Professor to student looking for a job] You've no business looking for work with a child that age.

We expect women who come here to be competent, good students, but we don't expect them to be brilliant or original.

Women are intrinsically inferior.

Any woman who has got this far has got to be a kook. There are already too many women in this department.

How old are you anyway? Do you think that a girl like you could handle a job like this? You don't look like the academic type.

Why don't you find a rich husband and give all this up?

Our general admissions policy has been if the body is warm and male, take it; if it's female, make sure it's an A–from Bryn Mawr.

[To a young widow who had a five-year-old child and who needed a fellowship to continue at graduate school] You're very attractive. You'll get married again. We have to give fellowships to people who really need them.

Somehow I can never take women in this field seriously.[16]

One graduate student in French tells of the discouraging comments and attitudes held by the two heads of her department. They believed that women were not suited to academic life, that they did not have the mental capabilities to achieve the doctorate, and if they somehow did manage to get a Ph.D., they would never publish. After two frustrating years, she dropped out of graduate school, although she had a fine academic record, and applied to a social work school, seeking a career "more compatible with woman's role in society."[17] This is but one incident. There are countless versions of the story. More than a third of the women students who responded to a University of Chicago survey report that they had been discouraged by faculty members or had heard of other women being discouraged about women's capabilities in various academic fields or for various jobs.[18]

Sex bias not only pervades social interaction but it is in texts as well. Discrimination in curricular materials has already been described in some detail in Chapters 5 and 6, and at the college level, the patterns are similar. There are the sins of omission—pages of material without mention of an individual woman or without reference to women as a group. And there are the sins of commission—stereotypes of women, particularly in literature—as castrating bitches, as sirens, sexually alluring and deceitful, and as madonnas, passive and ethereal. When one considers curricular materials within the general social context, the situation borders on the ludicrous.

UNIVERSITY OF ILLINOIS
AT URBANA-CHAMPAIGN

YOU WILL BE PLEASED TO LEARN THAT
*Jane Abbott**

Is a participant in the James Scholar Program in engineering for the 1971–1972 academic year. Our congratulations are extended to you on his superior academic performance.

Dean of Engineering

*Although this name is fictitious (changed upon the student's request) this is the standard form and permanent pronoun used to recognize excellence in engineering.

The woman student will spend the major portion of her academic studies reading material about male protagonists, written for the most part by male authors, taught to her for the most part by male professors, in a university that is operated and controlled by men.

One option available to the female student is to avoid the totally male perspective by attending a woman's college. There is much potential power lying dormant in the concept of the woman's college. This could be at least one preserve that men can't overrun, one training ground for future leadership where women can gain experience in student government, where they need not remain dutifully submissive and quiet while males take the lead in classroom discussions. Unfortunately, women's colleges frequently do not achieve their inherent potential. In the 1967–1968 Gourman Report ratings for academic excellence, the top five women's colleges were rated far below the top five men's colleges.[19] In comparing men's women's, and co-educational colleges, women's colleges receive the lowest ratings in the nation. Moreover, women's colleges stress the humanities and courses related to children, and they are strikingly weak in science offerings.[20]

Statements of school objectives give some indication of why there is this difference in quality. When stating goals and purposes, men's colleges indicate that their mission is to prepare the nation's future leaders. Often women's colleges offer goals that, if you read between the lines, indicate that leadership will not be the function of their graduates. The goals of Sullins College are particularly explicit:

Within a few years after graduation, most Sullins girls establish their own homes and assume the role of wife, mother, homemaker and community citizen. To meet these responsibilities today, students urgently need to develop positive and attractive personalities, social competence and assurance, sound cultural values, and a sense of personal and social responsibilities.[21]

In higher education, there is a trend toward the disappearance of the single sex school, and as of 1971, only 16 percent of the institutions of higher education were limited to one sex.[22] However, Dr. Bernice Sandler noted in testimony before Congress that sexual segregation is still legal and still has devastating effects on students;

Racial segregation of our education system was outlawed by the Supreme Court in 1954, yet as recently as 10 years ago, the Supreme Court declined to hear a case in which the Texas Court of Civil Appeals upheld the exclusion of women from a state college, Texas A & M. . . . In another court case under the 14th amendment in February 1970, a three judge federal court dismissed as "moot" a class action in which women sought to desegregate all male and all female public institutions in Virginia. . . . To give you an idea of the results of a sex segregated university and college system, let me quote from the Report of the Virginia Commission for the study of Education Facilities in the State of Virginia, 1964: "2,000 women were turned down for college entrance in the state of Virginia; during the same period of time, NOT ONE application of a male student was rejected."[23]

Years of functioning as a minority group in the male university take their toll. Aspirations are lowered and options are constrained. It had been found that college women are more likely than are men "to have an initially low level of aspiration (for graduate school training and for obtaining the doctorate) and to change to a lower level during the four years."[24] One study illustrates how totally and completely college women have learned to internalize an inferior role. At the University of Michigan, 90 women and 88 men were asked to make up a story about the following sentences: "After first-term finals, John (Anne) finds himself (herself) at the top of his (her) medical school class." The women wrote about Anne, the men about John. Here are some representative stories:

Boys' Stories

"John has worked very hard and his long hours of study paid off. . . . He is thinking about his girl, Cheri, whom he will marry at the end of medical school. He realizes he can give her all the things she desires after he becomes established. He will go on in medical school and be successful in the long run."

"John is a conscientious young man who worked hard. He is pleased with himself. John has always wanted to go into medicine and is very dedicated. . . . John continues working hard and eventually graduates at the top of his class."

Girls' Stories

"Anne is an acne-faced bookworm. She runs to the bulletin board and finds she's at the top. As usual she smarts off. A chorus of groans is the rest of the class's reply. . . . She studies 12 hours a day, and lives at home to save money. 'Well, it certainly paid off. All the Friday and Saturday nights without dates, fun—I'll be the best woman doctor alive.' And yet a twinge of sadness comes thru— she wonders what she really has. . . ."

"Anne has a boyfriend, Carl, in the same class and they are quite serious. . . . She wants him to be scholastically higher than she is. Anne will deliberately lower her academic standing the next term, while she does all she subtly can to help Carl. His grades come up and Anne soon drops out of medical school. They marry and he goes on in school while she raises their family."

"Anne is talking to her counselor. Counselor says she will make a fine *nurse*."

The stories were scored to assess whether there were any negative feelings associated with being successful. In their stories, only eight of the men, fewer than 10 percent, showed any motive to avoid success. Indeed, as the sample quotes indicate, the men wrote glowingly and with open delight at John's achievements. In contrast, over 65 percent of the college women showed negative reactions toward the successful female medical student. Some tried to solve what they considered to be the dilemma of Anne's success by insisting that she give up her career and get married, evidently the only real achievement possible for a woman. These matchmakers at least could accept the fact that Anne was in medical school. For others, such a circumstance was too preposterous, and misreading the cues, they placed Anne at the top of her *nursing class*.[25]

College women's inability to accept women who achieve academic success was also pointed up in an article by Philip Goldberg entitled, "Are Women Prejudiced Against Women?" He gave college women sets of booklets containing six identical professional articles in fields that are traditionally considered male, female, and neutral. The articles were identical, but the names of the authors were not. For example, an article in one set would bear the name John T. McKay, and in another set the same article would have Joan T. McKay as the author. Each booklet contained three articles by "women" and three by "men." The students rated these articles on value, persuasiveness, and profundity and the authors for style and competence. The male authors were rated the highest in every dimension, even in areas such as dietetics and homemaking. Goldberg concluded that "women are prejudiced against female professionals and, regardless of the actual accomplishments of these professionals, will firmly refuse to recognize them as the equals of their male colleagues."[26]

And still another study demonstrates how women have internalized a role devoid of success and exhibit prejudice toward other women who fail to conform to the lowered standards. In this study, 128 female college students were asked to evaluate 8 paintings. The students were given fictitous information about the painter—half of the time the students were told that the art work was done by a male, and the other half of the time that it was the work of a female artist. The students were also given fictitious information as to whether or not the painting was an acknowledged success. Sometimes they were told that the painting shown to them had already won a prize at an art exhibit, and at other times that the painting was simply an entry in a contest. When informed that the art work had not yet been judged by professional standards, women students consistently rated paintings signed by "male artists" more highly than paintings signed by "female artists." Only when a painting had previously been evaluated as prize winning was it accorded equal respect regardless of the gender of the artist.[27]

PREJUDICED POLICIES

The undercurrent of sexism that pervades university life surfaces more formally and blatantly in policies, procedures, and structure that are custom-tailored to suit the needs of the male student. One way policy works against the university woman is to make an education more expensive for her than for her male classmate. Discrimination in terms of cost appears not only in lesser financial aid allotment, but also in college policy that often insists that she live in a campus dormitory and pay full room and board fees. The university usually does not play at surrogate parent for the male student, and he can escape some of the burdensome college expenses by getting a cheaper room off campus and eating where he pleases. Lack of gynecological services at many university health centers also results in increased expense for the woman because she is forced to go off campus to obtain medical care.

Moreover, the university with its rigid course timetable and lack of adequate day care facilities shows little understanding or concern for the needs of women who have children. If we observe a student-mother as she tries to continue her education, perhaps we can get some sense of the frustration she experiences:

Mary Ellen lifted ten-month-old Tommy out of the car seat and hoisted him under one arm while she tucked his diaper bag and her psychology and history texts under the other. It was a heavy load, and she was relieved when she finally arrived on the third floor where she could hear the professor beginning his lecture on minority groups. She slipped into a chair by the door, opened the diaper bag and drew out some toys and a cookie for her son. She hoped that he would be content and quiet; this was an important lecture.

The topic may have been important, but the lecturer was dull, and for a moment Mary Ellen's mind wandered. She thought, a little bitterly, of how much easier it would be if there were some extra money to hire a baby sitter, or if her husband, who was also a student, would take equal responsibility in caring for Tommy—or if only the university would open a good day care center as many of the women students had been demanding. Then quickly her mind snapped back to the lecture and her son who, becoming restless and noisy, was beginning to distract the other students.

Mary Ellen is a fictional character, but she represents thousands of mothers who need good child care services provided if they are to complete their education in any kind of reasonable and satisfactory manner. Too often universities fail to provide day care services, or if facilities are available, they will only admit children who have reached a certain age, typically three. The determined student-mother must resort to a variety of unsatisfactory makeshift arrangements. If there is a little extra money (and usually this is not the case), she can hire a babysitter; if she has friends in the same predicament, she can band with them in an informal day care arrangement. If these options are not available, she can bring her baby to class with her, get a seat near the door, and steel herself for frequent interruptions and possible instructor hostility. If this proves too trying, she can drop out.

A comprehensive day care program is only one option that universities could, but often do not, provide. Classes are for the most part offered during the day, at the very time when the married woman is busiest with household responsibilities. Most universities do offer some evening courses, but they are often minimal and frequently end early. If the student-mother is lucky, she can squeeze in an hour lecture between the time she tucks her children into bed and the time the university closes its doors. If she needs particular, required courses to graduate, she may have to wait several semesters until the courses are offered at night, thereby dragging out her college attendance for several years.

College libraries, too, close early, and sometimes books are locked up by 10:00 or 11:00 in the evening. For the woman with both family and research responsibilities, this may mean the hectic experience of arriving at the library at about 8:00, hurriedly tracing down appropriate references, and just settling into the reading, only to be interrupted by the jarring, closing bell, telling her that she has fifteen minutes to vacate the premises.

Another obstacle the married female must face if she tries to be responsive to mobility demands of her husband's career, is starting college or graduate school in one university and completing it in another. In this process of transfer, she may meet inflexible transfer requirements that cause her to lose numerous hard-earned credits, particularly at the graduate level. Even if she does not have to cope with changing locations, she may meet a university requirement of taking nine or twelve credits each semester in order to graduate. This demand, combined with home and child care responsibilities, can create a pressured learning situation, one that finally results in a dead end, as the woman, exhausted from trying to balance conflicting roles, leaves school. Of course, many of these obstacles also deter males who do not follow the traditional pattern of uninterrupted education and who try to combine work with continuing education. However, societal pressures more frequently force women into this position.

Higher education must become more aware of and responsive to

Conditions Affecting Women's Decisions to Attend Graduate School

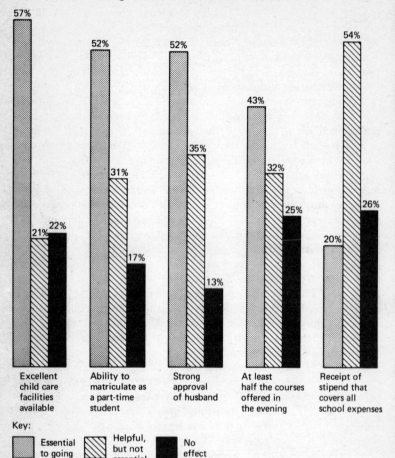

Key:

Essential to going   Helpful, but not essential   No effect

SOURCE: "Special Report on Women and Graduate Study," U.S. Department of Health, Education and Welfare, Washington, D.C., June 1968.

the needs of women students, just as it is beginning to be more concerned about other disadvantaged and minority groups. The graph on this page highlights these needs, and colleges and universities must—with sensitivity and concern—respond.

There is another group whose needs are not thoroughly reflected in this graph. They are the women who leave school to raise their children, and then ten or twenty years later, try to resume their university careers. This is a pattern that a growing number of women are following: Between 1950 and 1969 school enrollment rose from 26,000 to 311,000 among women 25 to 29 years of age and from 21,000 to 215,000 among women 30 to 35 years of age.[28] These women often bring enormous talent, enthusiasm, and drive with them when they return to the campus, as can be seen in the responses of a group of mature women graduate students at the University of Chicago when they were asked about their academic work:

I'm very excited, very stimulated and enthusiastic. It's very, very hard work. I have never spent so much time so aggressively fighting for every minute to get one more article read before I fall asleep. But it's great.

I feel so fulfilled in my work, so intellectually stimulated that I don't have to lean on my husband for that which I need. And I think if I just did not have to work quite so hard at home I would be a very happy human being. I say this quite humbly.

It was enormously demanding and very joyful, and painful, and a growing experience in every kind of way. . . . And it comes to you, it's just poured into you, the energy to do this, because you love it. Just the pain of having to start all over again was wonderfully healthy too. Women are able to make a world, in middle age, where they are hardly threatened at all . . . . where there is no engagement, no painful, naked confrontation of real personalities or minds that's distressing and wonderful. . . . (But) I think the cost of this in human values has been excessive. I'm not at all sure I would just say to everybody, just run out and do this. I think it is impossible to know when you begin what the price is going to be. What it's been for myself I don't begrudge. What it's been for my family I feel guilty about, I really do.[29]

The comments also give some hint of the special problems mature women face. They may feel torn from trying to fulfill their family's needs as well as their own academic pursuits. They may feel ill at ease on a campus surrounded by younger students, and they may suffer worry and concern that years away from the classroom have left them incapable of doing rigorous academic work. Their problems vary, and mature women who return to college will need special advising, counseling, and placement services—help that universities too often do not supply. Indeed, results of the recent AAUW survey show that 46 percent of the 454 universities in the sample had *no programs* related to the special educational needs of women on campus.[30]

University placement policies are insufficient not only for the mature woman—but for all women students. When a female college senior enters the placement office, she may find the opportunities for future employment very different for her than for her male counterpart. One woman summed up the placement situation she encountered with: "No one asks a male college graduate if he can type." Unfortunately, it is the rare placement office that rejects recruiting literature and firms that discriminate against women or that advertise positions specifying the sex of the applicant.

Discriminatory admissions and placement services, increased financial burdens, inflexible requirements, scanty assistance offered to the perseverance of a woman who tries to combine raising a family with attending classes or her determination to return to college after years of absence—such are the potential obstacles that lie ahead of the high school woman who is filling out college application forms. Considering the roadblocks, it is little wonder that only 39 percent of the women who begin the college route ever make it through to the B.A., and that of Ph.D's earned in 1968, only 13 percent were acquired by women.[31]

A NICE PLACE TO VISIT—
BUT DON'T TRY TO WORK THERE

Some women, however, manage to shut eyes and ears to the discriminatory messages and complete the obstacle path that confronts an aspiring female doctoral candidate. When these women try to put to use their hard earned degrees, they are confronted with a variety of Do Not Trespass signs that guard against their encroachment on the male domain of higher education.

The first warning immediately appears in the shape of discriminatory hiring practices. In a 1970 experiment, eight paragraphs summarizing the professional accomplishments of a young psychologist were sent to chairmen of every degree granting psychology department in the country. Two forms were used, one to indicate a male applicant and the other a female. They were identical except in name and the sex reference pronoun. The departments rated the "women" less desirable than men in six of the eight instances.[32] In another study, using a sample of college teachers who had previously been Woodrow Wilson Fellows, it was found the men had received three times as many initial job offers as had the women.[33] Other researchers who have recently investigated discrimination in the hiring of male and female professors summarize the situation: "When all variables were equal except sex, the male candidate was typically chosen for employment."[34]

The justification for failure to hire academic women frequently takes the following form: A woman is not fully committed to her career; she may get pregnant and leave work for an extended period of child care; it will be better to hire a male whose career pattern is more stable.

Research into career patterns of female professors shows that this justification is founded on myth. Approximately 90 percent of women with doctorates are working. Of these women, 81 percent work full time and 79 percent have not interrupted their careers in the past ten years. Moreover, the more education a woman has, the more likely it is that she will be in the labor force.[35]

Despite such findings, the position of the academic woman has actually been getting worse. In 1870, women made up one-third of the faculty in institutions of higher learning; in 1970, they composed less than a quarter.[36] In the more prestigious universities, the figure drops to 10 percent or less.[37] With the growing surplus of Ph.D.'s, Doris Pullen in "The Educational Establishment: Wasted Women" suggests that higher education will become more and more a male domain.

Say she is one who makes it. With her new Ph.D. where can she go? In its January 12, 1970, issue, The Chronicle of Higher Education *reported that the academic marketplace was tighter than it had been in recent memory, that some 49 percent of 1969 Ph.D.'s in physics were still looking for jobs. That the chairmen of modern language departments of several major universities reported receiving more than 600 applications for 5 openings, that 2000 history teachers are job hunting; that one university planning to graduate 70 Ph.D.'s in English in June 1970 expects to hire only one new faculty member in September. No one really expects the lucky person will be a woman. John Rumbargo, assistant executive secretary of the American Historical Association, noted that in a tight market "Women don't get hired."[38]*

A particularly effective roadblock to feminine employment in higher education is the nepotism clause. Nepotism clauses, both formal and informal, prevent a faculty appointment of more than one member of a family to the same department, or in some cases, to the same college or university. These nepotism clauses disqualify professionals, not on the basis of degree qualifications, or teaching competence, or publishing history, or in fact anything remotely related to academic qualifications. A family relationship, in practice usually that of marriage—two people legally living together—becomes the basis for disqualification. It is usually the talent and scholarship of the wife that are placed on the sacrificial altar of the nepotism god. Here's an example of the way the nepotism clause works.

> *Nepotism rules often lead to farcical situations. One of the more famous cases is that of Dr. Maria Goeppert Mayer, the first woman to receive the Nobel Prize for physics since Marie Curie. Her husband is also a physicist. Department after Department hired him, while graciously allowing her to use the laboratory facilities free. . . . Another recent case known to me illustrates both sexual discrimination and covert nepotism rules (many institutions claim not to have them and do not print them in official literature). A brilliant European couple were invited to teach in one department, for they specialize in different areas. He did not have a Ph.D.; she did. He had not published a book; she had. He was hired as a visiting Associate Professor; she, after considerable hassle, as a visiting Assistant Professor. Throughout the negotiations, they were told that the nepotism rule would prevent the institution's offering her a full-time position in the same department as her husband, although, in reply to a questionnaire circulated by the AAUW a few years ago, the institution declared that it did not have any nepotism rules.*[39]

An equally absurd situation recently occurred in a California university. There, a man and woman each on the teaching staff decided to get married; they soon learned, however, that if they did so, the university's nepotism policy would force one member of the couple to relinquish his or her appointment. Faced with the untenable alternative of sacrificing one career, they were forced to abandon their marriage plans and to live together in a common law arrangement.

Even if a woman is not blocked from obtaining an initial university position, a new roadblock soon appears after she is hired.

> *Dr. Ellen Berg is a dedicated and productive assistant professor of history and also the only woman in her department. During six years at the university, she has proven to be extremely concerned about her students, preparing conscientiously for her classes, counseling students in school and often inviting them to her home where, after dinner, she helps them sort out career and social problems. The students respond warmly to her, and for two years have voted her the*

university's outstanding teacher. Besides this teaching involvement, she has compiled an impressive record in research and publication.

Nevertheless, each year Dr. Berg grows increasingly disheartened and angry as she watches younger, newer men in the department, with qualifications equal to hers or not as fine, promoted to positions above her.

This account is again fictional but again representative. Typically, the academic woman is not promoted at a rate equal to that of her male colleague. "The national makeup of college and university faculties by rank is 21.6 percent professors, 20.7 percent associate professors, 28.3 percent assistant professors, and 19.9 percent instructors. If one assumes that this distribution is a reasonable facsimile of the way the ranks should be divided among a given faculty, the percentages of women who hold positions at every level except assistant professor are quite discrepant."[40] Connecticut College is a case in point. There, at each academic rank, women were more likely than men to have the doctorate when appointed, yet they had to wait longer before being promoted to the next rank than men.[41] Alice Rossi studied 188 major departments of sociology across the country. This is the academic breakdown that she found:

Women formed: 30 percent of the doctoral candidates
            27 percent of the full-time instructors
            14 percent of the assistant professors
            9 percent of the associate professors
            4 percent of the full professors
            less than 1 percent of the deparment chairmen.[42]

The field of sociology is not special. This pattern of women swelling the ranks of the lower academic levels is a typical one. It has been estimated that 90 percent of the men with doctorates and 20 years of academic experience will have won the title of full professor. For women with identical qualifications, barely half will be full professors.[43]

In administration, too, women are missing at the top. In a recent analysis of top administrative positions in universities, researchers found that in their sample, 100 percent of the presidents, 97 percent of the graduate deans, 96 percent of the deans of students, 95 percent of the directors of admissions, 86 percent of the registrars and 100 percent of the directors of development were men.[44] Another survey, conducted for the AAUW also notes the very conspicuous absence of women as administrative leaders.[45]

TABLE 3. Women in College Administration (1967–1970)

Position	Coed schools (376)			Women's colleges only (59)		
	% Men 3 years	% Women 2–3 years	Total responses	% Men 3 years	% Women 2–3 years	Total responses
President	94.5	4.7	366	50.0	46.6	56
Vice President	97.1	1.6	246	69.0	17.3	29
Director of Development	97.1	1.8	314	86.0	6.0	50
Business Manager	93.0	4.9	362	66.1	32.2	56
College Physician	81.8	7.0	325	81.8	12.7	55
Director Financial Aid	78.5	14.9	364	21.0	66.7	57
Director Placement	71.8	20.7	355	22.0	72.7	55
Director Counseling	82.0	12.6	273	30.0	66.6	30
Dean of Students	82.2	11.5	343	12.2	82.5	57
Head Librarian	62.7	29.4	368	22.8	61.4	57
Academic Dean	76.0	10.1	359	30.9	61.8	55
Assoc., or Asst. Academic Dean	73.5	11.9	223	32.0	44.0	25
College Counselor	37.7	17.2	265	26.8	51.3	41

SOURCE: *AAUW Journal*, November 1970.

Table 3 summarizes the AAUW study and demonstrates more explicitly the breakdown of males and females in administration and the minor role women generally have in policy making decisions.

Another Do Not Trespass sign is unequal pay for equal work. In one study it was found that there was a clear and decisive gap between male and female professor's salaries. At the three lower ranks of instructor, assistant professor, and associate professor, the gap was $500, whereas at the rank of professor, the disparity was a striking $1,400.[46] It seems that the longer a woman remains in higher education, the greater her rank and her professional experience, the more likely she is to experience economic discrimination. Another group of researchers summarize their findings: "Generally, the woman Ph.D. does the same type of work. . . . But she does it as a slightly lower rank and for an average of about $700 per year less than her male colleagues."[47]

Do Not Trespass signs also emerge more subtly as a result of the academic woman's occupying a disadvantaged position in the communications system of her discipline. It has been found that academic women do not enjoy full colleagial relationships with male faculty members with whom they work,[48] and that these male colleagues, responding to sex status rather than occupational status, deny her experiences that might further her professional development.[49] Moreover, women faculty members are denied easy social access to and communication with publishers and editors, who are usually male, and frequently it is during such social occasions that requests to chair a panel or to write an article or a book are made.[50]

Higher education cannot be left without mentioning bias against women that can be seen very clearly in the intensified microcosm of the Phi Delta Kappa Controversy. Phi Delta Kappa is an honorary society for educators. Consisting of 85,000 members, it is the largest professional fraternity in the world. Despite clamoring from women without and clamoring from some men within (the Harvard chapter has withdrawn from the main body), this organization limits membership to "males of good character." Can it be that Phi Delta Kappa fears the corrupting influence of women on its upstanding young men? One can only speculate in bewilderment at its discriminatory exclusiveness.

This chapter has a personal meaning because it deals with the level of education in which I am involved and touches upon prejudice that I have recently experienced. As a doctoral student with an infant, I went through the frustrating search for a trustworthy babysitter, the hectic rush from daytime classes to home and family responsibilities, and the anger at the 10 o'clock voice on the loudspeaker announcing that the library was closing and that my research for that evening would be terminated. I remember, too vividly, the agonizing job hunting at conventions where my husband, who was also a doctoral student, and I were informed time and time again by various universities: "We'd really like to get both of you, but we have this nepotism policy. . . ." And I remember the conference with our dean when advising on our nepotism problem, he recommended that my husband should get a position in a metropolitan area, and then if I were lucky I might be able to pick something up in a year or two. This advice was proffered at a dissertation nadir, and several despondent weeks went by before I could force myself to begin work on the dissertation again or to feel that it would be worthwhile to finish.

In too many cases discrimination actually does prevent women from finishing. For example, another women who had survived the educational system until she had reached a point where she needed financial assistance to go on, learned too late that the aid was to be denied her because of a policy that prefers men. She summed it up this way, "I feel like I've been operating with my head in a guillotine for about twelve years and the blade finally came down." Policies that cause such stories of frustration and failure must be ended, and the cruel deterrents that discourage the academic woman and too often cause her to drop out must be torn down. Discrimination against women must not be allowed to remain a professionally accepted policy throughout our system of higher education.

In 1959, Caplow and McGee stated in *The Academic Marketplace*, "Women Scholars are not taken seriously and cannot look forward to a normal professional career. . . . Women tend to be discriminated (against) in the academic profession not because they have low prestige but because they are outside the prestige system entirely."[51] An analysis of the present situation shows that the past fourteen years have done little to improve the position of academic women. It is only recently that the women's movement has drawn national attention to the inequities and has begun the encouraging process of change.

RECOMMENDATIONS FOR CHANGE

WE DEMAND: That the right of women to be educated to their full potential equally with men be secured by Federal and State

legislation, eliminating all discrimination and segregation by sex, written and unwritten, at all levels of education, including colleges, graduate and professional schools, loans and fellowships and Federal and State training programs such as the job corps.
National Organization for Women Bill of Rights, adopted at NOW's first national conference, Washington, D.C., 1967.[52]

In education, in marriage, in everything, disappointment is the lot of women. It shall be the business of my life to deepen this disappointment in every woman's heart until she bow down to it no longer.

Lucy Stone, 1855

There is a developing awareness among women on campuses across the country of the prejudice that is encompassing and suffocating them; along with this realization there is anger, hostility, a new sense of pride, and a demand for change.

Colleges and universities are in key positions to bring redress to long standing inequities against women. According to Audrey Cohen, creator and President of the New College for Human Services in New York City, there are three major areas in higher education in which change must come about:

1. Policy and structural changes to promote increased involvement of women in academic life at all levels and in all fields.
2. Program and service changes to facilitate life on campus for women, including provision of child care facilities on campus and campus health services for women.
3. Academic changes, including the institution of courses or major programs in female studies.[53]

Policy and structural changes

This category encompasses the need for equality in the criteria used in policies for admission and financial aid. Adjustments and tamperings to insure that each freshman class will have more places for men than for women must no longer be tolerated. One result may be that in institutions now heavily male there will be an equal number of women or perhaps even more women than men in classes. Academic quality and talent—not gender—must be the criteria on which admission is based.

Also included in this category is the need for greater flexibility and freedom in residence requirements. The in loco parentis attitude toward college women—restricting them to dormitories where they are locked up during the night hours—not only restrains women more severely than men and causes them greater expense, but also denies them the responsibilities of adulthood. It is another manifestation of the reprehensible double standard.

Staffing patterns should be equitable, and this includes, as reform begins, an intensive search for competent females. Every effort must be made to appoint qualified women to faculty and administrative positions and to university governing boards. This effort may entail establishing special recruiting committees to hire competent women. When equality of opportunity is a reality in our institutions, such compensatory actions will not be necessary. In the meantime, schools of higher education must concentrate on providing, among other benefits, strong and positive female role models for graduate and undergraduate women. Nepotism rules, which almost always harm the female member of a married couple, must be rescinded. Employment interviewers should no more ask about a female's marital or child bearing plans than they should ask a male applicant whether he intends to have a heart attack in the near future. Once hired, women should receive equal pay for equal rank and be promoted on an equal basis with male faculty members.

Continuing education for mature women must be facilitated by a variety of structural changes. Every effort must be made so that women do not have to choose between education and family, but, as men can, have their share of both worlds.

Students should have the ability to matriculate on a part-time basis and flexibility to transfer without excessive credit loss. Moreover, the university, instead of becoming a night-time ghost town, or at best, the scene of a limited number of course offerings, could be transformed into a vital learning and resource center during the evening hours. Upon entering this university resource center, a student would be offered a wide variety of evening courses as well as audiotapes and videotapes of daytime lectures and presentations. There should also be easily accessible cassette tapes, films, and programmed materials, on a variety of topics to help students attain course credits in independent study and learning contract arrangements.

An approach to learning called competency based education might be particularly helpful in providing continuing education for women. In this approach, objectives are clearly spelled out and shown to students so that they know from the beginning the competencies they are expected to reach. There are a variety of learning opportunities that can be taken to reach each objective, and typically, classroom attendance is but one way to satisfy each objective.

Other ways the university could provide continuing education would be to increase the number and variety of correspondence offerings and to give credit for life experiences. For example, in a course in early childhood, it would be irrational for the instructor to assume that a woman who has raised six children knows no more about the subject than a nineteen year-old sophomore whose experience with infants is limited—and who in fact may not have been near a baby in years.

Across the country there are a growing number of experimental programs that provide continuing educational opportunities for women. Among the earliest and best known of these is a facility organized at the University of Minnesota specifically committed to making the resources of the university more useful to adult women. Now called the Minnesota Planning and Counseling Center for Women, it highlights individual counseling and informational services for women at all levels of education, scholarship aid for adult women, nursery facilities, and job placement services.[54]

Another program called Project SELF has been initiated by the Continuing Education Program of the University of Massachusetts. In Project SELF, women who have left school at various points during their education and for a variety of reasons are given an opportunity to begin again and even change the direction of their professional or personal inclinations. This is an important innovation both for the woman who has devoted herself to childrearing for a number of years and needs to step back into the world and to the high school dropout who has new hopes that her world can open up.

Program and service changes

Women will be better able to pursue studies and academic careers on the same basis as men when child care facilities are made available at universities. Such child care centers would not only free women to live richer lives and participate more fully in professional and community activities, but also could be of profound benefit to children. Rapidly accumulating evidence indicates that the years of early childhood are crucial in the impact they have on later intellectual and psychological development. These facilities should not be mere baby-sitting centers. Rather, staffed by competent personnel, equipped with an abundance of toys and materials, perhaps operated in conjunction with departments of psychology and education, they could play a vital role in encouraging the child's full intellectual and emotional development—including his or her attitudes toward sex stereotypes.

These facilities, offering maximum flexibility in hours of operation and in ages of the children admitted, should be controlled by the parents themselves. Some universities might wish to go further and experiment with situations similar to the kibbutz of Israel: Parental visiting would be done after work and on weekends, and daily care would be carried out within the child care facility. Such a full-time service would indeed enable women to pursue studies and careers on a more equitable basis with men.

University Health Services should provide as full and complete care of women as of men. This means making a gynecologist and an obstetrician available, dispensing birth control information and contraceptives, providing prenatal care, and taking a realistic stand on abortion and treatment of venereal disease. The following is an article that was recently published in the newspaper of a large university:

Pregnancy—how to cope

Few women talk about it, but it's a common problem. On a campus the size of the University of Massachusetts, many women will think they may be pregnant in a space as short as a week.

Many times it's a false alarm. Psychological factors (a low grade, a roommate problem) and some physical problems unrelated to pregnancy can delay a woman's menstrual period. Before you deal with a pregnancy you may not want, be sure. A simple urine test for pregnancy becomes effective six weeks after the first day of your last menstrual period. . . .

If you are fairly certain that you are pregnant, and have any idea that you might want to have the pregnancy terminated, have your pregnancy test as soon as it is effective. Do not be content to wait if your doctor tells you to "wait a couple of more weeks and see if you get your next period." If you don't want to be pregnant, it's better to be pregnant a short time than a long time.

If you are pregnant and you've had your test at the infirmary, chances are that a doctor there has already referred you to one of the two organizations that can inform you of all the legal alternatives—from having the child and raising it yourself, to legal termination of your pregnancy. The decision is up to you. . . .

A word about being afraid to ask for birth control or help with a problem pregnancy: don't be, it's no disgrace to admit that you're a sexual being or that you're pregnant.

There are other articles similar to this one appearing in campus newspapers across the country. In their direct and candid presentation, they reflect a significant change of attitude among college students, and they form a collective mandate for university health services to meet changing student needs. Where there are laws that make this difficult, educators and medical consultants should lend their support to bring pressure against these laws and to change them.

Academic changes

Sex bias in the curriculum is being challenged, and one of the most exciting results is the concept of women's studies. Shelia Tobias has defined women's studies as the "intellectual examination of the absence of women from history; the fresh look in a non-freudian way at the social psychology of women; in the study of women in literature and the images of women in the Arts; the economic and legal history of the family and speculations about androgeny defined as societies, utopian, primitive, or revolutionary, where sex differences have been minimized."[55]

According to Florence Howe and Carole Ahlum, "Women's studies as a curricular mode is part of a broad spectrum of developing interdisciplinary studies. In particular, it is related to ethnic studies in its focus on the history, culture, and status of a social group. . . . The immediate justification for women's studies is the traditional male-dominated curriculum."[56]

In 1970, San Diego State College approved a proposal to implement a program in women's studies. It was the nation's first. Growing out of one of the small "rap groups" of San Diego Women's Liberation, the idea was at first opposed by an overwhelming number of administrators and faculty. When the San Diego program was finally implemented, it consisted of ten courses: Socialization Process of Women, Self-Actualization of Women, Contemporary Issues in the Liberation of Women, Women in History, Women in Education, Women in Comparative Cultures, Women under Various Economic and Political Systems, and Field Experience.[57]

Since this initiation in 1970, courses have mushroomed on campuses throughout the country. Only a year later there were 610 courses and 15 women's studies programs, and there is every indication that more and more courses are developing. One of the most unique and encouraging aspects of this rapid growth is the willingness of instructors to share teaching strategies, syllabi, and bibliographies. One hundred and thirty-seven course syllabi have been published in Female Studies I, II, and III (Tobias, 1970; Howe, 1970; Howe & Ahlum, 1971), eleven essays have been published in Female Studies II, and IV (Howe 1970, Showalter and Ohman, 1971) and another group of fifteen essays will be published in 1972 as Female Studies V.[58]

As an extremely important aspect of a women's studies program, or in fact, of any university program, there must be an intensive effort to encourage research on all topics concerning women. There is a dearth of information in so many areas, but for educators there is a particular need to investigate how female students can be helped to reach their fullest potential. What, for example, is the effect of male role models in the early grades and female role models in higher education? What changes are there in attitude and ability after students have participated in a women's studies program, and what changes in attitude and in physical ability take place after women participate in an integrated physical education program with challenging requirements and top notch facilities? Do counselors and teachers who have participated in consciousness raising sessions and are committed to a nonsexist perspective have a different effect on students than counselors and teachers who have not undergone such experiences and are not committed to this perspective? Special research institutes should be established at selected universities with a majority of the researchers female, for they will better know the questions that need asking and will be able to interpret the findings with increased understanding.

Many of the recommendations we have suggested are not only becoming a concern of conscience but of the courts as well. The Department of Health, Education and Welfare is demanding that colleges and universities stop discrimination against women or under Executive Order 11246, lose all federal contracts. The Women's Equity Action League (WEAL), a Washington-based group, has been prodding HEW to make sure that the sex discrimination provisions of the executive order will not collect dust. WEAL has presented HEW with hundreds of complaints from college campuses and has achieved some very real improvements—although many feel that the actions of HEW are too cumbersome and slow.

Over a hundred years ago, Henrik Ibsen wrote *The Doll's House*. In this play Nora rejects dependency and all assumptions that she needs to be taken care of and provided for by her husband. At one point, Helmer says to his wife, "Before all else you are a wife and mother." She replies, "That I no longer believe. I believe that before

all else I am a human being, or at least I should try to become one."
Higher education is changing and the campus is growing into a place
where that goal can be reached and where women will be able to
actualize their inherent potential.

For the most part we have presented a negative and a depressing
picture of women's opportunities in the male university. We feel that,
unfortunately, it is accurate, but like any picture—only for the moment. It is the university that offers the most hope for change—the
explosive growth of women's studies courses; the caucuses and committees of women starting and growing and expanding throughout
higher education; the hundreds of affirmative action cases initiated by
HEW; the increased interest in hiring women for teaching and administrative positions; and the involvement and concern about the
role of women by both males and females—that is beginning to per-
meate every aspect of university life.

All these very real harbingers of change make us hopeful and op-
timistic that a futuristic scenario of higher education will include
representative numbers of men and women as teachers and administrators; students of both sexes with aspirations to become engineers
or lawyers, doctors or writers, artists or political leaders; a nonsexist
curriculum concerned with both mankind and womankind; greater
flexibility in policy and structure allowing for varying life styles; and
fine, well-equipped day care centers where fathers and mothers,
faculty and students may go during breaks between classes to play
with, care for, and enjoy their children. Most importantly, there will
be a new norm of equality and a new spirit of honesty and openness
on the campus as women and men of all races and ethnic groups
relate to one another—without games of pretended inferiority and
superiority—humanely and with dignity.

NOTES

[1]Quoted in "Revolution II: Thinking Female," *College and University
Business*, 48, no. 2 (February 1970), 70.

[2]Quoted in Ruth Oltman, "The Evolving Role of the Women's Liberation Movement in Higher Education," paper presented at the American
Association of University Women, Chicago, Illinois, March 1971, Ed
049, 489.

[3]This summary is based on the work of Walter M. Matthews, "The
Development of Sexism in American Education," paper presented at the
American Educational Research Association, Chicago, Illinois, April 1972.

[4]Marguerite Johnson, "Situation Report: College Education," *Time*, 99,
no. 12 (20 March 1972), p. 91.

[5]Elaine Walster, Anne Creary, and Margaret Clifford, "The Effect of Race and Sex on College Admission," *Sociology of Education, 44,* no. 2 (1971), 237–244.

[6]Material presented by Bernice Sandler for the record to the Committee on the Judiciary, House of Representatives, 92nd cong., Hearings on Equal Rights for Men and Women, 31 March 1971.

[7]Johnson, *op. cit.*

[8]*The Chronicle of Higher Education, 6* (October 1971), p. 2.

[9]Sandler, *op. cit.*

[10]Ruth Oltman, "Campus 1970—Where Do Women Stand?"—*American Association of University Women Journal, 64,* no. 2 (November 1970) 14–15.

[11]Sandra Acker Husbands, "Women's Place in Higher Education?" *School Review, 80,* no. 2 (February 1972), 261–274, in reference to William Eobe, "Student Integration and Departmental Cohesiveness in American Graduate Schools," Ph.D. diss., University of Chicago, 1961.

[12]*Ibid.,* in reference to Kenneth Feldman and Theodore Newcomb, "The Impact of College on Students," San Francisco, Jossey Bass, 1969, pp. 107–108.

[13]Sandler, *op. cit.*

[14]Oltman, "Campus 1970—Where Do Women Stand?" *op. cit.*

[15]Husbands, *op. cit.,* in reference to Sandra Tangri, "Role Innovation in Occupational Choice Among College Women," Ph.D. diss., University of Michigan, 1969.

[16]Anne Sutherland Harris, "The Second Sex in Academe," *American Association of University Professors Bulletin, 56,* no. 3 (September 1970), p. 292. Reprinted by permission.

[17]Jane Gould and Abby Pagans, "Sex Discrimination and Achievement," *Journal of The National Association of Women Deans and Counselors, 35,* no. 2 (Winter 1972), 74–82.

[18]Husbands, *op. cit*

[19]Doris Pullen, "The Educational Establishment: Wasted Women," in Mary Lou Thompson, ed., *Voices of the New Feminism,* Boston, Beacon Press, 1970, pp. 135–155.

[20]Kate Millet *et al., Token Learning: A Study of Women's Higher Education in America,* New York, National Organization for Women, 1968, pp. 5–7.

[21]Pullen, *op. cit.,* p. 125.

[22]Sandler, *op. cit.*

[23]*Ibid.*

[24]Husbands, *op. cit.,* in reference to Alexander Astin and Robert Panos, *The Educational and Vocational Development of College Students,* Washington, D.C., American Council on Education, 1969, p. 51.

[25]Matinna Horner, "Woman's Will to Fail," *Psychology Today, 3,* no. 6 (1969).

[26]Philip Goldberg, "Are Women Prejudicial Against Women?" *Transaction, 5* (April 1968), pp. 28–30.

27G. J. Pheterson, S. B. Keisler, and P. A. Goldberg, "Evaluation of the Performance of Women as a Function of Their Set, Achievement, and Personal History," *Journal of Personality and Social Psychology, 19* (1971), 114–118.

28Jean Wells and Harriet Magruder, "Education Programs for Mature Women," *Education Digest, 37*, no. 5 (1972), 42–45.

29Quoted in Carol Le Fevre, "The Mature Woman as Graduate Student," *School Review, 80*, no. 2 (1972), 281–297. Reprinted by permission of the University of Chicago Press.

30Oltman, "Campus 1970—Where Do Women Stand?" *op. cit.*

31Pullen, *op. cit.*

32Lora Robinson, "The Status of Academic Women," ERIC Clearinghouse on Higher Education, Washington, D.C., April, 1971, Ed 048, 523, in reference to Linda Fidell, "Empirical Verification of Sex Discrimination in Hiring Practices in Psychology," *American Psychologist, 25* (December 1970), 1094–1098.

33*Ibid.* in reference to Jean Henderson, "Women As College Teachers," Ph.D. diss., University of Michigan, 1967.

34Lawrence Simpson, "Attitudes of Higher Education Agents Toward Academic Women," Ph.D. diss., Pennsylvania State University, 1968.

35Facts About Women in Education, prepared by Women's Equity Action League, Cleveland, Ohio. Can be obtained from WEAL, 1253 4th St. S.W., Washington, D.C.

36Sandler, *op. cit.*

37*Ibid.*

38Pullen, *op. cit.*, pp. 120–121.

39Harris, *op. cit.*

40Robinson, *op. cit.*, p. 4.

41*Ibid.*, p. 4.

42Alice Rossi as quoted in Sandler, *op. cit.*

43*Ibid.*

44Edith Painter, "Women: The Last of the Discriminated," *Journal of National Association of Women Deans and Counselors, 34*, no. 1 (1971), 50–62.

45Oltman, "Campus 1970—Where Do Women Stand?" *op. cit.*, pp. 14–15.

46Michael LaSorte, "Academic Women's Salaries: Equal Pay for Equal Work?", *Journal of Higher Education, 42*, no. 4 (April 1971), 265–278.

47Robinson, *op. cit.* quoting James Simon, Simon Clark, and Kathleen Galway, "The Woman Ph.D.: A Recent Profile," *Social Problems, 15* (Fall 1967), 221–236.

48Husbands, *op. cit.* in reference to Jessie Bernard, *Academic Women*, University Park, Pennsylvania, State University Press, 1964, pp. 59–60, 80, 83.

49*Ibid.* in reference to Cynthia Epstein, *Woman's Place: Options and Limits in Professional Careers*, Berkeley, University of California Press, 1970.

[50]Beatrice Dinerman, "Sex Discrimination in Academia," *Journal of Higher Education*, 42, no. 4 (1971), 253–264.

[51]Theodore Caplow and Reece J. McGee. *The Academic Marketplace*, Garden City, N.Y., Doubleday, Anchor Books, 1958, as quoted in Robinson, *op. cit.*

[52]Quoted in Robin Morgan, ed., *Sisterhood Is Powerful*, New York, Random House (Vintage), 1970, p. 513.

[53]Audrey Cohen, "Women and Higher Education: Recommendations for Change," *Phi Delta Kappan*, 53, no. 3 (November 1972), p. 166.

[54]Jean Wells and Harriet Magruder, "Education Programs for Mature Women," *The Education Digest*, 37, no. 5 (January 1972), 42–45.

[55]Shelia Tobias, "Female Studies: Its Origins, Its Organization and Prospect," a paper distributed at the Modern Language Association, 1970, New York City.

[56]Florence Howe and Carole Ahlum, *Academic Women on the Move*, Alice Rossi, ed., New York, Russell Sage, 1973.

[57]Roberta Salper, "The Theory and Practice of Women's Studies," *Edcentric*, 3, no. 7 (1971), p. 5.

[58]Howe and Ahlum, *op. cit.*

8
The anatomy of change: a positive approach for educators

*Dear, Dear! How queer everything is today! And yesterday
things went on just as usual. I wonder if I've been changed
in the night? Let me think: was I the same when I got up
this morning? I almost think I can remember feeling a little
different. But if I'm not the same, the next question is, "Who
in the world am I?" Ah, that's the great puzzle.*

> *Lewis Carroll*
> Alice's Adventures in Wonderland[1]

The confusion of Alice during the early moments of her trip
through Wonderland also expresses the strange feelings, the
disorientation we experience, males and females, as we come to
recognize the depth to which the only culture we have known
has distorted our perspective and growth. Often, after the first
immersions into the research material describing the perpetuation
of sexism in our society, it is as though our minds had been
stripped of a very fine protective layer. Every cell becomes a
superconductor and amplifier of ideas and situations in which
discrimination exists. The world never looks quite the same again.

But it is our conviction that this is just the first step and that
the next steps will lead to change. The overall change in cultural
values can only come about satisfactorily if the most important

of all our institutions, the institution of education, understands the need to build toward a nonbiased school system.

There is a great deal that is valuable and to be respected in our educational system. This must be preserved. And foremost among that which is good is flexibility, a flexibility that will, in fact, allow for alterations. Positive action can begin right away, leaving intact that which is valuable and attacking that which is bad.

It is often said that our schools reflect our society, that the values that the community or the country accept are those values that are taught in schools. Society has begun to establish some of the needed reforms. Educators have a choice—to wait for the pressure of social change to be exerted on them or to take the initiative. Rather than mirror social values, educators have the option and we believe, the responsibility to lead the way. And we anticipate that, as they become aware of the harmfulness of sexism, they will be not only willing but anxious to do so. After all, it is nothing less than justice, freedom, and equality of opportunity that are in question.

Awareness that there is a problem is the first step. In this we hope we have provided sufficient evidence of how society and schools fail to serve both sexes equally well. The main objective of education, stated in countless ways but nonetheless generally agreed upon, is to provide all children with maximum opportunity to enrich their own lives and the life of their community and country. Ralph Tyler, director emeritus of the Center for Advanced Study in the Behavioral Sciences, has focused on the needs of our postindustrial society. He points out that only 5 percent of our labor force is unskilled and that during just one generation employment opportunity in technical, professional, managerial, and service occupations has increased more than 100 percent. Identifying potential talents and furnishing them with an opportunity to develop through education is the means of satisfying these news needs. To do so, says Dr. Tyler, "schools can be encouraged to help *all students* learn rather than to serve primarily in screening and sorting [italics mine]."

Dr. Tyler goes on to indicate that it is against the postindustrial background that efforts to assess school performance must be viewed. In this context he states: "From the standpoint of an individual student, *the criterion of an educational institution is one in which the student gains a wider range of alternatives in his [or her] life choices with each increment of education* [italics mine]." Moreover, the student is "aided to find new doors rather than being trained ever more narrowly to fit into a specific societal niche."[2] It is not intrinsic to the design of these new doors that they discriminate according to sex.

However, like Alice in Wonderland, the first time we explore the room, the doors may all be locked and the key we find may not fit. When we finally manage to open a door, we may have to alter in size or shape (or mind set) to get through the passageway. But that is when the adventure really begins, and it will be worth every effort.

Having established that sexism is bad and that it should be eradicated, we must provide concepts and a program which will accomplish the goal of a nonsexist school system. We reinforce our devotion to this task with the realization that a generation of children educated with freedom from this discrimination will become the first generation of adults in a more healthy society.

As adults, especially educators, there are several general recommendations that must be heeded: We must develop a new sensitivity to our interactions with and our reactions to children of all ages and adults. Rather like a self-disciplinary game of "freeze," we must recognize when we are reacting according to typical sex stereotypes or biases and *stop* ourselves. Our sex-based attitudes and expectations must be jettisoned, and although at first the conscious effort to overcome these prejudices may require rethinking our actions and redoubling our efforts, we can look forward to eventually breaking some of our own sexist habits and limitations. Our reward will come, not only in observing a population of young people liberated from conventional boundaries but also in discovering new freedom for ourselves.

If we had millions of dollars to spend on new workbooks, texts, and nonfiction for our schools, we still would not find the books we need for teaching without prejudice. Publishers are becoming aware of pressure for nonsexist books, and as individuals we can contribute to keeping the pressure on until we find biased books satisfactorily replaced by those free from bias. When a member of the Committee to Eliminate Sexual Discrimination in the Public Schools of Ann Arbor, Michigan, questioned the publishers of a new math book for elementary schools about the bias they display, she received a reply from the editor-in-chief. It read in part:

> I'm afraid I will have to agree with your general remarks about the illustrations on the pages you cite. . . . I am sure this happened quite unintentionally and unconsciously, though that may merely tend to confirm how deep and instinctive such stereotypes go. . . .
> I would also agree that textbook companies have a particularly great responsibility to avoid stereotyping of any kind, just as we now attempt to do in depicting members of minority groups, and that we

should also endeavor to provide all children with the most positive self-image that we can. In line with your suggestion, I will ask our authors and editors to see if the pages you list can be changed in the next printing of the book. . . .[3]

This is encouraging, and many such queries have received similar reactions that indicate that publishers are examining their offerings with this new dimension in mind. Certainly it helps to refuse to buy the worst offenders, and certainly for economic reasons if none other, publishers will be glad to find a new market opening up.

However, until the new books are available, we must conscientiously analyze the materials we have for teaching. We must offer students interpretive alternatives and try to provide supplementary material. When we are using biased books, we can point out those biases and initiate discussions about them. Supplementary material in monographs and magazines if not books is being produced at a tremendous rate.

We must also inform ourselves and others of some of the legal resources at hand to combat sexism. Feminists have been asked why it took so long after the women's movement gained substantial strength for movement women to direct their attention to the perpetuation of sexism in elementary and secondary school education. One answer is that attention was concentrated in the beginning on such overt discriminations as salary and promotional inequities. In many ways these problems are more tangible, and the legal weapons to fight them have been improving. However it should be noted that such giant steps as the Equal Rights Amendment to the Constitution, which is currently awaiting ratification, set the bold direction for equality. The specifics of its application—that is, how it will work for individuals—will be determined by litigation. Similarly, other new laws that will be mentioned await the tests of their strengths and weaknesses in court.

Although the federal laws which did include a sex discrimination ban (the Civil Rights Act of 1964 and the Equal Pay Act of 1963) did not include teachers and school administrators, many educators who have felt discriminated against because of their sex were able to find legal backing in state legislation or through educational organizations. And if, for example, a school system employs more than fifty people and receives $50,000 or more in federal funds, that school must comply with the federal contracts regulations in regard to hiring, promotions, salaries, fringe benefits, supplementals, tenure, and maternity leave policy. These regulations, prohibiting discrimination based on sex, were set out by an executive order of President Lyndon Johnson that became effective in 1968. That order could, however, be repealed at the discretion of succeeding presidents.[4]

In the summer of 1972 further recourse against discrimination was written into the Education Amendments (Public Law 92–318) extending coverage of the Equal Pay Act, part of the Fair Labor Standards Act (FLSA) to academic administrative personnel and teachers in elementary and secondary schools. According to Richard J. Grunewald, one of the people responsible for administering the FLSA, "One of our important objectives is to eliminate discriminatory wage practices based on sex." There is a further provision in the 1972 Education Act that "no person in the United States shall, on the basis of sex, be excluded from participation in, be denied the benefits of, or be subjected to discrimination under any education program or activity receiving Federal financial assistance." This covers public or private preschool, elementary, and secondary schools and institutions of vocational, professional, and higher education. Moreover, in 1972 the Equal Employment Opportunity coverage of the Civil Rights Act of 1964 was amended to include employees of public and private institutions.[5]

What is important to note is this: While laws are taking shape and being defined, educators do have more power than they may realize when it comes to fighting sex bias. And the more frequently discrimination is successfully challenged, the more incisive those laws against it should become. Also, as such legal actions take place they will have the additional effect, by their implications at least, of making inroads into the amorphous hidden curriculum.

As for policies that are discriminatory toward students, some states also have laws that insist that no student, regardless of sex, shall be deprived of the opportunity to take advantage of all the benefits of a public school:

Dear Miss Kocik:
We have investigated the problem of sex discrimination in the course selection at Greenfield High School, both with regard to the Health Education course and the shop courses. As a result, I am assured by the Superintendent of Schools . . . that you are not obliged to select the Health Education course if you do not wish to, and that you may sign up for a shop course if you do wish to. . . . Needless to say, if you run up against some kind of difficulty, you should contact me immediately.

This letter, signed by David Matz, chairman of a chapter of the Civil Liberties Union of Massachusetts, was written to a high school sophomore who, with support and direction from the women's movement, had taken her complaint to the CLU. The summer of that same year (1971) the Massachusetts legislature had passed a law stating that schools could not discriminate on the basis of sex, and when the school that Judy Kocik attended was made aware of the law, their policy was changed without litigation.[6]

Sensitivity, good books, and real equality of opportunity and reward are the most general of recommendations to all concerned about the process of education. But even as we consider students and teachers, elementary, secondary, and schools of higher education, we must keep in mind that in each of our categories we are talking about individuals, people from many different backgrounds, and schools in many different environments, with a variety of problems. Across-the-board recommendations must be tailored to fit special situations. This was made clear by the principal of one inner-city elementary school. He told us, in confidence, "Our playgrounds are segregated and our lunch lines are, too. But we have to do this because parents complained about the kinds of things which were going on." He was referring, rather ambiguously, to the fact that the children were uninhibited in their sex play and exploration. Perhaps there are some instances in which this kind of segregation seems valid as a temporary, emergency measure. But it should certainly last no longer than is absolutely necessary, while some of the deeper problems are being sorted out.

Among these problems is that a culture develops attitudes in its young people and then blushes when it sees young people mimic what they have learned. These "misbehaving" children had simply not yet learned the difference between public and private "misbehavior." What they had successfully assimilated was the attitude of adults who consider females little more than sex objects, and they were acting accordingly. The degree to which this attitude manifests itself may vary in different socioeconomic or ethnic environments. If, however, all children are taught in school to respect the talents and qualities of people as individuals, they will learn to live and work together as equals, and their interest in the opposite sex is likely to change into more desirable relationships. In an elementary school nearby, for example, there is a nine-year-old girl of unsuppressable energy and ambition. She insists on joining the boys in kickball and baseball and she is as skilled as the best of her male colleagues. Boys respect her; they would not dream of pinching or demeaning her because she is a girl. In fact, the mother of one of her male classmates told us that her son admires this girl tremendously and wishes he could relate to all girls similarly. It is only the other young girls who are unsure how to relate to this "tomboy." Most of them would like to have the same freedom she has.

An analogous problem is that encountered by male teachers or administrators. An assistant superintendent of schools, recalling when he went into teaching, described the first lessons that he was given, and they were all "don'ts": Don't take a little girl to the bathroom. Don't take a sick girl home from school. Don't leave the door closed when you are talking to a girl. And these don'ts were backed up with horror stories about male teachers whose careers had been ruined because of intimations of sexual seduction. Here are more signs of a basic sickness in our society, and to reiterate, if we can cure the disease as we educate our children, then such unhealthy prohibitions will be unnecessary.

PRESCHOOL THROUGH ELEMENTARY SCHOOL

From the moment young children enter any social or learning situation, be it a child care center or a play group or the first grade, they should be given every opportunity to see themselves as individuals relating to other individuals, rather than as boys or girls relating to members of the same or the opposite sex. Not that sex differences do not exist, it is just that they must be put into the proper perspective as one of the small contributions to a person's individuality.

There is some question as to whether there will be more or fewer sex-based restrictions on children in a traditional school setting as compared to an innovative one. For example, part of the structure of traditional schools includes the investment of great authority in the teacher as she conducts subject-oriented classes. If in such a situation, the teacher has assumed responsibility for dispelling the limitations of sex stereotyping, will she be especially effective in providing ideas and materials specifically designed to overcome such stereotyping? In innovative or open schools, on the other hand, the stress is on the freedom of the individual's development, and the teacher is a facilitator rather than an authoritative director. Can we assume that the natural outcome, even without teacher intervention, will be to reflect the truth that stereotypical roles are not innate but rather imposed by cultural restrictions? Will students with greater freedom choose to reject stereotypical roles? Or will the hidden curriculum in these schools be just as pervasive if not more so than in other schools? We can only speculate at this point, because there has nowhere been the kind of commitment that would allow us to gauge the relative success of one system or another.

There has, however, been some investigation of the attitudes of students who are currently attending schools that range along the "traditional-modern continuum." Patricia Minuchin, an educational psychologist, has been particularly interested in the relationship between educational environments and cognitive and personality development. She conducted a study of nine-year-old, fourth-grade, middle-class, urban children in four schools. Each school occupied a different place along the continuum. In reference to sex role assumptions, expectations, and concept, Minuchin and her colleagues found that girls in "modern" schools "departed most from the conventional expectations and patterns." She points out, however, that those girls were also coming from families with less restrictive attitudes and that it is difficult to "separate clearly the reflective effects of school and home."[7]

But there is no doubt that the socializing influence of schools is great. Because of that all classrooms—from traditional and self-contained to innovative and integrated—should allow no discrimination according to sex. Children should be encouraged to work and play together, and they should be further stimulated to try and test their skills in categories that they may have already learned to exclude. The intervention and encouragement of an adult, a well-placed comment, can do much to extend the horizons and enhance the self-esteem of young people.

In simple, day-to-day activities in elementary school, we can begin to abolish sexism by avoiding any situation in which activities are divided by sex. Children should not be lined up by sex to go out to recess, to lunch, or to meet the school bus. There are few gestures as obscene as punishing a boy by making him sit with the girls, and yet it often happens. A class should not be greeted with "Good morning, girls and boys" (any more than "blacks and whites"), when it can be addressed with "Good morning, children." No classroom activity should be divided into competitive male and female groupings, whether a spelling bee, a debating team, or a race to solve math problems. (In fact, this kind of competition in learning is usually undesirable. For if we want children, as individuals, to develop their individual potential, we do not want them to judge their accomplishments in competition with others.)

To balance the above restrictions, it is important to conscientiously open up the aspirations and understanding of all children. It may cause discomfort when a small boy is first invited to play the role of a nurse or a young girl is asked to be the general of a Civil War army, but eventually both will begin to understand and reject limitations placed on their own and each other's aspirations.

The enjoyable ways children learn can be even more productive if, at the same time the curriculum is taught, the hidden curriculum is unwound and the implicit and insidious sexism therein is replaced with a strong nonsexist bias. If this is questioned for its compensatory nature, it is admittedly so—for it will require enormous effort to overcome the established pattern.

■ In a kindergarten a boy and girl were busy at the workbench hammering nails. When the teacher came over, he patted the little boy on the head and said, "That's it, give it another whack." He was about to say to the little girl, "Here, let me give you a hand," but he stopped himself and instead said, "Good work, keep at it." The message he had imparted to the boy was "You can do it," and the message he almost automatically gave the girl was "You need help." By his fortunate second thought, he was able to give the same message of self-reliance to both children.

■ An elementary school spent a week on a project called "A Trip to Washington." The entire school participated. By acting out roles, they learned about the process of our government, the history of the United States, national monuments, and since they had to make a bus to catch their airplane to the capital, they learned about transportation. They could, but did not, have a female pilot on the plane and a male steward (although they had a mixed bunch of hijackers who almost succeeded in diverting the plane to Cuba). They did not project a female for President of the United States, nor did they pay much attention to some of the important women in our history. They may have alluded to Martha Washington and Betsy Ross, but they ignored Sojourner Truth and Susan B. Anthony.

■ It was the day of the Christmas program at a small elementary school. A kindergarten teacher was seasonably joyous. She had managed to have deleted from a skit a line about Santa bringing guns for boys and dolls for girls. She mentioned her victory to a parent also committed to the eradication of sex stereotyping in school, and they laughed together at the thought that, next year, Santa Claus might be a female.

■ In a public elementary school, a young girl borrowed a newly published library book that was designed to show that mothers have other jobs besides the conventional ones. The child flipped through

Mommies at Work by Eve Merriam and Beni Montresor when she got home and was unimpressed by the pictures of women repairing radios, directing television plays, looking through giant telescopes, punching tickets on trains, or building enormous bridges.[8] But when she came to the picture of a mother with her head under the hood of a car, she had a strong reaction. "Look, Mommy," she pointed out to her own, " this *proves* women's liberation."

■ The mother of two small boys and a seven-year-old girl was visiting the private, co-educational school her children attend in Brooklyn, New York. "In the kindergarten there were two rooms," she later reported. "The blocks, trucks, and all the doing toys were in one room; the dolls and ornamental things were in another room. I said to my daughter one day, 'Do you have a girls' room and a boys' room?' And Eva said, 'Oh no, the girls are allowed to go into the boys' room, too.' " In September 1970, this mother and about fifteen to twenty others formed a group that they called the Sex Roles Committee. Working with the school they have managed to break through a good deal of the sex role stereotyping that was, albeit unconsciously, perpetuated. Here is one parent's report of the satisfactory results of their efforts: "My son had a doll that he loved a lot and wanted to take to school when he was in kindergarten last year. But he was afraid the girls would tease him. The first day in school this year, he took the doll with him and openly hugged and kissed it." The response of the school's staff to the Sex Roles Committee is also interesting. At first, when approached by the mothers, their reaction was "Who, me?" according to the school director. "But now I think even the most resistant staff member has moved. I think even if people are not ready to be different, they're ready to act differently," she concluded.[9]

In many ways the director's conclusion is evidence for one of our main contentions—*that even if educators are not ready or willing to change their own beliefs about sex roles, they should nevertheless behave in nonsexist ways.* And although we can describe sexism in intellectual or abstract terms, the above are ways in which it was, should, or could be dealt with in real, everyday situations.

Included in the attitudinal shift asked of educators is a purposeful devotion to eradicate hostile aggression, often displayed by competitiveness, in all children. This is obviously one of the most subtle and most difficult dimensions of behavior modification. Underlying it is the moral imperative that our culture cannot survive the rigors of technological advance and sophisticated weaponry until the energy expended on aggression and competition is channeled into positive action in the area of cooperation on a worldwide scale. R. Buckminster Fuller has been discussing this dimension of universal survival by describing our world as the Spaceship Earth hurtling through the universe. He has written:

> *Our innocent, trial-and-error-sustaining nutriment is exhausted. We are faced with an entirely new relationship to the universe. . . . We have discovered that it is highly feasible for all the human passengers aboard Spaceship Earth to enjoy the whole ship without any individual interfering with another and without any individual being advanced at the expense of another, provided that we are not so foolish as to burn up our ship and its operating equipment. . . . Most importantly we have learned that from here on it is success for all or for none. . . .*[10]

These are ideas that can be taught to children, and often in those very terms. Even though there are some who insist that, rather like a computer, man (although not woman) has been irrevocably programmed for aggression, and even though we have no more concrete evidence to disprove their contention than they have evidence that man is machinelike, it is imperative that we gamble on those mechanists being wrong.[11] Consider this in the terms of the wager put forth by Blaise Pascal, a philosopher of the seventeenth century. Pascal, discussing whether God does or does not exist, postulated that, if He does exist and we act as though He doesn't we have all to lose; if He does not exist but we act as though He does, we lose nothing; but if He does exist and we act as though we know He does, then we have all to gain. Revising this postulate in nonsexist terms: We have nothing to lose and all to gain if we believe that aggression is not innate and act as though we believe that children can grow up with their minds set on cooperation and not on competition. This may prove that boys can be, not only as cooperative as girls, but can cooperate with girls.

Before we picture some noncompetitive scenes, we would like to offer a special suggestion. Girls who wear dresses to school do not have the same freedom as those who wear slacks. It is a sign of progress that in many schools, "dress codes" are being reexamined. If, in subtle ways, girls who do wear slacks to school are encouraged, more will follow suit, and this will help alleviate some of the sexual inhibitions and curiosities that tend to limit the activities of females as well as males.

■ A good recess scenario would show girls pushing boys and boys pushing girls on the swings. Rotating softball games where everyone gets a chance at bat and at pitching, until each child manages to hit a ball. And each child is encouraged by all the others to succeed. A relay race that does not match teams but integrates the fastest and the slowest in one race against the most neuter of all adversaries—time.

■ A positive classroom scenario could include the entire class applauding an individual who overcomes a difficulty with his or her math or reading book assignment. And that individual then working with another student with a similar problem. This, too, could be on a continuing, rotating basis. Or a physical education program where children do exercises in body movement and learn folk dances, and partners are matched, not by sex, but by such arbitrary frivolities as the colors in their clothes, the first initial or the third letter in their names.

Of utmost importance in our relations with school children is that we find a variety of ways to stress and reward cooperation while we try to eliminate aggressive competition or impotent docility. And also in this context, we cannot tolerate incidents in which children demean other children, even in such typical exchanges that are so widespread that we tend not to notice them. Such as: "He's a sissy." "She's just a girl."

When children repeat in the classroom the negative judgments that they have already assimilated, an astute educator can use them in a positive learning situation. Carol Ahlum, a young woman who taught in an elementary school, described to us how she coped with one such situation:

We were planning a play for a videotape project and my third grade class was thinking up funny conversations between animals and farmers. A boy suggested that one scene could be a mouse scaring a farmer's wife.

"Why not have the mouse scare the farmer?" I immediately asked.

"No," he replied, "farmers aren't afraid of mice, only farmers' wives are."

I asked why.

"Because all women are afraid of mice," he answered.

I then asked if any of the girls in the class were afraid of mice. They all yelled "NO!"

"See, Glen, we aren't afraid of mice and we're women. But why have you always thought that women are afraid of mice?"

"Because that's what the comic books say."
"Why do you think they show women afraid of mice?"
"Because otherwise, it wouldn't be funny," Glen concluded.

A teacher can also systematically and intelligently berate harmful jingles such as the one that says that litle girls are made of sugar and spice. Teachers and children can, in fact, have fun inventing and substituting positive-image jingles of their own. And in the earliest grades, as children prepare and begin to learn reading, both teachers and students should examine the materials and techniques used, and avoid such confusion as this:

One high school girl recently told her adult-living class about an experience she had as a kindergartner. When she pasted a picture of a man holding a baby on the page of her workbook entitled "Fathers' Jobs," the teacher marked this wrong—even though the girl explained that she had seen her father holding a baby many times.[12]

For the sake of argument, look with your class through the workbooks and texts used in teaching. Count the number of times male figures appear in comparison to females. Even such a simple statistical compilation provides a surprise. Fantasize that you all had come from a distant planet with a unisex population, and your spaceship landed in an elementary school yard. Pretend you then went into an empty classroom and started leafing through a workbook to figure out what kind of culture you had come to. You would easily reach the conclusion that something like 80 percent of its population was male. Pursuing this cultural analysis with more sophistication in looking at the pictures, you would also conclude that the small percentage of females in this population were born with aprons on and had never learned to run, to go anywhere, to do anything (certainly nothing adventurous), and only served by standing and waiting and watching.

The individuals and feminist groups who have been similarly examining the sexism in school texts have persuaded local and state officials to do the same. In Boston, the Commission to Improve the Status of Women, established by Mayor Kevin White in 1970, set up a task force to analyze the books used in the Boston public schools. Both in text and in pictures they found the traditional, that is "the 'passive' orientation of females . . . rather heavily reinforced throughout."[13] In California, a bill was put before the state legislature requiring that the texts used in the public elementary and secondary schools include "accurate portrayals of both men and women in all types of roles, including professional, vocational, and executive."[14] Such actions are going on across the country.

The bitter taste of sex bias in school texts is also reflected in the books stacked in the schools' libraries. *Mommies at Work* is just one small contribution in providing a satisfactory image of females, and many, many more such books are needed. Small presses such as the Feminist Press are trying to bring out new books with positive images for girls. The Feminist Press operates with conviction, as a nonprofit organization, and hopes to encourage female writers, artists, designers, and editors. For educators who have no current alternatives but to use the texts available, the least they should do is pose the question to students: "I wonder why . . . ?" And as the dialogue begins and the old assumptions are questioned, the minds of children will become more open and fertile.

An interesting perspective is provided by Masha Rudman whose course on teaching reading in the School of Education at the University of Massachusetts has for more than two years included an investigation of sex stereotyping in children's literature. She points out that the stress on boys' achievements is often the very purposeful intention of publishers who are aware of the fact that boys seem to have more difficulty learning to read than do girls. "I don't dispute the fact that we do a bad job teaching reading, nor that we hamper boys even more than we hamper girls," she told us, but she feels the entire method of teaching reading needs revision. She would "bombard" students with every variety of printed materials, from newspapers and comic books to canned goods and printed packages, rather than censor materials. She prefers to "use everything," so that students will themselves gain insight and discrimination in their reading. Rudman even suggests as one of many devices providing children with the small stickers used by the women's movement that read, "This Ad is Offensive to Women," and with the development of their own critical judgment, children will learn where those stickers belong. In ways such as these, she would look forward to eliminating such distortions as racism and sexism "and all the other things we hate."

Martha Batten is an inspired teacher who also has a feminist consciousness. Because she has a fine reputation as an educator we interviewed her to find out some of the ways in which she goes about abolishing sexism in her fourth- and fifth-grade classes. "I want to affect kids, not by telling them what to do, or having them do something because I would do it, or would want them to," she said. For that approach she believes, "misuses" the power of a teacher.

Instead, Martha Batten takes advantage of, and even creates, situations in which children can gain new perspectives on themselves and their colleagues. She also talks, not *at*, but *with*, her students a great deal. For example, one day the conversation settled on the subject of what it would be like when the students continue on to high school. Batten described some of her own high school experiences. Then the class went on to discuss "the hell a school dance can be both for the girl who waits around to be invited and for the boy who must suffer the torment or embarrassment of asking. In both cases there is the potential humiliation of rejection."

As an outcome of their discussion her class planned a dance at which there were to be no partners. Anyone who wanted to come simply came (attendance was 100 percent), and anyone who wanted to dance, alone or with a partner, did so. It was great fun and a great success. There was one especially humorous moment when a boy came up and asked Martha Batten to dance, not, as he put it, "because you're a woman, but because you're a teacher." Recalling the incident she laughed and said, "That's another form of discrimination I'll have to deal with."

Believing in the importance of a nonsexist working atmosphere Batten says to her students, "You can sit wherever you want to as long as there are both sexes at the table." Because of such efforts many students themselves have begun to reject baiting and teasing such as "he has a girlfriend," or "she likes you." "Look," Batten has heard a number boys reply defiantly, "this girl is my *friend*." And she recognizes such comments as a direct result of *individuals* working with other *individuals* who share a common interest, be it chemistry, cooking, engineering, or art.

Although Martha Batten feels she still hasn't "found the answer," and is herself continually learning as she teaches, there is substantial evidence that she has hit a responsive note with her students. "In terms of the *vocabulary* of sexist behavior I see great success. Almost all of the students are aware enough to avoid it, at least in the classroom. In terms of changing their behavior I feel varying success." She can count twenty out of one hundred students who have "*really*" been touched, whose "options have been opened up," and there are as many boys as there are girls.

To us a measure of her good working relationship with students was reflected in this: Scheduled for the weekend following our interview was the Amherst, Massachusetts, fair, an annual event that takes place on the town common. Usually its the kind of event at which girls and boys divide camps, with boys throwing water balloons and girls running away. This year several of her students of both sexes asked Martha Batten if she would join them—as a friend.

Educators who feel they have a responsibility to work toward change cannot, of course, work in a vacuum. The single teacher who got one instance of sex bias taken out of the school's Christmas play will take a hundred years to get the system changed if she has no support. The involvement of the community, other educators, administrators, and parents is needed. When individuals are working together for a common purpose, not only can they encourage and support one another, but obviously they are more likely to see their cause recognized.

One woman with enormous courage started by herself and gathered support along the way. Dorin Schumacher, in a monograph called "Changing the School Environment: A Progress Report," describes some of the frustration and sometimes the humiliation she had to undergo in order to make her point. Her point was that even in a "progressive" community where the school is associated with a university school of education, there is blatant discrimination against females. Her first meeting with the assistant principal during which she asked for a small PTA discussion group about sexism got this response: "After all, this school already stands for individual development. There is no prejudice here. Besides, most parents would not want their daughters to have careers." Schumacher risked her own as the battle continued uphill:

Some of the teachers—the males—in the name of the "faculty" challenged the fathers to play a basketball game to raise money for the school. I decided to do an action on my own to draw attention to the attitudes of the school administration and faculty, particularly as it was manifested in the sports program. I signed myself up for the father-teacher basketball game.

When my team showed up for the practice session, I discovered that two of the fathers were professional football players and several of the others had played varsity basketball in college. I played junior varsity basketball one year in high school, girls' rules, of course. I did manage to make a basket during the practice session and no one was more surprised than I.

The week of the big game I underwent a series of personal trials which included Ph.D. orals and I got what felt like the flu. But I *played the big game anyway, wiped out as I was. And my daughter was terrific. She came out and encouraged me saying, "Just try, Mommy, you don't have to get a basket, just try." Several of the mothers and the girl students came up and said, "We know what you're trying to do and we think it's great. You've got a lot of guts." And I was wondering what the hell I was doing out there making a fool of myself and dealing with side issues.*

I never did learn men's basketball rules and I ran around the court feeling as though I was in a Kafka-esque world of confused and jumbled visual impression where everyone understood what to do but me. The next day at school my daughter played baseball with the boys for the first time.

A discussion group and a committee did form at the above school, and the school began to make efforts toward following some of the recommendations of the committee. Once she had put herself forward as a person willing to fight for equality in the school, Dorin Schumacher found support and encouragement. And a good measure of success. For, in July, 1972, as a member of the Joint Task Force on Education in Pennsylvania, she saw the recommendations of their report, *Sexism in Education*, adopted by the state's Secretary of Education. He committed the Department of Education to making the elimination of sexism in education a priority.[15]

A program to eliminate sexism in school cannot be conducted as a one-shot effort to keep some "pressure group" quiet for a while. In one school system visited by a group of feminists who were anxious to see changes made, an official said: "The population flux and the time involved become critical. At one point, in one of our schools, we had a population of two hundred black students. We began to get the wheels rolling for a black studies program and then, by the time we had a full-fledged program ready, the population had shifted and there were only forty black students left." One of the women pointed out to him that, regardless of the potential racial or ethnic shifts that might take place over the next one hundred years, he could rest assured that about 50 percent of the school population would remain female.

When the Holyoke, Massachusetts, school system opened its ears to the rumblings of feminists, it agreed that the concept of sexual equality was one that they would institute on a permanent, far-reaching basis. An interesting possibility that other systems might adopt was the suggestion that the schools' audiovisual resources be used to tape a dialogue among local feminists and educators. This tape would be used for in-service training of teachers, and the educators themselves, after viewing the tapes, could continue the discussion.

Another important step would be to ask parents to speak to the student body about their professions, especially mothers who are professional doctors, lawyers, scientists, politicians, or bus drivers or businesswomen. It would help to counter unhappy stories such as this:

> Last summer . . . my sister was accepted into medical school. Naturally there were congratulations and comments from neighbors, friends, and relatives. After a few days of this, she found her son (age six) and her daughter (age five) crying real tears for no apparent reason. When she at last got to the cause of their grief, she found that they thought if she were going to become a doctor, she would first have to turn into a man and they wouldn't have a mother.[16]

Finally, within the staffing pattern of a school, and this refers to preschool personnel all the way through the highest levels of higher education, an equitable staffing pattern is imperative. All educational institutions need females in the highest administrative positions, otherwise it will remain impossible to persuade girls that they will not necessarily stay at the lowest levels of the professional and economic continuum. Females can hardly unlearn deference to males when they see, at the earliest moments of their education, women teachers continually looking to a man principal for authority. Nor can males overcome the unfortunate impression that it is their destiny to dominate others.

Children have not been tracked and socialized for so long that their destinations are irrevocably set, nor are their options permanently limited. Remembering that the course of history must favor a nonsexist society, consider that those children who are educated into the rigid stereotyping of yesterday are undergoing something that in many industries has been called planned obsolescence. This seems all right to the manufacturers until the customers rebel; but meantime the product suffers. It should not be the purpose of education to build obsolescence into young people.

SECONDARY SCHOOLS

When young people begin their secondary school education, the problems of sex roles and gender identification become, as in the adult world, either painful or rewarding. It is during this period, as we noted in Chapter 6, that females begin to underachieve and often exhibit the will to fail. It is here that the tracks narrow and that the circumspect young woman becomes aware that society does not expect her to do much more than marry and raise a family, or if she must work, to do much more than be satisfied with some of the least

> High school is closer to the core of the American experience than anything else I can think of. . . . We have all been there. While there, we saw nearly every form of justice and injustice, kindness and meanness, intelligence and stupidity which we were likely to encounter in later life.
>
> Kurt Vonnegut, Jr., in *Our Time Is Now*[17]

satisfying jobs. Although we can reiterate most of the basic recommendations for elementary school—desegregating courses and activities (and of course, schools), providing positive role models for females, investigating texts and libraries, in short, widening the options of all young people—all these recommendations take on a new dimension. For now students are becoming increasingly responsible for their own education:

■ In New York City in 1969 Alice de Rivera brought suit against the city to ban the segregation of a vocational school. She succeeded in becoming the first female student at Stuyvesant High School.[18]
■ Three students in New York City went before hearings of the National Commission on Population Growth and the American Future to ask that sex education in high schools include information on contraception as well as provide free contraceptive devices for anyone who wants them. One of the students, a 16-year-old high school woman described what took place in her "hygiene" class when she asked the teacher to discussion contraception:

"The teacher wrote on the blackboard all the methods that she knew. 'What method would you recommend to a 16-year-old girl?' a student asked. 'Sleep with your grandmother,' the teacher replied."
Ten months later, according to the testimony, one of the girls in the class became pregnant.

The young woman who described the incident above was a member of the High School Women's Coalition. This group of several hundred students from New York City high schools has appealed to their city's Board of Education to make birth control information available in secondary schools.[19]

■ Students at a school in Long Island, New York, requested a course about women. Their request was honored—"Women in Society" was offered in the fall semester of 1970-71. The students, including males, talked about sex role socialization in general and in their own lives.

During the first semester the class wrote and produced a musical skit called "You've Come A Long Way, Baby" for fellow students. During the next semester they performed their second skit, "Some Of My Best Friends Are Women," at the New York State Conference on the Social Studies. After their performance the students conducted workshop discussions in which they educated some 100 teachers, curriculum developers, and textbook editors about the value of their course.[20]

But even as students win some of their demands, they lose others. In New Haven, Connecticut, a young woman brought suit against the Connecticut Interscholastic Athletic Conference, Inc., which was prohibiting her from entering in the athletic activities of cross-country running and indoor track. The State Commisisoner of Education informed the court that it would not be in the interest of the state to have girls competing in interscholastic competition. The court agreed, and in its rather incredible opinion, wrote:

The present generation of our younger male population has not become so decadent that boys will experience a thrill in defeating girls in running contests, whether the girls be members of their own team or of an adversary team. It could well be that many boys would feel compelled to forego entering track events if they were required to compete with girls. . . . The mere fact that that crosscountry running and indoor track do not involve bodily contact, a point stressed by the plaintiffs, is not the answer. In the world of sports, there is ever present as a challenge, the psychology to win. With boys vying with girls in cross-country running and indoor track, the challenge to win, and the glory of achievement, at least for many boys would lose incentive and become nullified. Athletic competition builds character in our boys. We do not need that kind of character in our girls, the women of tomorrow, by the conduit of putting them in athletic competition with the opposite sex.[21]

We hardly need comment on such a perversion of ideology, although we can easily recognize that brand of sexism. At this point the question is: What to do about it?

In secondary school athletics we would repeat the point made about elementary school physical education—that both sexes be allowed to develop their skills together, especially stressing the non-competitive aspect of the skill. In swimming, tennis, skiing, and folk dancing, trampoline, or calisthenics, the joy of proficiency, the toning up and appreciation of the body can be emphasized above the desire and anxiety to win. And when it is insisted that competition or rivalry can provide a stimulus for reaching higher levels of proficiency, then the latter should be the most important goal, mindful of the useful cliché—it isn't whether you win or lose that counts; it's how you play the game.

The budget for boys' and girls' athletic programs should be the same, if not synonymous. That is, when there must be separate programs they should at least receive equal funds. Girls should not have to vacate an area when the boys move in, be it the basketball or volleyball courts or the baseball diamond. Furthermore, it is suggested that male and female athletics directors be hired on equal terms to work together, both with females and males. And as an additional means of overcoming the fear that males might be tempted to take physical liberties with females (an apprehension often voiced), it is strongly suggested that the coaches be coached and also that courses be provided for women that give them the physical strength and training that they need to become assured that when necessary, they can defend themselves. The women's movement has initiated courses in self-defense, and schools should do the same so that women can gain self-confidence in their ability to protect their physical safety.

If coaches need to be coached, counselors need some counseling. When students begin to ask questions about courses and professional aspirations, sexist answers should be outlawed. When Judy Kocik first went to her counselor, a male, about her desire not to take the health course but rather to opt for shop, he laughed her out of his office. When she went to the health education teacher she was told, "In ten years from now when you are a mother you will be grateful to us." Fortunately, Judy was not persuaded.

Vocational testing should be seriously questioned before it is ever administered. Just as it is patently foolish to test the IQ of students whose home environment includes no locks on doors by asking them

to unlock a door lock, so it is useless to test the professional qualifications of a female student who has been successfully dissuaded
from anticipating anything other than housework, a secretarial job,
or nursing in her future. Counseling young women should be done
only by individuals particularly sensitive to the pressures of sex bias
and committed to encouraging young women to see and consider a
wide variety of options.

And one of the special roles of counselors of women should be
to find a better mesh among desire, expectation, and reality. They can
assist a student who needs to explore her own economic resources
and possibilities, from part-time work to scholarship assistance.
Counselors can further help students seek out the widest variety of
opportunities to enhance the number of options that may be available
in the continuation of education. A student's chances for success are
sure to multiply in direct ratio to the increment of choices that become accessible to her.

In extracurricular activities, females should be strongly supported
to take leadership roles when they have the inclination or ability.
And above all, in all areas of the curriculum, when teachers teach,
the exclusion of women should be examined. Gena Corea, a reporter
for the *Holyoke Transcript,* took the initiative of examining the history texts used in the Holyoke school system in the fall of 1971.
The bias excluding the contributions of women was more than
amply illustrated by her sample. Corea wrote a series of articles
for her newspaper that eloquently questioned the sexism manifested in what the high school students were being taught. Subsequently, juniors and seniors in a Holyoke high school were asked
for essay comments on those articles. The comments were given to
Corea and she showed them to us. Mostly unsigned they ranged the
spectrum:

*I think they should throw it away. All it is is women feeling sorry
for themselves. Because no one else will do it for them.*

*True. All on paper is true. But why not. . . . Do we read into the
private lives of Black Slaves, or how hard they fought for their independence. Woman, Man, Black, White—we on earth are supposedly
created equal. Women have come very far in this world and have
gained many honors which we never dreamt possible. Doesn't this
woman realize our world has enough problems without us adding
more. It's one way to arouse [indignation?] from women if this is
her purpose. If her purpose was simply to have people notice this*

discrimination of the female—fine. She is a fine writer and got her point across.

Women shouldn't even have the rights and privileges they have. I am prejudiced, but I believe women were put here to serve men.

I believe leaving women out of history was wrong. Now they are getting their chance. They better make it good.

Some of the information on women left out of the history books should be put in the new editions, but a lot of the informatoin is not that important.

I think that Gena Corea has a grudge against males.

Women were never given equal rights, and were never treated very good by men. They are used as servants really. Men always thought that they were better in ways of strength and intelligence. Women seem to be much kinder and pleasant to be with than most men. In the years to come women will dominate the lives of men more than they do now. [Signed by a male.]

The fact that the modern history books ignore the accomplish-ments of women is a testimonial to the fact that the majority of men think women's rights is a farce. [Also signed by a male.]

RIGHT ON! . . . More and more women are beginning to realize the total absurdity of their roles in life, in the past and now. Women have been taken for granted and treated as second-class citizens long enough. There is no female democracy in today's pro-male society. . . . Women at least deserve the right to show if they are really com-petent or not. They shouldn't be pushed aside and called silly, or dumb broads. Give us a chance! . . .

The comments of these students are instructive of where our society is today. Educators must make a conscientious effort in every area of the curriculum, whether by using supplementary material or by assigning special projects to students, to promote the exploration of the areas where women have made contributions. It is not only in history, but in science, social sciences, and the arts that the roles and potential roles of females can be considered. Much material is already available, and much more is being published, for feminists have set themselves the task of researching the neglected papers, biographies, and autobiographies of women. And many exciting dis-coveries are being made. For example, it was actually a woman,

Catharine Greene, who invented the cotton gin in 1792. However, because "custom frowned upon" women taking out patents in their own names, Eli Whitney is credited with the invention.[22]

A series of multimedia programs that will provide much of the needed information is currently being produced by NOW education coordinator Anne Grant West and her colleagues. They have done an exciting history series entitled "Our North American Foremothers," which asks educators and students to consider why "we remember the warnings of Paul Revere, but . . . have forgotten the longer, all-night ride of Sybil Ludington? We remember Lewis and Clark, but how have we forgotten Sacajawea, who led them? We remember Ulysses Grant, but how have we forgotten Anna Ella Carroll, whose military maps and strategy led to the Union victory?"[23]

The NOW education project is not stopping with answers to those provocative questions, however. They are also working on an educational aids project designed to "encourage young women to think seriously about their skills and interests and to plan their schooling with an appreciation of themselves as human beings with unique personal goals." They plan a series of film strips called "Women in the World of Work" covering possibilities in fields as diverse as publishing, medicine, religion, engineering, architecture, government, building trades, and education. In each area a full range of options will be discussed. In publishing, for example, they will include women involved in writing, editing, and printing, and those women will talk not only about their work, but also about how they coped with the kinds of discrimination that they encountered. The NOW group intends to set up a distribution network across the country to make their materials available to schools.

There is a special area of discrimination in high school curriculum that requires great sensitivity on the part of all concerned. It was alluded to earlier when we mentioned the group of high school women in New York who went to the Board of Education asking for contraceptive counseling. Schools must no longer treat sexual relations between individuals in terms of victorian or puritanical ideals. Where education courses coming under such umbrellas as "family living" discuss sexuality, they should no longer condone any implications of double standards. Males and females are responsible for their own behavior (even when it includes homosexuality), and an unbiased discussion of physiological realities and consequences of behavior should be available to them in education, as should an inquiry into the moral framework in which such behavior occurs.

Moreover, pregnant students should no more be dismissed from school than should the fathers of the children they may bear. And when a young mother is absent for the delivery of her baby, the school should make special provisions to enable her to continue her education. These young women, who are likely to be alone, require even more support than others—the kind of educational involvement that permits them to maintain self-esteem and to look forward to the economic independence that they will badly need.

Clearly, this is a hasty discussion of some of the elements that must be introduced into courses and policies that deal with sexuality, and the subject is far from exhausted. The emphasis for educators here, as throughout, is that they should approach this and all phases of education with a new attitude. In this case it is an attitude that will, as early as possible, provide preadolescents with some knowledge of the changes taking place in their bodies, will help them later to be comfortable with their bodies and its changes, and will teach them to be responsible individuals who understand their responsibilities toward other individuals.

In several high schools, and even an occasional junior high, female studies courses have been initiated to explore such questions as:

1. Are women born or made? Are they formed by their biology or their culture?
2. Are women oppressed? If so, by whom or what? If not, why are they complaining and what do they want?
3. Do women have a history and a culture of their own?
4. What alternatives do women have now? How will or should women's lives change in the future?

The above is part of an outline developed by June Slavin for a course in the social studies department of a Newton, Massachusetts, high school. After embarking on this course, Slavin recognized difficulties—breaking down the traditional age barriers between students and teachers, and the school's responses, which range from hostility to dismay to the rationale that such courses are a fad, among others. And she also believes it should be pointed out that outlines such as hers must not be considered an easy recipe, a formula, or a right way to do it, for the group dynamics in the class itself often redirects the plan with which one set out.

Where special courses of the female studies genre seem appropriate, the question of the role that male students should play in those courses is also appropriate. A female studies course should not be allowed to become another arena in which competition between the sexes takes place. Its obvious purpose should be to inform and to provide both males and females with encouragement in breaking through the traditional limitations set by stereotyping.

As throughout the educational system, the staff should be kept current with the nonbiased material that is available. And in secondary schools, not only should professional women be invited to address the student body, but also feminists (and perhaps antifeminists) should be invited to have discussions with students and the faculty, administrators, and parents. Female students should be included on committees that are responsible for organizing such events. It is further suggested that an ombudswoman be appointed in every school to work with a committee of parents and educators so that the progress in equality throughout the school will be monitored. There should be in every school some recourse for a student or teacher who feels she (or he) is suffering discrimination because of her (or his) sex.

When trying to make these breakthroughs one often meets strong resistance. In the outstanding report, "Let Them Aspire," compiled by Marcia Federbush for the Ann Arbor, Michigan, Committee to Eliminate Sexual Discrimination in the Public Schools, many good recommendations were put to school officials. One section of the report reads:

Unjustifiable excuses for omitting girls
In our various encounters with school-related personnel, we have come across the following justifications (among others) for keeping girls out of certain courses or activities:
"There's no place for a girl to take a shower."

"What about insurance. What if a girl fell off a sixteen-foot ladder?"

"Where would a girl go the toilet?"

"But a girl might get her hair caught in the machinery."

"We can't let girls do metal work because they have to wear masks and work with sparks."

"The unions won't let them in, so why should we train girls for jobs they won't be able to get?"

"But boys have to swim nude."

"If girls were in the class, we'd have to make crafts instead of real woodwork."

"The weights are too heavy for girls to carry."

"Girls aren't interested in that sort of thing."

"Girls wouldn't want to take off their jewelry and tie back their hair for that course."

We submit that NONE of these reasons is valid.

If the room is not equipped with a shower, then one of the sexes will have to use the gym shower, wash with soap and water, or remain greasy. If teachers are worried about long hair, then long-haired girls (and boys) should be required to fasten it back in some way. (Teachers have never expressed to us their worry about boys with long hair.)

At any rate, no interested student, regardless of sex, color, weight, or any other physical feature, should be refused admittance into any course in which she (he) is interested. Changes may have to be made in conventional thinking patterns, but these will be necessary if our schools are to be humane to all students and are to bring out the best potential that each person has to offer."[24]

This, again, is part of the general attitudinal shift being demanded today of educators. Perhaps it may be achieved by inservice training that would give educators a wider perspective of the role women may play. There should be discussion groups in which teachers examine their own prejudices, and these should be used as a basis for investigation of the individual's own experiences and expectations of life. And most important, much of the training should be done in schools of education as students prepare to assume the role of educators. Unless adults can break some of the patterns of their own sexist conditioning, they are unlikely to provide an unbiased education for young people.

SCHOOLS OF EDUCATION

More than any of the other departments, it is the schools of education that have the greatest responsibility and opportunity to effect long-range and overall change in the educational systems of this country. What they can achieve is awesome; what they currently fail to achieve is perhaps even more so. Considering that 88 percent of elementary and about 50 percent of the secondary school teachers are female, it should be astounding that in a typical graduate school of education where as many as 95 percent of the students are female, not even one member of the permanent faculty is a woman![25] In the context of this book, this is one of the greatest sins.

It is not, however, a sin that is easily expiated. Happily the past several years have shown a positive trend in reevaluating and upgrading the role of the teachers and in considering education a profession of special social consequence. It is to be hoped that concurrently, as the profession is upgraded, it will not, as most professions with status do, be preempted by men. It is important that males and females share equally in this social responsibility.

Sex stereotyping and sexism in school and society must become the special area of concern in schools of education. It should enter the curriculum in at least three ways: incorporation into all of the courses within the school; retraining or in-service education of practicing educators; and as a special discipline in itself. The first two areas are most obvious, for in order that educators teach subjects or purvey attitudes that are nonsexist, they themselves must have some special instruction on the roles, contributions, and possibilities of women.

We have investigated means of achieving a nonsexist education throughout this chapter, and we have talked about the attitudinal change that must come about. We recommend also the reeducation of those who educate teachers. In this context it seems highly advisable that everyone in the field of education be required to take a survey course on women and education, a course which would make them aware of the bias that exists and that must be overcome. One such course has been taught by Susan Bereaud at Cornell University. Here is part of the original syllabus for that course:

Women and Education
  I. What are the effects of the female majority on the profession of education?
   A. What kinds of women choose teaching as a career?
      1. What is their self-image?
         a. What is their attitude toward risk taking?
         b. How do they view themselves as professionals?
   B. Why do women choose teaching as a career?
      1. Is it a temporary job until marriage and/or children?
      2. Is elementary -or secondary school teaching a second choice?
   C. What are their expectations from the profession for personal fulfillment?

   D. What are the effects of the female majority in teaching on the male attitude toward teaching as a profession?

   E. Why does the percentage of women in teaching decrease as the academic level increases?

     1. Are there different attitudes among the women in the different levels of teaching?

     2. Why do these differences exist?

II. How has the uneven distribution of women in teaching affected the educational process?

   A. Does school reinforce preschool training with reference to sex roles?

   B. Is school a haven for "good little girls" without role models for boys because of the low number of males in the first six years of school?

   C. How is the low level of achievement of American school children related to the preponderance of female teachers?

   D. How has the lack of career commitment among female teachers affected teaching?

III. Are there differences toward the traditional sex roles in radical schools, and what role do women play in these schools?[26]

After more than a year of concentrated research on the problems of sexism in school and society, the recommendations in this chapter have come to seem obvious, many even conservative. Yet we realize that to others they may appear radical or revolutionary. Whatever adjective is chosen is unimportant, for what they are, above all, is *necessary*. As a new consciousness and self-esteem spreads among women (and liberated men), it is better than certain that more and more women will reject the second-class citizenship that had almost become second nature. Their first nature, their human nature, is advancing with the thrust and irrevocability of an idea whose time has come, a movement whose moment is now—a credo so deep and all-encompassing that it can never be cancelled. The era for positive change is here, and the measure of success lies in the affirmation and encouragement of all good men and women.

NOTES

[1]Lewis Carroll, Introduction and notes by Martin Gardner, *The Annotated Alice*, New York, Clarkson N. Potter, 1960, p. 37. Reprinted by permission of the publisher.

[2]Ralph Tyler, "National Assessment: A History and Sociology," *School and Society*, *98*, no. 2325, (December 1970), 471–483.

[3] Marcia Federbush, *Let Them Aspire: A Plea and Proposal for Equality of Opportunity for Males and Females in the Ann Arbor Public Schools.* Copies available from 1000 Cedar Bend Drive, Ann Arbor, Michigan 48105.

[4] See Karen Branan, "What Can I Do About Sex Discrimination," *Scholastic Teacher*, November 1971, p. 20, which suggests specific avenues of recourse; also, Sonia Pressman Fuentes, "University Women and the Law," *College English*, May 1971, provides legal guidelines and background; and Louis Fischer and David Schimmel, *The Civil Rights of Teachers*, New York, Harper and Row, 1973.

[5] "Brief Highlights of Major Federal Laws and Orders on Sex Discrimination," and "Education Act Extends Sex Discrimination and Minimum Wage Provisions," Legislative Series 2, July 1972, Women's Bureau, U.S. Department of Labor, Employment Standards Administration, Washington, D.C. 20210.

[6] The Commonwealth of Massachusetts, Acts, 1971, Chap. 622, Section 5: "Every child shall have a right to attend the public schools of the town where he actually resides, subject to the following section. No child shall be excluded from or discriminated against in admission to a public school of any town, or in obtaining the advantages, privileges and courses of study of such public school on account of race, color, sex, religion or national origin." Approved 5 August 1971.

[7] Patricia Minuchin, "The Schooling of Tomorrow's Women," *School Review*, 80, no. 2 (February 1972) pp. 199–208.

[8] Eve Merriam and Beni Montresor, *Mommies at Work*, New York, Scholastic Book Services, 1971.

[9] Lisa Hammel, "Mothers Carry Women's Lib Message to Grade School," *New York Times*, 8 January 1971.

[10] R. Buckminster Fuller, *Operating Manual for Spaceship Earth*, Carbondale, Southern Illinois University Press, 1969.

[11] For a mechanist point of view see, for example, Lionel Tiger and Robin Fox, *The Imperial Animal*, New York, Holt, Rinehart and Winston, 1971.

[12] Gail T. McLure *et al.*, "Sex Discrimination in Schools," *Today's Education*, 60 (November 1971), p. 33.

[13] Boston Commission to Improve the Status of Women, Education Task Force Report, December, 1971.

[14] Rose M. Somerville, "Women's Studies," *Today's Education*, 60 (November 1971), p. 36.

[15] Dorin Schumacher, "Changing the School Environment: A Progress Report." Since writing this report Dorin Schumacher has received her Ph.D. A copy of the Joint Task Force Report on Sexism in Education is available from the Pennsylvania Department of Education, Harrisburg, Pa.

[16] Aileen Pace Nilsen, "Women in Children's Literature," *College English*, 32 (May 1971), pp. 918–926.

[17] Kurt Vonnegut, Jr., "Introduction," in John Birmingham ed., *Our*

Time Is Now, New York, Praeger, 1970, p. x. Reprinted by permission of the publisher.

[18]Alice de Rivera, "On De-Segregating Stuyvesant High," in Robin Morgan, ed., *Sisterhood Is Powerful,* New York, Random House (Vintage), 1970.

[19]Jane Brody, "High Schools Are Urged to Assist Birth Control" *New York Times* 28 September 1971.

[20]This information comes from Carol Ahlum and Jackie Fralley who are compiling a handbook of high school feminist studies curriculums to be published by KNOW Press, Box 86031, Pittsburgh, Pa.

[21]*Hollander* v. *Connecticut Interscholastic Athletic Conference, Inc.* Superior Court, New Haven County, Conn., 29 March 1971.

[22]See Aileen S. Kraditor, ed., *Up From the Pedestal,* Chicago, Quadrangle Books, 1968, p. 87.

[23]Information on these programs is available from Anne Grant West, 453 7th St., Brooklyn, N.Y. 11215; or NOW, New York City Chapter, 28 East 56th St., New York, N.Y. 10022.

[24]Federbush, *op.cit.,* p. 13.

[25]Janet Emig, "Another Prejudice, One Woman in Academe Fights Back," *Mount Holyoke Alumnae Quarterly,* Fall, 1970. It is to be noted that, whether the school of education provides a graduate, undergraduate, or postgraduate staff will change the ratio somewhat, but it can usually be documented, in any case, that women have less prestige, permanence, and pay.

[26]The syllabus for this course was drawn up by Arlene Ryan and Jane Camhi of the Cornell Studies Program. They used it successfully to convince the Education Department of the University to initiate a course on women and education. Susan Bereaud has been teaching the course since the fall of 1970 (Ryan and Camhi were filling other positions) and has subsequently drawn up her own syllabi and course outlines.

Appendix A
Selected annotated bibliography on the women's movement and sexism in education

In this brief and by no means inclusive bibliography, we have listed a few of the more important books and articles that we have used as references and sources, and we have also tried to include books and collections that are now in manuscript form and therein go beyond current bibliographies.

For background on the women's movement both *Feminism, The Essential Historical Writings*, edited by Miriam Schnier (New York: Random House, 1972), and *Up From the Pedestal*, edited by Aileen S. Kraditor (Chicago: Quadrangle Books, 1968), provide the historical context in which women have struggled for full human rights and include fine selections of the writings of those women who have led such struggles.

For sociological interpretations of the current position of women and an understanding of how and why women are anxious to change their status, Eva Figes' *Patriarchial Attitudes* (New York: Stein and Day, 1971) and Elizabeth Janeway's *Man's World Woman's Place: A Study in Social Mythology* (New York: William Morrow, 1971) should be included.

Sisterhood is Powerful, An Anthology of Writings From the Women's Liberation Movement, edited by Robin Morgan (New York: Random House, Vintage, 1970) includes a wide span of women's writings, from experiential to empirical, with authors ranging from black women and high school students to aging women. Also *Black Woman*, edited by Toni Cade (New York, Signet, 1970), provides a much-needed perspective on minority women.

There are interesting points of view from all sides and some amusing reading in the Congressional Hearings of the Committee on the Judiciary on the Equal Rights For Men And Women amendment prior to its passage in 1972. Copies can be ordered from the U.S. Government Printing Office in Washington, D.C.

The winter 1972 issue (*8*, no. 1) of the *Massachusetts Review* (Amherst, Mass.) is devoted to women. Included are Bella Abzug on politics, Anais Nin on feminism, Penina Glazer on women in the labor movements, Cynthia Wolff on women in literature, and Anne Halley with a fictional account of women in graduate school.

A new interdisciplinary journal *Women's Studies*, currently being put together, will be an important contribution as a "forum for presentation of scholarship and criticism about women in the fields of literature, history, art, sociology, psychology, political science, economics, anthropology, law and the sciences." For more information write the editor, Wendy Martin, Department of English, Queens College of the City University of New York, Flushing, New York.

There are some educational journals that have devoted entire issues to sex bias in education. "Women and Education," a special issue of *School Review*, *80* (February 1972), is a collection of articles on the socialization of women both in and out of schools. There is ample coverage of the socialization process in young children and some analysis of the role of women in higher education in it. Unfortunately, it has no discussion of women at the high school level.

"Women in Education," a special issue of *Edcentric 3* (December 1971), offers some excellent articles, including Roberta Salper on "The Theory and Practice of Women's Studies"; The Feminists on Children's Media on "Sexism in Children's Literature"; and Anne Sutherland Harris on "The Second Sex in Academe." This issue also includes a list of women's groups and pertinent publications. Again, there is no information on high school women.

Although in the issue devoted to "Sex Differences and the School," the *National Elementary Principal 46* (November 1966), the perspective is decidedly not a feminist one, some valuable information is presented. Two articles in this issue that are particularly helpful are "Teacher Interactions with Boys and Girls," by Pauline Sears and David Feldman, and "Sex Differences in Children: Research Findings in an Educational Context," by Patricia Minuchin.

There are a number of articles that analyze sexism in children's books. In "Male and Female in Children's Books—Dispelling All

Doubts," by Mary Ritchie Key, in the *American Teacher* (February 1972), a variety of studies concerned with sex typing in school readers is summarized. Janice Trecker's "Women in U.S. History Texts," *Social Education 35* (March 1971), presents an excellent analysis of women, and of the lack of them, in high school history books. "A Feminist Look at Children's Books, by The Feminists on Children's Literature, *School Library Journal 17* (January 1971) offers one of the best discussions of this topic.

"Sex Discrimination in the Elementary School," by Myra and David Sadker, *National Elementary Principal,* (October 1972) gives a succinct review of the various forms of discrimination that affect the elementary school girl.

"Discriminating Against the Pregnant Teacher," sponsored by the NEA Du Shane Emergency Fund Division and found in *Today's Education 60* (December 1971), is a brief but informative discussion of various forms of discrimination against pregnant teachers as well as a description of court actions in progress.

Report on Sex Bias in the Public Schools (Education Committee, NOW, New York, 1971) is an excellent compilation of data collected from elementary and secondary schools throughout New York City, as well as some pertinent discussion of the way sex bias operates in schools. This report consists of articles on segregation, sex stereotyping in school readers, sex education, guidance, personnel, and administration, as well as recommendations for change. It also includes letters from parents and teachers concerning sexism and excerpts from court testimony by high school women who have experienced discrimination.

For a fascinating account of the work of a small group of people interested in a nonsexist education for their children, *Let Them Aspire* can be ordered from editor Marcia Federbush, 1000 Cedar Bend Drive, Ann Arbor, Michigan 48105.

Conspiracy of the Young by Paul Lauter and Florence Howe describes channeling and tracking of young people and has a chapter concerning "The Female Majority" (New York: World, Meridian paperback, 1970.)

College Influences on the Role Development of Female Undergraduates, by Carole Leland and Marjorie Lozoff and published by The Institute for the Study of Human Problems (Stanford University, January 1969, Ed 026 975) surveys two decades of research on the educational, occupational, and sociopsychological development of undergraduate and·adult women. It offers an excellent review of the literature in this area.

For a comprehensive report on women in higher education, there is *The Status of Academic Women* by Lora Robinson, published by Review 5, ERIC Clearinghouse on Higher Education (Ed 048 523). This report includes three parts: Section I presents reviews of *Academic Women* by Jessie Barnard, *The Woman Doctorate in America* by Helen Astin, *Women and the Doctorate* by Susan Mitchell, and *Women as College Teachers* by Jean Henderson. Section II consists of fifty-four annotated campus reports that cover employment conditions for women. Section III describes twenty-five projects, including committees, task forces, and study groups formed to collect and disseminate information on employment conditions for women at various academic institutions and within various professional organizations.

Academic Women on the Move, edited by Alice Rossi and scheduled for publication late in 1972 (New York: Russel Sage Foundation), will be a collection of the writings of people with intriguing ideas about education. Included are articles by Florence Howe, Jo Freeman, Helen Astin, Alan Bayer, Bernice Sandler, and Alice Rossi.

For some hard, statistical information on where the female fits into academe, three research reports issued by the American Council on Education provide access to some figures that, because there are breakdowns according to sex, provide fuel for independent interpretations and research. They are *The American Freshman: National Norms for Fall 1971 6*, 6 (1971); *The American Graduate Student: A Normative Description 16*, 5 (1971); and *College and University Faculty: A Statistical Description 5*, 5, (1970). Copies can be ordered from the ACE office at 1 Dupont Circle, Washington, D.C.

A look at the contribution of women to education is the intention of *Dauntless Women in Childhood Education 1856–1931*, to be published in 1972 by the Association for Childhood Education International.

In addition to the above there are several selected bibliographies available. There is, for example, a bibliography of literature on, by, and about women in *Sisterhood is Powerful*, mentioned above. Also, the *Library Journal* of 1 September 1971 has a fine, annotated bibliography divided into categories such as "Economic and Legal Status" and "Mythology and Psychology."

Know Press, which publishes reprints, has an extensive list of articles on various issues, which can be ordered from KNOW, Inc., P.O. Box 10197, Pittsburgh, Pennsylvania 15232. KNOW is also distributing the invaluable *Female Studies Guide*, as well as a series of course syllabi and bibliographies on women.

Women's Studies Abstracts is a new venture, first edition coming out in Winter 1972, which will be published quarterly. It can be ordered from P.O. Box 1, Rush, New York 14543.

A list of liberated reading for children is called *Little Miss Muffet Fights Back* and can be obtained from Children's Media Project, P.O. Box 4315, Grand Central Station, New York. "Reducing the Miss Muffet Syndrome: An Annotated Bibliography," by Diane Stavn, *School Library Journal,* 18 (January 1972) offers another selection of nonsexist children's books. A number of other lists are also available.

A bibliography of articles that disscusses *Sexism in Children's Books,* compiled by Florence Howe and Carol Ahlum, is available from the Clearing House on Curriculum, SUNY College at Old Westbury, Old Westbury, New York 11568.

And finally, the Women's Bureau of the U.S. Department of Labor in Washington, D.C. will provide a list of their publications that can be ordered from the Superintendent of Documents. They have a series of pamphlets under the heading Career Opportunities for Women, Why Not Be—an Engineer; an Optometrist; a Pharmacist, etc., which expands the traditional vision of women's jobs and would be useful to educational counselors.

Appendix B
Sex bias questionnaire*

copyright 1972 by
Myra Pollack Sadker

Teachers' Form

		A	B
1.	When you meet a new class of students do you expect girls to do well in spelling, reading, and language arts and boys to do well in math, science, and mechanical skills?	Yes——	No——
2.	Do you ever use sex as a basis for separating students for classroom activity (asking students to line up by directing boys to one side of the room and girls to the other; organizing girls against boys in academic competition)?	Yes——	No——
3.	Do you discuss sex typing with your students—its causes and possible effects?	No——	Yes——
4.	When you ask students to help you with school chores, do you usually expect boys to run film projectors and move books from room to room, and girls to keep attendance and banking records?	Yes___	No___

*In constructing this questionnaire, there has been no attempt to assess its statistical reliability and validity. It is simply meant to be a list of questions that may reflect sexist practices in schools.

                                                        A   B

5. When report cards are given out, do girls
usually receive the A and B grades? (Do these
grades truly reflect academic achievement, or are
they a reward for more submissive and controll-
able behavior?)   Yes___   No___
6. Do you expect girls to become teachers, nurses,
and secretaries, whereas for boys, is the range
of occupations that comes to mind much greater?   Yes___   No___
7. Do you usually analyze curricular materials to
see if female characters are represented and
portrayed in a nonstereotyped manner?   No___   Yes___
8. Do you give more of your classroom attention
to boys, both disciplining them more and talk-
ing with them more about the subject matter?   Yes___   No___
9. Do you stop one sex from making demeaning
comments about the other such as, "I don't
want to read any dumb girl's book"?   No___   Yes___
10. Would you rather have a male than a female
principal or superintendent?   Yes___   No___

Administrators' Form
1. When you interview new teachers for your
school staff, do you feel that you would rather
hire a competent male than a competent female
teacher?   Yes___   No___
2. Are all courses and activities in your school
open to both males and females?   No___   Yes___
3. If your school has segregated sports programs,
are more monies, facilities, and attention given
to the men's physical education program than
the women's?   Yes___   No___
4. When students are brought to you for discipli-
nary action, do you discipline males more severely than females—even when both are guilty
of the same or equivalent misdemeanors?   Yes___   No___
5. Does your school have a policy that forces
female employees to leave at some officially
designated time during pregnancy?   Yes___   No___
6. Are there committees established in your school
to report on sex stereotyping in books and other
curricular materials?   No___   Yes___

	A	B
7. Are there any programs for students scheduled during the school year that focus on sex discrimination?	No___	Yes___
8. Does your school offer workshops for faculty and staff in which the effects of sex bias on students are discussed?	No___	Yes___
9. (If you are associated with a high school) does your school allow pregnant teenage women to attend their regular classes if they wish to do so?	No___	Yes___
10. Is the majority of administrative personnel (team leaders, department chairpeople, principals, superintendent, etc.) in your school district male?	Yes___	No___

Scoring: A statistically valid scoring procedure has not been developed for this questionnaire, nor are labels such as "Sexist Teacher" or "Nonsexist Administrator" assigned to various scores. However, it may be useful for you to reexamine those items that were responded to by a check in Column A. Each response marked in Column A may reflect a tendency toward sex bias in that particular area. A prevalence of responses in that column may reflect a generalized set toward sex bias in your classroom or your school system.